TALMUD AND MIDRASH

Jacob Neusner

Studies in Judaism

University Press of America,® Inc.
Lanham · Boulder · New York · Toronto · Plymouth, UK

Copyright © 2007 by
University Press of America,® Inc.
4501 Forbes Boulevard
Suite 200
Lanham, Maryland 20706
UPA Acquisitions Department (301) 459-3366

Estover Road
Plymouth PL6 7PY
United Kingdom

All rights reserved
Printed in the United States of America
British Library Cataloging in Publication Information Available

Library of Congress Control Number: 2006931834
ISBN-13: 978-0-7618-3592-9 (paperback : alk. paper)
ISBN-10: 0-7618-3592-X (paperback : alk. paper)

Studies in Judaism

EDITOR

Jacob Neusner
Bard College

EDITORIAL BOARD

Alan J. Avery-Peck
College of the Holy Cross

Herbert Basser
Queens University

Bruce D. Chilton
Bard College

José Faur
Bar Ilan University

William Scott Green
University of Rochester

Mayer Gruber
Ben-Gurion University of the Negev

Günter Stemberger
University of Vienna

James F. Strange
University of South Florida

Contents

Preface vii

1. Hosea in the Mishnah, tractate Abot, and the Tosefta 1
2. Hosea in Sifra, the two Sifrés and the Mekhilta Attributed to R. Ishmael 3
3. Hosea in the Yerushalmi 25
4. Hosea in Genesis Rabbah, Leviticus Rabbi, and Pesiqta deRab Kahana 39
5. Hosea in Esther Rabbah I, Ruth Rabbah, Song of Songs Rabbah, Lamentations rabbah and The Fathers According to R. Nathan 85
6. Hosea in the Bavli 113

Preface

> A language community is not just a group marked out by its use of a particular language: it is an evolving communion in its own right, whose particular view of the world is informed by a common language tradition. A language brings with it a mass of perceptions clichés, judgments and inspirations. In some sense, then, when one language replaces another, a people's view of the world must also be changing.
>
> Nicholas Ostler[1]

I

What happens to a religious community when its first language is replaced by a second, yet a third, and onward through time? Whether or not the new language marks a change in world-view remains to be seen. Continuities of culture despite variations of language demand deep deliberation. The communities that inherited the holy Scriptures of ancient Israel, Rabbinic Judaism and catholic, orthodox Christianity, found themselves possessed by divine writings in a language other than their own — writings dictated by God to prophets, for example. They nonetheless regarded themselves as those of, and to, whom in their day God through Scripture spoke, those that continued and now constituted the community of ancient Israel. And that was so even though they did not form a language community coherent with the language of Scripture. But how to form a community of "perceptions, clichés, judgments and inspirations" within an alien yet authoritative language-world? Here is a case, common in religious traditions, in which one language replaces another even while the holy writings in the replaced language remain authoritative.

The Rabbinic sages of the first six centuries C.E. for their part recognized the difference between the language of Scripture and the language of the sages, that of the Mishnah for example. Greek and Latin, Aramaic and Syriac, Mishnaic or Middle Hebrew — none of the principal languages of Judaic and Christian antiquity opened the door to the received Scripture, which required translation. Yet all these language communities made their own the received writings in an alien tongue.

Theology trumps culture. For their heirs the ancient Israelite Scriptures represented authoritative accounts of God's messages in God's own wording. That is why the shift in language — from God's language, Hebrew as recorded by the prophets, to the languages of the faithful, now inheritors — challenged them to contemplate continuities from present to past. But they would say, from past to present. None could concede what is self-evident to modern historical linguistics, including those devoted to Scripture: when one language replaces another, views of the world must also be changing. But how were authoritative writings in one language to be received by communities speaking a different language? Conveyed by a divine language that no one now spoke and that many did not comprehend, Scripture, its law and theology, history and prophecy, enjoyed the privileged position in the faith- and language-communities of Judaism and Christianity. Both religious traditions faced the task of mediating God's word of old to language-communities that used other words altogether to say other things entirely.

How they did so forms a principal problem in the study of formative Judaism and Christianity. In general terms, the Christian solution, the organization of the Old Testament and the New Testament, and the Judaic solution to the same problem, the formation of the doctrine of the dual Torah, an oral Torah that amplified and complemented the written Torah of ancient Israel, run parallel. The New Testament found validation in the Old, as Christianity read backward from the Gospels to the Israelite prophets. The Rabbinic sages of the documents of the oral Torah received and recast the written one into wholly new modes of thought as well as of expression. They read forward from Scripture to the present moment. Nonetheless, that characterization of the reception of Scripture in formative Christianity and Judaism rests in general on episodic data, on mere examples and illustrations.

It is time for systematic work. This sourcebook and its companions represents the effort to collect and classify the hard facts in full detail of how Israelite Scripture was received and recast in the language-communities that produced the Bible in two Testaments of Christianity and the dual Torah of Judaism. Take the prophets, for example. Everyone knows that verses of prophecy figure prominently in the Gospels' narratives, and that they figure as proof-texts in Rabbinic exegesis of scriptural narratives as well. But to what end, and with what larger conception in mind? Biblical authority in Christianity forms a staple topic of theological inquiry. But I do not know of a systematic survey of how the Rabbinic *documents*, for their part, respond to the prophetic ones: select, explain, and utilize the received language of Scripture.

What is at stake in such a study is an account of how the Rabbinic system took over the prophetic writings and responded to their exhortations and theology — weighty issues. So far as prophetic Judaism challenges the covenantal nomism of Rabbinic Judaism, as some suppose it does, the wherewithal of evaluating that proposition, so critical to the history of Judaism, awaits. And these form only two important questions that a survey of Rabbinic readings of Israelite prophetic writings will help to resolve. This collection of Rabbinic comments on verses in the book of Hosea carries forward the presentation of Jeremiah and Amos. It will be followed by anthologies of Rabbinic readings of Isaiah, Ezekiel, and the other literary prophets.

To what end? I address the hypothesis that Rabbinic Judaism in its normative canon, from the Mishnah through the Bavli, not only formally through

Preface

proof-texts but theologically through normative propositions represents a continuation and realization of Prophetic Judaism.

II

The Rabbinic sages of the first six centuries of the Common Era recognized that that Scripture's language was not their own, the Hebrew of the prophets and the Hebrew of the Mishnah and Midrash-compilations of Rabbinic Judaism being distinct forms of Hebrew. Here is a protracted account of their engagement with distinct linguistic usages and the meanings imputed to the differences, with italics signifying the use of Aramaic, plain type, of Hebrew:

BAVLI QIDDUSHIN 4:1-2 70A-B/V.5

A. *There was a man from Nehardea who went into a butcher shop in Pumbedita. He said to them, "Give me meat."*
B. *They said to him, "Wait until the servant of R. Judah bar Ezekiel gets his, and then we'll give to you."*
C. *He said, "So who is this Judah bar Sheviskel who comes before me to get served before me?"*
D. *They went and told R. Judah.*
E. He excommunicated him.
F. *They said, "He is in the habit of calling people slaves."*
G. He proclaimed concerning him, "He is a slave."
H. *The other party went and sued him in court before R. Nahman.*
I. *When the summons came, R. Judah went to R. Huna, he said to him, "Should I go, or shouldn't I go?"*
J. *He said to him, "In point of fact, you really don't have to go, because you are an eminent authority. But on account of the honor owing to the household of the patriarch [of the Babylonian Jews], get up and go."*
K. *He came. He found him making a parapet.*
L. *He said to him, "Doesn't the master concur with what R. Huna bar Idi said Samuel said,* 'Once a man is appointed administrator of the community, it is forbidden for him to do servile labor before three persons'*?"*
M. *He said to him, "I'm just making a little piece of the balustrade."*
N. *He said to him, "So what's so bad about the word, 'parapet,' that the Torah uses, or the word 'partition,' that rabbis use?"*
O. *He said to him, "Will the master sit down on a seat?"*
P. *He said to him, "So what's so bad about 'chair,' which rabbis use, or the word 'stool,' which people generally use?"*
Q. *He said to him, "Will the master eat a piece of citron-fruit?"*
R. *He said to him, "This is what Samuel said,* 'Whoever uses the word "citron-fruit" is a third puffed up with pride.' *It should be called either etrog, as the rabbis do, or 'lemony-thing,' as people do."*

S. *He said to him, "Would the master like to drink a goblet of wine?"*
T. *He said to him, "So what's so bad about the word 'wineglass,' as rabbis say, or 'a drink,' as people say?"*

The story further meanders in a variety of directions, but what is important for the present argument is clear: language-choices signaled social and cultural differences. Nor only so, but the use of Aramaic, rather than Hebrew, is attributed to God himself, by the prophets:

Genesis Rabbah LXXIV:XIV.

1. A. "[Laban called it Jegar-sahadutha, but Jacob called it Galeed. Laban said, 'This heap is a witness between you and me today. Therefore he named it Galeed, and the pillar Mizpah, for he said, 'The Lord watch between you and me when we are absent one from the other. If you ill-treat my daughters or if you take wives besides my daughters, although no man is with us, remember, God is witness between you and me'"]" (Gen. 31:47-50): "Laban called it Jegar-sahadutha:"
   B. Said R. Samuel bar Nahman, "Let the Aramaic language not be a minor one in your view, for in the Torah, the Prophets, and the Writings, the Holy One, blessed be he, paid all due respect to it.
   C. "In the Torah: 'Jegar-sahadutha.'
   D. "In the Prophets: 'Thus shall you say to them' (Jer. 10:11), [given in Aramaic].
   E. "In the Writings: 'Then spoke the Chaldeans to the king in Aramaic' (Dan. 2:4)."

The passage has God dictate to Jeremiah a prophesy in Aramaic, and this is a mark of the importance of that language.

How these differences in not only word choice but the entirety of language were sorted out affords perspective on the religious systems — Rabbinic Judaism, catholic, orthodox Christianity — that with Scripture in hand would emerge from late antiquity. The uses to which they put the heritage of the past reveal much about the traits of mind and theological program that characterized the heirs of Scripture. To be sure issues that provoke interest have tended to focus on whether the later generations impose upon the scriptural heritage their own concerns or attempt to replicate the original, historical message and perspective of the Scriptural writers. So Scripture as a historical resource has been made to stand in judgment upon the systematic theological readings of the heirs of Scripture in later times. But such a perspective imposes upon the Judaic sages and Christian theologians issues of historical authenticity that did not preoccupy them — they took for granted the historical facticity of Scripture's narratives and the authority of its laws — and obscures the issues that did concern them.

It is easier to invoke the notion that the sages and theologians possessed clear programs of inquiry than exactly to define of what those programs consisted.

Preface

It is common to impute to them issues important to contemporary learning, pertinent to, if not historical, then theological or philological-exegetical topics. So debates in the Judaic framework pursue the issues of whether exegesis is provoked by traits of language and expression of the text or responds to issues of a systematic character pervading the documents in which the particularities of detailed exegesis figure. Such debates, which yield interesting results for the contemporary hermeneutics of Scripture, do not greatly advance our systematic knowledge of the way in which the sages and theologians received Scripture and responded to it. That knowledge depends upon comprehensive surveys of details and the categorization of the details. These desiderata await realization. We cannot now on the basis of a full corpus of data define the range of concerns that drew sages and theologians to Scripture: what they were likely to ask Scripture to reveal, to demonstrate, to elucidate.

My purpose here and in the companion anthologies is to create a data base for analytical studies of Rabbinic Judaism and ancient Israel prophecy. I collect and classify the corpus of comments on specific verses of Scripture embedded in the writings of the ancient rabbis and theologians. When we have accomplished the work of hunting and gathering the data and inductively ordering it by its interior categories, we shall have established solid foundations for generalization. Then we may say what the sages and theologians proposed to accomplish in their engagement with Scripture. We may begin to outline the authority of Scripture as that authority imposed structure and order upon the sages' and the theologians' systems: for what was Scripture likely to be interrogated, and what were the issues important in late antiquity on which Scripture was not invited to testify. To answer these questions of large-scale characterization and generalization requires a kind of work of collecting and arranging facts that until now has not been done — a reference book on Rabbinic readings of Israelite prophecy.

III

My ambition here accordingly is modest. This is a source book produced by grunt work, just a collection and classification of facts meant to provide documentation for the future study of how one particular kind of ancient Israelite Scripture, the prophetic books, found a place in the new language-community formed by the Rabbinic sages and documented in their canon from the Mishnah, ca. 200 C.E., through the Talmud of Babylonia, a.k.a., the Bavli, ca. 600 C.E. I have collected from my translations and arranged in sequence document by document the references to the principal prophets set forth in the Rabbinic writings of late antiquity. In the companion studies I classify the uses of prophecy undertaken by the rabbis: the evidences of the movement from language to language, world view to world view. The present collection carries forward *Jeremiah in Talmud and Midrash* (Lanham, 2006: University Press of America. Studies in Judaism series), and its companion *Rabbi Jeremiah*, and *Amos in Talmud and Midrash* (Lanham, 2006: University Press of America. Studies in Judaism series).

The sources and reference system derive from my translations of the canon of formative Judaism. In those translations I consulted prior versions of the same documents. These derive from the British translations published by Soncino Press, London. Where these are used, I cite the name of the translator and the page in the Soncino translation where the work appears. The reference system I have devised signals the sentence, paragraph, completed unit of thought, plus the document and its conventional divisions, e.g., chapter and subchapter. The use of Aramaic type faces signals Aramaic, plain type, Hebrew, and bold face type, the citation of the Mishnah or the Tosefta by a later document.

The Mishnah. A New Translation. New Haven and London, 1987: Yale University Press. *Choice* Outstanding Academic Book List, 1989. Second printing: 1990. Paperbound edition: 1991. CD Rom edition: Logos, 1996. CD Rom/ Web edition: OakTree Software, Inc. Altamonte Springs, FL.

Editor: *The Law of Agriculture in the Mishnah and the Tosefta.* Leiden, 2005: E. J. Brill.

    I.   *A History of the Mishnaic Law of Agriculture. Berakhot, Peah.*
    II.   *Demai, Kilayim., Shebiit*
    III. *Terumot, Maaserot, Maaser Sheni, Hallah, Orlah, Bikkurim*

The Tosefta. Translated from the Hebrew. N.Y., 1977-1980: Ktav. II-VI.

    I.   Editor: *The Tosefta. Translated from the Hebrew. I. The First Division Zeraim.* N.Y., 1985: Ktav.
    II.   *The Tosefta. Translated from the Hebrew. The Second Division. Moed.* Second printing: Atlanta, 1999: Scholars Press for USF Academic Commentary Series.
    III. *The Tosefta. Translated from the Hebrew. The Third Division. Nashim.* Second printing: Atlanta, 1999: Scholars Press for USF Academic Commentary Series.
    IV. *The Tosefta. Translated from the Hebrew. The Fourth Division. Neziqin.* Second printing: Atlanta, 1999: Scholars Press for USF Academic Commentary Series.
    V.   *The Tosefta. Translated from the Hebrew. The Fifth Division. Qodoshim.* Second printing: Atlanta, 1997: Scholars Press for USF Academic Commentary Series.
    VI. *The Tosefta. Translated from the Hebrew. The Sixth Division. Tohorot.* Second printing: Atlanta, 1990: Scholars Press for *South Florida Studies in the History of Judaism.* With a new preface.

Preface

Reprint: *The Tosefta in English.* I. *Zeraim, Moed, and Nashim.* Peabody, 2003: Hendrickson Publications. With a new introduction.
Reprint: *The Tosefta in English.* II. *Neziqin, Qodoshim, and Toharot.* Peabody, 2003: Hendrickson Publications.

The Babylonian Talmud. Translation and Commentary. Peabody, 2006: Hendrickson Publishing Co. Second printing of *The Talmud of Babylonia. An Academic Commentary.*

i. Berakhot
ii. Shabbat
iii. Erubin
iv. Pesahim
v. Yoma-Sukkah
vi. Taanit-Megillah-Moed Qatan-Hagigah
vii. Besah-Rosh Hashanah
viii. Yebamot
ix. Ketubot
x. Nedarim-Nazir
xi. Sotah-Gittin
xii. Qiddushin
xiii. Baba Qamma
xiv. Baba Mesia
xv. Baba Batra
xvi. Sanhedrin
xvii. Makkot-Abodah Zarah-Horayot
xviii. Shebuot-Zebahim
xix. Menahot
xx. Hullin
xxi. Bekhorot-Arakhin-Temurah
xxii. Keritot-Meilah-Tamid-Niddah

The Talmud of Babylonia. A Complete Outline. Atlanta, 1995-6: Scholars Press for *USF Academic Commentary Series.* Now: Lanham, MD. University Press of America

I.A. *Tractate Berakhot and the Division of Appointed Times. Berakhot, Shabbat, and Erubin.*
I.B. *Tractate Berakhot and the Division of Appointed Times. Pesahim through Hagigah.*
II.A. *The Division of Women. Yebamot through Ketubot*
II.B. *The Division of Women. Nedarim through Qiddushin*

III.A. *The Division of Damages. Baba Qamma through Baba Batra*
III.B. *The Division of Damages. Sanhedrin through Horayot*
IV.A. *The Division of Holy Things and Tractate Niddah. Zebahim through Hullin*
IV.B. *The Division of Holy Things and Tractate Niddah. Bekhorot through Niddah*

The Talmud of the Land of Israel. An Academic Commentary to the Second, Third, and Fourth Divisions. Atlanta, 1998-1999: Scholars Press for *USF Academic Commentary Series.* Now: Lanham, MD. University Press of America.

I. *Yerushalmi Tractate Berakhot*
II.A. *Yerushalmi Tractate Shabbat. Chapters One through Ten*
II.B. *Yerushalmi Tractate Shabbat. Chapters Eleven through Twenty-four. And the Structure of Yerushalmi Shabbat*
III. *Yerushalmi Tractate Erubin*
IV. *Yerushalmi Tractate Yoma*
V.A. *Yerushalmi Tractate Pesahim. Chapters One through Six.*
V.B. *Yerushalmi Tractate Pesahim. Chapters Seven through Ten. And the Structure of Yerushalmi Pesahim*
VI. *Yerushalmi Tractate Sukkah*
VII. *Yerushalmi Tractate Besah*
VIII. *Yerushalmi Tractate Taanit*
IX. *Yerushalmi Tractate Megillah*
X. *Yerushalmi Tractate Rosh Hashanah*
XI. *Yerushalmi Tractate Hagigah*
XII. *Yerushalmi Tractate Moed Qatan*
XIII.A.*Yerushalmi Tractate Yebamot. Chapters One through Ten*
XIII.B.*Yerushalmi Tractate Yebamot. Chapters Eleven through Seventeen. And the Structure of Yerushalmi Yebamot*
XIV. *Yerushalmi Tractate Ketubot*
XV. *Yerushalmi Tractate Nedarim*
XVI. *Yerushalmi Tractate Nazir*
XVII. *Yerushalmi Tractate Gittin*
XVIII.*Yerushalmi Tractate Qiddushin*
XIX. *Yerushalmi Tractate Sotah*
XX. *Yerushalmi Tractate Baba Qamma*
XXI. *Yerushalmi Tractate Baba Mesia*
XXII. *Yerushalmi Tractate Baba Batra*
XXIII.*Yerushalmi Tractate Sanhedrin*
XXIV. *Yerushalmi Tractate Makkot*

XXV. *Yerushalmi Tractate Shebuot*
XXVI. *Yerushalmi Tractate Abodah Zarah*
XXVII. *Yerushalmi Tractate Horayot*
XXVIII. *Yerushalmi Tractate Niddah*

The Talmud of The Land of Israel. An Outline of the Second, Third, and Fourth Divisions. Atlanta, 1995-6: Scholars Press for USF Academic Commentary Series. Now: Lanham, MD. University Press of America

- I.A *Tractate Berakhot and the Division of Appointed Times. Berakhot and Shabbat*
- I.B *Tractate Berakhot and the Division of Appointed Times. Erubin, Yoma, and Besah*
- I.C *Tractate Berakhot and the Division of Appointed Times. Pesahim and Sukkah*
- I.D *Tractate Berakhot and the Division of Appointed Times. Taanit, Megillah, Rosh Hashanah, Hagigah, and Moed Qatan*
- II.A. *The Division of Women. Yebamot to Nedarim*
- II.B. *The Division of Women. Nazir to Sotah*
- III.A *The Division of Damages and Tractate Niddah. Baba Qamma, Baba Mesia, Baba Batra, Horayot, and Niddah*
- III.B. *The Division of Damages and Tractate Niddah. Sanhedrin, Makkot, Shebuot, and Abodah Zarah*

The Two Talmuds Compared. Atlanta, 1995-6: Scholars Press for USF Academic Commentary Series. *The Talmud of the Land of Israel. An Academic Commentary to the Second, Third, and Fourth Divisions.* Atlanta, 1998-1999: Scholars Press for *USF Academic Commentary Series.* Now: Lanham, MD. University Press of America.

- I.A. *Tractate Berakhot and the Division of Appointed Times in the Talmud of the Land of Israel and the Talmud of Babylonia. Yerushalmi Tractate Berakhot*
- I.B. *Tractate Berakhot and the Division of Appointed Times in the Talmud of the Land of Israel and the Talmud of Babylonia. Tractate Shabbat.*
- I.C. *Tractate Berakhot and the Division of Appointed Times in the Talmud of the Land of Israel and the Talmud of Babylonia. Tractate Erubin*
- I.D. *Tractate Berakhot and the Division of Appointed Times in the Talmud of the Land of Israel and the Talmud of Babylonia. Tractates Yoma and Sukkah*

- I.E. *Tractate Berakhot and the Division of Appointed Times in the Talmud of the Land of Israel and the Talmud of Babylonia. Tractate Pesahim*
- I.F. *Tractate Berakhot and the Division of Appointed Times in the Talmud of the Land of Israel and the Talmud of Babylonia. Tractates Besah, Taanit, and Megillah*
- I.G. *Tractate Berakhot and the Division of Appointed Times in the Talmud of the Land of Israel and the Talmud of Babylonia. Tractates Rosh Hashanah, Hagigah, and Moed Qatan*
- II.A. *The Division of Women in the Talmud of the Land of Israel and the Talmud of Babylonia. Tractates Yebamot and Ketubot.*
- II.B. *The Division of Women in the Talmud of the Land of Israel and the Talmud of Babylonia. Tractates Nedarim, Nazir, and Sotah.*
- II.C. *The Division of Women in the Talmud of the Land of Israel and the Talmud of Babylonia. Tractates Qiddushin and Gittin.*
- III.A. *The Division of Damages and Tractate Niddah in the Talmud of the Land of Israel and the Talmud of Babylonia. Tractates Baba Qamma and Baba Mesia*
- III.B. *The Division of Damages and Tractate Niddah in the Talmud of the Land of Israel and the Talmud of Babylonia. Baba Batra and Niddah.*
- III.C. *The Division of Damages and Tractate Niddah. Sanhedrin and Makkot.*
- III.D. *The Division of Damages and Tractate Niddah. Shebuot, Abodah Zarah, and Horayot.*

The Components of the Rabbinic Documents: From the Whole to the Parts. I. *Sifra.* Atlanta, 1997: Scholars Press for USF Academic Commentary Series.

- Part i. *Introduction. And Parts One through Three, Chapters One through Ninety-Eight*
- Part ii. *Parts Four through Nine. Chapters Ninety-Nine through One Hundred Ninety-Four*
- Part iii. *Parts Ten through Thirteen. Chapters One Hundred Ninety-Five through Two Hundred Seventy-Seven*
- Part iv. *A Topical and Methodical Outline of Sifra*

The Components of the Rabbinic Documents: From the Whole to the Parts. II. *Esther Rabbah I.* Atlanta, 1997: Scholars Press for USF Academic Commentary Series.

Preface *xvii*

The Components of the Rabbinic Documents: From the Whole to the Parts. III. *Ruth Rabbah.* Atlanta, 1997: Scholars Press for USF Academic Commentary Series.

The Components of the Rabbinic Documents: From the Whole to the Parts. IV. *Lamentations Rabbati.* Atlanta, 1997: Scholars Press for USF Academic Commentary Series.

The Components of the Rabbinic Documents: From the Whole to the Parts. V. *Song of Songs Rabbah.* Atlanta, 1997: Scholars Press for USF Academic Commentary Series.

    Part i.   *Introduction. And Parashiyyot One through Four*
    Part ii. *Parashiyyot Five through Eight. And a Topical and Methodical Outline of Song of Songs Rabbah*

The Components of the Rabbinic Documents: From the Whole to the Parts. VI. *The Fathers Attributed to Rabbi Nathan.* Atlanta, 1997: Scholars Press for USF Academic Commentary Series.

The Components of the Rabbinic Documents: From the Whole to the Parts. VII. *Sifré to Deuteronomy.* Atlanta, 1997: Scholars Press for USF Academic Commentary Series.

    Part i.   *Introduction. And Parts One through Four*
    Part ii. *Parts Five through Ten*
    Part iii. *A Topical and Methodical Outline of Sifré to Deuteronomy*

The Components of the Rabbinic Documents: From the Whole to the Parts. VIII. *Mekhilta Attributed to R. Ishmael.* Atlanta, 1997: Scholars Press for USF Academic Commentary Series

    Part i.   *Introduction. Pisha, Beshallah and Shirata*
    Part ii   *Vayassa, Amalek, Bahodesh, Neziqin, Kaspa and Shabbata*
    Part iii. *A Topical and Methodical Outline of Mekhilta Attributed to R. Ishmael.*

The Components of the Rabbinic Documents: From the Whole to the Parts. IX. Atlanta, 1998: Scholars Press for USF Academic Commentary Series. Now: Lanham, University Press of America.

Part i. *Introduction. Genesis Rabbah Chapters One through Twenty-One*
Part ii. *Genesis Rabbah Chapters Twenty-Two through Forty-Eight*
Part iii. *Genesis Rabbah Chapters Forty-Nine through Seventy-Three*
Part iv. *Genesis Rabbah Chapters Seventy-Four through One Hundred*
Part v. *A Topical and Methodical Outline of Genesis Rabbah. Bereshit through Vaere, Chapters One through Fifty-Seven*
Part vi. *A Topical and Methodical Outline of Genesis Rabbah. Hayye Sarah through Miqqes. Chapters Fifty-Eight through One Hundred*

The Components of the Rabbinic Documents: From the Whole to the Parts. X. *Leviticus Rabbah*. Atlanta, 1998: Scholars Press for USF Academic Commentary Series.

Part i. *Introduction. Leviticus Rabbah Parashiyyot One through Seventeen*
Part ii. *Leviticus Rabbah Parashiyyot Eighteen through Thirty-Seven*
Part iii. *Leviticus Rabbah. A Topical and Methodical Outline*

The Components of the Rabbinic Documents: From the Whole to the Parts. XI. *Pesiqta deRab Kahana*. Atlanta, 1998: Scholars Press for USF Academic Commentary Series.

Part i. *Introduction. Pesiqta deRab Kahana Pisqaot One through Eleven*
Part ii. *Pesiqta deRab Kahana Pisqaot Twelve through Twenty-Eight*
Part iii. *Pesiqta deRab Kahana. A Topical and Methodical Outline*

The Components of the Rabbinic Documents: From the Whole to the Parts. XII. *Sifré to Numbers*. Atlanta, 1998: Scholars Press for USF Academic Commentary Series.

Part i. *Introduction. Pisqaot One through Eighty-Four*
Part ii. *Pisqaot Eighty-Five through One Hundred Twenty-Two*
Part iii. *Pisqaot One Hundred Twenty-Three through One Hundred Sixty-One*
Part iv. *Sifré to Numbers. A Topical and Methodical Outline*

The Rabbinic Midrash. Peabody, 2006: Hendrickson Publishing Co. Second printing, in twelve volumes, of *The Components of the Rabbinic Documents: From the Whole to the Parts*.

Preface

The plan of the project as a whole is as follows:

Jeremiah in Talmud and Midrash. A Source Book. Lanham, 2006: University Press of America STUDIES IN JUDAISM SERIES.

Amos in Talmud and Midrash. A Source Book. Lanham, 2006: University Press of America STUDIES IN JUDAISM SERIES.

Hosea in Talmud and Midrash. A Source Book. Lanham, 2006: University Press of America STUDIES IN JUDAISM SERIES.

Joel in Talmud and Midrash. A Source Book. Lanham: University Press of America STUDIES IN JUDAISM SERIES

Obadiah in Talmud and Midrash. A Source Book. Lanham: University Press of America STUDIES IN JUDAISM SERIES

Jonah in Talmud and Midrash. A Source Book. Lanham: University Press of America STUDIES IN JUDAISM SERIES

Micah in Talmud and Midrash. A Source Book. Lanham: University Press of America STUDIES IN JUDAISM SERIES

Nahum in Talmud and Midrash. A Source Book. Lanham: University Press of America STUDIES IN JUDAISM SERIES

Habakkuk in Talmud and Midrash. A Source Book. Lanham: University Press of America STUDIES IN JUDAISM SERIES

Zephaniah in Talmud and Midrash. A Source Book. Lanham: University Press of America STUDIES IN JUDAISM SERIES

Haggai in Talmud and Midrash. A Source Book. Lanham: University Press of America STUDIES IN JUDAISM SERIES

Zechariah in Talmud and Midrash. A Source Book. Lanham: University Press of America STUDIES IN JUDAISM SERIES

Malachi in Talmud and Midrash. A Source Book. Lanham: University Press of America STUDIES IN JUDAISM SERIES

Isaiah in Talmud and Midrash. A Source Book. Lanham: University Press of America STUDIES IN JUDAISM SERIES

Ezekiel in Talmud and Midrash. A Source Book. Lanham: University Press of America STUDIES IN JUDAISM SERIES

I thought I would analyze the results of the anthologies prophet by prophet and so produced *Rabbi Jeremiah* (Lanham, 2006: University Press of America. But it quickly became apparent that I could not answer my analytical questions on the basis of the data pertaining to individual prophets, and the results were obviously anomalous. Since my purpose is to clarify the character of Rabbinic Judaism, with prophecy as the variable and Rabbinic Judaism as the base, I had to create my database and collect and arrange the data on all the prophets before I could formulate my program of inquiry.

I am pleased to acknowledge the advice in planning this project of colleagues in biblical studies, in particular Richard E. Friedman, University of Georgia; Alan Cooper, The Jewish Theological Seminary of America; Bernard Levinson, University of Minnesota; and Jon Levenson, Harvard University. Their advice is always valuable. For planning the project as a whole I further consulted William Scott Green, University of Rochester, Herbert Basser, Queen's University, and Bruce D. Chilton, Bard College.

Jacob Neusner
Research Professor of Theology
Senior Fellow, Institute of Advanced Theology
Bard College
Annandale-on-Hudson, New York 12504 5000

ENDNOTE

[1] Nicholas Ostler, *Empires of the Word. A Language History of the World* (N.Y. 2005: HarperCollins), p. 13.

1

Hosea in the Mishnah, Tractate Abot, and the Tosefta

MISHNAH

Nothing pertains.

TRACTATE ABOT

I find no references to Hosea.

TOSEFTA

TOSEFTA SHABBAT
7:4. A. He who asks his staff, saying, "Shall I go? Shall I not go?" — lo, this is one of "the ways of the Amorites."
B. Even though this is no direct proof [in Scripture] for this proposition, there is at least a hint about it:
C. "My people inquire of a thing of wood, and their staff gives them oracles" (Hos. 4:12).

Treating the staff as a source of prophesy is explicitly condemned by Hosea.

TOSEFTA SOTAH
7:2. A. The oath imposed by judges — how so?
E. In regard to all the transgressions which are mentioned in the Torah, they exact retribution from the man himself. But with reference to this one, they exact retribution from the man and from the entire world, so that the transgression of the entire world is blamed on him,

F. since it is said, "Swearing and lying . . . therefore does the land mourn, and every one who dwells therein does languish" (Hos. 4:2-3).
G. In regard to all the transgressions which are mentioned in the Torah, they exact retribution from the man himself, but in this case, they exact retribution from him and from his relatives,
H. as it is said, "Suffer not your mouth to bring your flesh into guilt" (Qoh. 5:5), and flesh refers only to one's relative, as it is said, "From your flesh do not hide yourself" (Is. 58:7).

The one who takes a false oath brings down punishment not only on himself but on the land and all its inhabitants by reason of falsely swearing and lying, so Hosea.

2

Hosea in Sifra, the Two Sifrés and the Mekhilta Attributed to R. Ishmael

SIFRA

I find no reference to Hosea.

SIFRÉ TO NUMBERS

SIFRÉ TO NUMBERS XXI:III
1. A. "The man shall be free from iniquity " (Num. 5:29-31):
   B. [The husband should not feel guilty if the wife dies, and he should not say,] "Woe is me, for I have put an Israelite woman to death.
   C. "Woe is me, for I have caused the humiliation of an Israelite woman.
   D. "Woe is me, for I used to have sexual relations with a woman who was in fact unclean."
   E. Therefore it is said, ." ..The man shall be free from iniquity."
   F. Ben Azzai says, "Scripture speaks of a case in which the woman emerges as clean. Since she has brought herself into this affair, she too should not escape some sort of punishment. Therefore it is said, 'The man shall be free from iniquity, but the woman shall bear her iniquity.'"
   G. R. Aqiba says, "Scripture comes to teach you the lesson that the end of the matter is death: 'Her body shall swell and her thigh shall fall away' (Num. 5:27).
   H. "Why then is it said, 'The man shall be free from iniquity, but the woman shall bear her iniquity'?
   I. "The man is free of sin, but that woman will bear her sin.
   J. "It is then not in accord with the statement, 'I shall not visit your daughters when they turn into prostitutes, nor your daughters-in-law when they commit adultery, for men themselves go aside with harlots and sacrifice with cult prostitutes, and a people without understanding shall come to ruin' (Hos. 4:14).

3

K. "He said to them, 'Since you run after whores, the bitter water will not put your wives to the test.'
L. "That is why it is said, 'The man shall be free from iniquity' — that is with reference to that sin [of which Hosea spoke. The husband is not guilty of having had sexual relations with a whore, though his wife is guilty, because he did not realize it, and, when he did, he took the correct action.]"

Hosea treats female and male sexual deviance as equivalently deplorable, and that requires harmonization with Num. 5:29-31.

SIFRÉ TO NUMBERS XXIII:III
1. A. "..he shall separate:"
   B. The sense of the word "separate oneself" in every passage is only abstinence, and so Scripture states [using the same word], "And they shall keep themselves separate from the holy things of the children of Israel" (Lev. 22:2).
   C. And it further says, "You shall not harvest the crop that grows from fallen grain nor gather in the grapes from the unpruned vines" (Lev. 25:5).]
   D. And again: "They resorted to Baalpeor and consecrated themselves to a thing of shame" (Hos. 9:10).
   E. And again: "Am I to lament and abstain in the fifth month as I have done for so many years?" (Zech. 7:3).
   F. So, in all, the sense of the word "separate oneself" in every passage is only abstinence.

Hosea contributes to a philological discussion.

SIFRÉ TO NUMBERS XLII:II
3. H. R. Eleazar Haqqappar says, "Great is peace, for the seal of all blessings is only peace, as it is said, 'The Lord bless you and keep you, the Lord make his face to shine upon you and be gracious to you,] the Lord lift up his countenance upon you [and give you peace.'"
   I. R. Eleazar, son of R. Eleazar Haqqappar, says, "Great is peace, for even if the Israelites worship idols but keep the peace among them, it is as if the Omnipresent says, 'Satan shall never touch them,' as it is said, 'Ephraim is joined to idols, let him alone' (Hos. 4:17).
   J. "But when they are divided by dissension: 'They love shame more than their glory' (Hos. 4:18 [RSV).
   K. "Lo, great is peace and despised is dissension."

Even though the Israelites worship idols, God ignores their sin if they live in peace, but if they give way to dissension, they are shamed.

2. Hosea in Sifra, the Two Sifrés and the Mekhilta Attributed to R. Ishmael

SIFRÉ TO NUMBERS CXXXI:II

2. A. Now they came and dwelt in Shittim — in a place of foolishness.
   B. At that time the Ammonites and Moabites went and built for themselves enclosures from Beth Hajeshimoth to the Snowy Mountain, and they installed there women selling every kind of delicacy. The Israelites would eat and drink.
   C. He made tents for them from the snowy mountain to Beth Hajeshimoth [north to south] and put women in them, selling all manner of goodies] [B. San. 106b: whores in them, old women outside, young women inside.
   D. "When an Israelite was eating and drinking and carousing and going out for walks in the market to buy something from the old lady, [the old lady would say to him, 'Don't you want some linen clothes?"]
   E. The old lady would offer them at true value, and the girl would call him and say to him from inside, "Come and buy it for yourself for less."
   F. So he would guy it from her. This would happen two or three times, and then [the young one] would say to him, "Come on in, you are at home here. Sit down and make a choice for yourself." He would come in. Gourds of Ammonite wine would be set near her. (At this point the wine of gentiles had not yet been forbidden to Israelites.) She would say to him, 'Do you want to drink a cup of wine?'
   G. "When he had drunk a cup of wine, he would become inflamed. He said to her, "Submit to me." She would than take her the image of Peor from her bosom and said to him, "Worship this."
   H. He would say to her, "Now am I going to bow down to an idol?" [Sanhedrin: "Am I not a Jew?'
   I. She would say to him, "What difference does it make to you? Do they ask anything more from you than that you bare yourself?" [Sanhedrin:] But he did not know that that was how this idol was served.] So he would bare himself to it.
   J. On this basis, sages have said: **He who bares himself to Baal Peor — lo, this is the proper manner of worshipping it. And he who tosses a stone to Hermes — that is the proper manner of worshipping it [M. San. 7:6].**
   K. "'And not only so, but I shall not let you do so until you deny the Torah of Moses, your master!'
   L. "As it is said, 'They went in to Baal-peor and separated themselves unto that shame, and their abominations were according as they loved' (Hos. 9:10)."
   M. So he would become inflamed. He said to her, "Submit to me." She would say to him, "If you want me to submit to you, separate yourself from the Torah of Moses, and he did just that, as it is said, "But they came to Baal Peor and consecrated themselves to Baal and became detestable like the thing they loved" (Hos. 9:10).

N. In they end they arrange idolatrous banquets for them, and they called them and they ate, as it is said, "These invited the people to the sacrifices of their gods, and the people ate and bowed down to their god."
O. R. Eleazar b. Shammua says, "Just as it is not possible for a nail to be removed from the door without splinters, so it was not possible for the Israelites to separate from Peor without the loss of life."

Hosea indicts the Israelites for their idolatry at Baal Peor.

Sifré to Numbers CXXXI:I

1. E. R. Aqiba says, "Every passage contiguous to another provides an appropriate occasion for a lesson to be derived therefrom."
   F. Rabbi says, "There are many passages near one another or distant from one another as east from west [that provide occasions for lessons to be learned]."
   M. And along these same lines, you say, "Because you are not my people, and I am not your God" (Hos. 1:9).
   N. And it says, "Yet the number of the people of Israel shall be like the sand of the sea, which can be neither measured nor numbered, and in the place where it was said to them, [You are not my people,'] it shall be said to them, 'sons of the living God'" (Hos. 1:10).
   O. Now what has one thing to do with the other?
   P. The matter may be compared to the case of a king who got mad at his wife. He sent for a scribe to come and write a writ of divorce for her. Before the scribe got there, however, the king was reconciled with his wife. Said the king, "It is impossible that the scribe should go forth from here empty-handed. But say to him, 'Come and inscribe that I double for her the value of her marriage-settlement [should I die or divorce her].'"
   Q. That is the point of the statement, "Because you are not my people, and I am not your God" (Hos. 1:9), followed by "Yet the number of the people of Israel shall be like the sand of the sea, which can be neither measured nor numbered, and in the place where it was said to them, [You are not my people,'] it shall be said to them, 'sons of the living God'" (Hos. 1:10).
   R. Along these same lines, you say, "Samaria shall bear her guilt because she has rebelled against her God; they shall fall by the sword, their little ones shall be dashed in pieces, and their pregnant women ripped open" (Hos. 13:16).
   S. And it further says, "Return, O Israel, to the Lord your God, for you have stumbled because of your iniquity. Take with you words and return to the Lord" (Hos. 14:1).
   T. Now what has one thing to do with the other?
   U. The matter may be compared to the case of a city that rebelled against the king. The king sent a general to destroy it. The general was shrewd and capable. He said to them, "Take some time [about

2. Hosea in Sifra, the Two Sifrés and the Mekhilta Attributed to R. Ishmael

this rebellion of yours and stop it], for if not, I shall do to you what I did to such and such a city and its allies, to such and such a district and its allies."

V. So Scripture states, "Samaria shall bear her guilt because she has rebelled against her God; they shall fall by the sword, their little ones shall be dashed in pieces, and their pregnant women ripped open" (Hos. 13:16)., but further, "Return, O Israel, to the Lord your God, for you have stumbled because of your iniquity. Take with you words and return to the Lord" (Hos. 14:1).

Hosea's juxtapositions at Hos. 1:9, 10 are interpreted. Because the Israelites reconciled with God, "You are ot my people" becomes "the number of the people shall be like the sand of the sea, and instead of 'you are not my people' you are 'sons of the living God.' Hosea's prophecy of Samaria is contrasted with his counsel "return Israel," and these represent contrasting choices for Israel, illustrating Aqiba's general principle.

SIFRÉ TO DEUTERONOMY

SIFRÉ TO DEUTERONOMY XXXIX:II

6. A. Another matter: just as rain is a blessing, so dew is a blessing.
   B. And so Scripture says, "So God give you of the dew of heaven" (Gen. 27:28).
   C. And Scripture further says, "My doctrine shall drop as the rain" (Dt. 32:2).
   D. "I will be as the dew to Israel" (Hos. 14:6).
   E. "And the remnant of Jacob shall be...as dew from the Lord" (Mic. 5:6).

Hosea contributes a case for the catalogue on dew.

SIFRÉ TO DEUTERONOMY XLI:II

1. A. "That you may learn them and observe to do them" (Dt. 5:1):
   B. The phrasing of this clause indicates that deed depends on learning, and learning does not depend on deed.
   C. And so we find that a more severe penalty pertains to [neglect of] learning more than to [neglect of doing required] deeds.
   D. For it is said, "Hear the word of the Lord, you children of Israel. For the Lord has a controversy with the inhabitants of the land, because there is no truth nor mercy nor knowledge of God in the land" (Hos. 4:1).
   E. "...there is no truth:" truthful words are not said: "Buy the truth and do not sell it [also wisdom, instruction, and understanding]" (Prov. 23:23).
   F. "...nor mercy:" merciful words are not said: "The earth, O Lord, is full of your mercy" (Ps. 119:64).

G. "...nor knowledge of God in the land:" knowledgeable words are not said: "My people are destroyed for lack of knowledge [because you have rejected knowledge, I will also reject you, that you shall not be a priest of mine, seeing that you have forgotten the law of your God, I also will forget your children]" (Hos. 4:6).

Hosea 4:1 proves that Torah-learning takes priority over deeds.

Sifré to Deuteronomy XLVII:II
2. A. R. Simeon b. Yohai says, "Like seven kinds of happiness will be the faces of the righteous when they receive the face of the Presence of God in the age to come.
   B. "And these are they:
   C. "'But they who love him shall be as the sun when he goes forth in his might' (Judges 5:31).
   D. "'Fair as the moon shall they be, clear as the sun' (Song 6:10).
   E. "'And they that are wise shall shine as the brightness of the firmament and they that turn the many to righteous as the stars for ever and ever' (Dan. 12:3).
   F. "'They shall run to and fro like lightning' (Nahum 2:5).
   G. "'They shall be as the leader upon lilies' (Ps. 45:1).
   H. "'And his beauty shall be as the olive tree' (Hos. 14:7).
   I. "'A song of ascents' (Ps. 121:1).
   J. "That is, 'a song for the one who is destined to make ascents for those who serve him.'"

Hosea contributes one of the seven kinds of happiness that will shine from the faces of the righteous in the age to come.

Sifré to Deuteronomy XLVII:IV
1. A. Lo, Scripture says, "Yet the number of the children of Israel shall be as the sand of the sea, which cannot be measured or numbered" (Hos. 2:1).
   B. When the Israelites carry out the will of the Omnipresent: "...as the sand of the sea which cannot be measured or numbered."
   C. And if not, "yet the number of the children of Israel shall be."
2. A. And Scripture says, "[One thousand shall flee at the rebuke of one, at the rebuke of five shall you flee,] until you are left as a beacon upon the top of a mountain" (Is. 34 9:17).
   B. "For thus says the Lord God, the city that went forth a thousand shall have a hundred left" (Amos 5:3).
3. A. Another matter concerning the verse, "Yet the number of the children of Israel shall be as the sand of the sea, which cannot be measured or numbered" (Hos. 2:1):
   B. "Yet the number of the children of Israel:" this refers to the count done in heaven.

C. "...shall be as the sand of the sea:" this refers to the count done by man.

No. 1 contrasts Israel's fate when obedient and Israel's fate when disobedient. No. 3 has Israel counted in heaven and on earth.

Sifré to Deuteronomy XCVI:IV
1. A. "You are children of the Lord your God. You shall not gash yourselves or shave the front of your heads because of the dead. For you are a people consecrated to the Lord your God: the Lord your God chose you from among all other peoples on earth to be his treasured people" (Dt. 14:1-2):
   B. R. Judah says, "If you conduct yourselves in the way good children do, then you are children, and if not, you are not children [of the Lord your God]."
   C. R. Meir says, "One way or another, 'You are children of the Lord your God.'"
   D. And so Scripture says, "Yet the number of the children of Israel shall be as the sand of the sea...it shall be said to them, 'You are the children of the living God'" (Hos. 2:1).

Israel remains children of the living God whatever their moral condition, so Hosea.

Sifré to Deuteronomy CLXXI:III
2. A. "Let no one be found [among you who consigns his son or daughter to the fire, or who is an augur, a soothsayer, a diviner, a sorcerer, one who casts spells, or one who consults ghosts or familiar spirits, or one who inquires of the dead. For anyone who does such things is abhorrent to the Lord, and it is because of those abhorrent things that the Lord your God is dispossessing them before you. You must be wholehearted with the Lord your God. Those nations that you are about to dispossess do indeed resort to soothsayers and augurs; to you, however, the Lord your God has not assigned the like]" (Dt. 18:9-14). What is an augurer?
   B. It is one who takes hold of his staff and says, "...whether I should go, whether I should not go."
   C. So it is said, "My people ask counsel of their stock, and their staff tells them what to do" (Hos. 4:12).

Hosea supplies the sense of the indicated language.

Sifré to Deuteronomy CCCV:I
3. A. R. Nathan says, "Moses was distressed in his heart that one of his sons did not stand forth [as leader]. Said to him the Holy One, blessed be He, 'Why are you distressed in your heart? Is it that one of your sons has not stood forth?

B. "'Now are not the sons of your brother, Aaron, tantamount to your own sons.

C. "'And so too the man whom I am setting up over Israel will go and stand at the door of Eleazar [the priest, Aaron's son].'

D. "To what may this be compared? To a mortal king who had a son who was not worthy of the throne. He took the throne from him and gave it to the son of his ally.

E. "He said to him, 'Even though I have assigned greatness to you, go and stand at my son's door.'

F. "So said the Holy One, blessed be He, 'Even though I have assigned greatness to you, go and stand at the door of Eleazar.'

G. "That is in line with this verse of Scripture: 'And he will stand before Eleazar the priest' (Num. 27:21).

H. "At that moment Moses's strength returned, and he encouraged Joshua before the presence of all Israel, as it is said, 'And then Moses called Joshua and said to him in the sight of all Israel, 'Be strong and resolute, [for it is you who shall go with this people in the land that the Lord swore to their fathers to give them, and it is you who shall apportion it to them. And the Lord himself will go before you. He will be with you. He will not fail you or forsake you. Fear not and be not dismayed]' (Dt. 31:7-8).

I. "He said to him, 'I hand this people over to you. They are still lambs. They are still children. Do not go nitpicking for every little thing that they do. For even their Lord did not go nitpicking for every little thing that they do.'

J. "And so Scripture says, 'When Israel was a child, then I loved him' (Hos. 11:1)."

K. R. Nehemiah says, "'I do not have the right, but [if] I had the right, I should bring them in "beside shepherds' tents" (Song 1:8), to dwell therein.'"

Israel in the wilderness was like a child to God.

SIFRÉ TO DEUTERONOMY CCCVI:I

1. A. ["Give ear, O heavens, let me speak; let the earth hear the words I utter! May my discourse come down as the rain, my speech distill as the dew, like showers on young growths, like droplets on the grass. For the name of the Lord I proclaim; give glory to our God" (Dt. 32:1-3).]

B. "Give ear, O heavens, let me speak:"

C. R. Meir says, "When the Israelites enjoyed merit, they would give testimony against themselves.

D. "So it is said, 'And Joshua said to the people, "You are witnesses against yourselves"' (Josh. 24:22).

E. "When they went wrong, as it is said, 'Ephraim surrounds me with lies, and the house of Israel with deceit' (Hos. 12:1),

F. "the tribes of Judah and Benjamin gave testimony against them.

2. Hosea in Sifra, the Two Sifrés and the Mekhilta Attributed to R. Ishmael

G. "So it is said, 'and now, inhabitants of Jerusalem and men of Judah, judge, I ask, between me and my vineyard. What could have been done more to my vineyard?' (Is. 5:3-4).

H. "When the tribes of Judah and Benjamin went wrong, as it is said, 'Judah has dealt treacherously' (Mal. 2:11),

I. "the prophets gave testimony against them.

J. "So it is said, 'Yet the Lord forewarned Israel and Judah by the hand of every prophet' (2 Kgs. 17:13).

K. "When they did wrong to the prophets, as it is said, 'But they mocked the messengers of God' (2 Chr. 36:16),

L. "the heavens gave testimony against them.

M. "So it is said, 'I call heaven and earth to witness against you this day' (Dt. 4:26).

N. "When they did wrong to heaven, as it is said, 'Do you not see what they do...the children gather wood, the fathers kindle fire, the women knead the dough, to make cakes to the queen of heaven' (Jer. 7:17-18),

O. "the earth gave testimony against them.

P. "So it is said, 'Hear, O earth, see I will bring evil' (Jer. 6:16).

Q. "When they did wrong to the earth, as it is said, 'Yes, their altars shall be as heaps in the furrows of the field' (Hos. 12:12),

R. "the roads gave testimony against them.

S. "So it is said, 'Thus says the Lord, Stand in the ways and see' (Jer. 6:16).

T. "When they did wrong to the roads, as it is said, 'You have built your high place at every head of the way' (Ez. 16:26),

U. "the gentiles gave testimony against them.

V. "So it is said, 'Therefore hear, you nations, and know, O Congregation, what is against them,' (Jer. 6:18).

W. "When they did wrong to the gentiles, as it is said, 'But our fathers mixed with the nations and learned their works' (Ps. 106:35),

X. "he called the mountains to give testimony against them.

Y. "So it is said, 'Hear, O you mountains, the Lord's controversy' (Mic. 6:2).

Z. "When they did wrong to the mountains, as it is said, 'They sacrifice upon the tops of the mountains' (Hos. 4:13),

AA. "he called the oxen to give testimony against them.

BB. "So it is said, 'The ox knows his owner...' (Is. 1:3).

CC. "When they did wrong to the oxen, as it is said, 'Thus they exchanged their glory for the likeness of an ox that eats grass' (Ps. 106:20),

DD. "he called the fowl to give testimony against them.

EE. "So it is said, 'Yes, the stork in heaven knows her appointed times...' (Jer. 8:7).

FF. "When they did wrong to the domesticated beasts, wild beasts, and fowl, as it is said, 'So I went in and saw and behold, every detestable form of creeping things and beasts' (Ez. 8:10),

GG. "he called the fish to give testimony against them.
HH. "So it is said, 'Or speak to the earth and it shall teach you, and the fishes of the sea shall declare you' (Job 12:8).
II. "When they did wrong to the fish, as it is said, 'And make man as the fish of the sea' (Hab. 1:14),
JJ. "he called the ant to give testimony against them: 'Go to the ant, you sluggard...which provides her bread in the summer' (Prov. 6:6-8)."
KK. R. Simeon b. Eleazar says, "Sad indeed is the man who has to learn from an ant Had he learned and done what he learned, he would have been sad, but he had to learn from the ant's ways and did not even learn!"

Hosea testifies that Israel sinned against God and gives testimony against themselves. So too, when they sinned, the earth gave testimony against them, as did the mountains.

Sifré to Deuteronomy CCCVI:II

1. A. The Community of Israel is going to say before the Holy One, blessed be He, "Lord of the world, lo, my witnesses are present."
   B. For so it is said, "I call heaven and earth to witness against you this day" (Dt. 30:19).
   C. He will say to her, "Lo, I shall remove them."
   D. For so it is said, "For behold, I create a new heaven and a new earth" (Is. 65:17).
   E. She will say to him, "Lord of the world, lo, I see the places in which I did wrong, and I am ashamed."
   F. For so it is said, "See your way in the valley..." (Jer. 2:23).
   G. He will say to her, "Lo, I shall remove them."
   H. For so it is said, "Every valley shall be lifted up" (Is. 40:4).
   I. She will say to him, "Lord of the world, Lo, my [bad] name endures."
   J. He will say to her, "Lo, I shall remove it."
   K. For so it is said, "And you shall be called by a new name" (Is. 62:2).
   L. She will say to him, "Lord of the world, Lo, my name endures on account of my Baal-worship."
   M. He will say to her, "Lo, I shall remove it."
   N. For so it is said, "For I will take away the names of the Baalim" (Hos. 2:19).
   O. She will then say before him, "Lord of the world, none the less, children of my house make mention of it."
   P. He will say to her, "And they shall no more be mentioned by their name" (Hos. 2:19).

Hosea assures Israel that God will remove evidence of their Baal-worship.

2. Hosea in Sifra, the Two Sifrés and the Mekhilta Attributed to R. Ishmael

SIFRÉ TO DEUTERONOMY CCCVI:I CCCVI:III
1. A. The next day [the community of Israel[is going to say before him, "Lord of the world, in any event you have written, 'If a man puts away his wife and she leaves him and becomes another man's wife, may he return to her again?' (Jer. 3:1)."
   B. He will say to her, "Did I not write only 'a man'? But is it not also said, 'For I am God, not man' (Hos. 11:9)."
2. A. Another statement:
   B. "And are you divorcées in relationship to me, house of Israel?
   C. "And has it not been said, 'Thus says the Lord, where is your mother's writ of divorce, with which I sent her forth? Or which of my creditors is it to whom I have sold you?' (Is. 50:1)."

God has the power to reengage with Israel even after Israel was divorced from God and worshipped idols, so Hosea.

SIFRÉ TO DEUTERONOMY CCCVI:X
1. A. Another teaching concerning the verse, "Give ear, O heavens, let me speak:"
   B. R. Benaiah would say, "When someone is declared guilty in a trial, only the witnesses against him are the ones who lay hand on him first of all, as it is said, 'The hand of the witnesses shall be first upon him to put him to death' (Dt. 17:7).
   C. "And afterward everyone else comes along, as it is said, 'And afterward the hand of all the people' (Dt. 17:7).
   D. "So too, when the Israelites do not do what God wants them to, what is said concerning them?
   E. "'And the anger of the Lord be kindled against you and he shut up the heaven' (Dt. 11:17).
   F. "And afterward various punishments come along, as it is said, 'And you perish quickly from off the good land which the Lord gives you" (Dt. 11:17).
   G. "When the Israelites do what God wants them to, what is said concerning them?
   H. "'And it shall come to pass in that day, I will respond, says the Lord, I will respond to the heavens...and I will sow her unto me in the land' (Hos. 2:23-25)."

When Israel obeys God, God responds by bringing prosperity to the land.

SIFRÉ TO DEUTERONOMY CCCVI:XV
1. A. "May my discourse come down as the rain, [my speech distill as the dew, like showers on young growths, like droplets on the grass. For the name of the Lord I proclaim; give glory to our God]:"
   B. The meaning of "my discourse" is only "words of Torah, as it is said, "For I have given a good doctrine to you, my Torah, do not abandon it" (Prov. 4:2).

      C.   And further: "Receive my instruction and not silver" (Prov. 8:10).
      D.   "Instruction" means only "words of Torah," as it is said, "Hear, my son, the instruction of your father, and do not forsake the Torah of your mother" (Prov. 1:8).
      E.   And further: "Hear instruction and be wise, and refuse it not" (Prov. 8:33).
      F.   "Take fast hold of instruction, do not let her go" (Prov. 4:13).
      G.   "Take with you words and return to the Lord" (Hos. 14:34).
      H.   "Words" mean only "words of Torah:" "These words the Lord spoke to all your assembly" (Dt. 5:19).

God's discourse takes place in words of Torah, and that is his instruction, so Hosea.

SIFRÉ TO DEUTERONOMY CCCXIII:II

1. A. ["He found him in a desert region, in an empty howling waste. He engirded him, watched over him, guarded him as the pupil of his eye. Like an eagle who rouses his nestlings, gliding down to his young, so did he spread his wings and take him, bear him along on his pinions; the Lord alone did guide him, no alien god at his side" (Dt. 32:10-12).] Another teaching concerning, "He found him in a desert region:"
     B. This refers to Israel, as it is said, "I found Israel like grapes in a desert" (Hos. 9:10).
2. A. "...in an empty howling waste:"
     B. It was in a difficult situation, a place in which were marauding bands and thugs.
3. A. "He engirded him:"
     B. Before Mount Sinai, as it is said, "And you shall set a boundary for the people round about" (Ex. 19:12).
4. A. "...watched over him:"
     B. Through the Ten Commandments.
     C. This teaches that when the act of speech went forth from the mouth of the Holy One, blessed be He, the Israelites saw it and understood it and knew how much amplification was contained therein, how much law was contained therein, how many possibilities for lenient rules, for strict rulings, how many analogies were contained therein.

Hosea reinforces the Torah's reference to God's finding Israel in the desert.

SIFRÉ TO DEUTERONOMY CCCXIII:IV

1. A. Another teaching concerning, "He found him in a desert region:"
     B. This refers to the age to come.
     C. So Scripture says, "Therefore behold, I will seduce her and bring her into the wilderness and speak tenderly to her" (Hos. 2:16).

2. Hosea in Sifra, the Two Sifrés and the Mekhilta Attributed to R. Ishmael

In the age to come God and Israel will meet once more in the desert.

Sifré to Deuteronomy CCCXXIX:II
1. A. Another interpretation of the phrase, "I deal death and give life; I wound and I will heal, none can deliver from my hand:"
   B. This is one of the four promises in which to the Israelites is given an indication of the resurrection of the dead.
   C. [The others are these:] "Let me die the death of the righteous, and let my end be like his" (Num. 23:10)
   D. "Let Reuben live and not die" (Dt. 33:6)
   E. "After two days he will revive us" (Hos. 6:2).
   F. Might I suppose that the death applies to one person, the life to another?
   G. Scripture says, "I wound and I will heal."
   H. Just as the wounding and healing pertain to a single individual, so the death and life pertain to a single individual [thus showing that Scripture contains evidence for the belief in the resurrection of the dead].

Hosea explicitly speaks of the resurrection of the dead on the third day after death.

Sifré to Deuteronomy CCCXLII:I
1. A. "This is the blessing with which Moses, the man of God, bade the Israelites farewell before he died" (Dt. 33:1):
   B. Since Moses had earlier said to the Israelites harsh words, for example,
   C. "The wasting of hunger...without shall the sword bereave" (Dt. 32:24-5),
   D. "Also in Horeb you made the Lord angry" (Dt. 9:8),
   E. "You have been rebellious against the Lord" (Dt. 9:7),
   F. now he went and said to them words of comfort: "This is the blessing with which Moses, the man of God, bade the Israelites farewell before he died."
2. A. And from him did all of the prophets learn [how to conduct themselves].
   B. For they would first say to Israel harsh words and then go and say to them words of comfort.
   C. Now, for instance, you have among the prophets none whose words were more harsh than Hosea.
   D. When he began to speak, he said, "Give them, O Lord, whatever you will give. Give them a miscarrying womb" (Hos. 9:14)
   E. But then he spoke to them words of comfort:
   F. "His branches shall spread, his beauty shall be as the olive tree, and his fragrance as Lebanon. They who dwell under his shadow shall again make grain grown and shall blossom as the vine" (Hos. 144:7-8).

G. "I will heal their backsliding, I will love them freely...I will be as the dew to Israel, he shall blossom as the lily" (Hos. 14:5-6).

Hosea spoke harshly at first, then he comforted Israel, all in the model of Moses.

MEKHILTA ATTRIBUTED TO R. ISHMAEL

MEKHILTA ATTRIBUTED TO R. ISHMAEL XIII:III.
3. A. "So the people took their dough before it was leavened:"
   B. This indicates that they had kneaded the dough but had not sufficed to allow it to leaven before they were redeemed.
   C. And so it will be in the future redemption: "Who ceases to stir from the kneading of the dough until it be leavened. On the day of our king the princes make him sick" (Hos. 7:4-5).

The pattern of the first redemption, from Egyptian bondage, is matched by the pattern of the final redemption.

MEKHILTA ATTRIBUTED TO R. ISHMAEL XIV:I.
9. A. "And they baked unleavened cakes of the dough [which they had brought out of Egypt, for it was not leavened, because they were thrust out of Egypt and could not tarry, neither had they prepared for themselves any provisions]:"
   B. This indicates that they had kneaded the dough but had not sufficed to allow it to leaven before they were redeemed.
   C. And so it will be in the future redemption: "Who ceases to stir from the kneading of the dough until it be leavened. On the day of our king the princes make him sick" (Hos. 7:4-5).

Hosea is understood to speak of how the conditions of the original liberation from Egypt would be replicated at the redemption of the end of days.

MEKHILTA ATTRIBUTED TO R. ISHMAEL XXIII:I.
2. A. "Then the angel of God who went before the host of Israel moved [and went behind them; and the pillar of cloud moved from before them and stood behind them, coming between the host of Egypt and the host of Israel]:"
   B. R. Judah says, "Lo, this verse of Scripture is rich in many aspects.
   C. "The matter may be compared to the case of someone who was walking on the way, leading his son at the fore. If robbers came in front to kidnap the boy, he takes him and puts him at the rear. If a wolf comes at the rear, he takes him from behind and puts him to the fore. If robbers come before and wolves from behind, he takes him up into his arms.

2. Hosea in Sifra, the Two Sifrés and the Mekhilta Attributed to R. Ishmael

- D. "If the son begins to feel distress on account of the sun, his father stretches his cloak over him. If he gets hungry, he feeds him; thirsty, he gives him something to drink.
- E. "That is how the Holy One, blessed be he, did things:
- F. "'And I taught Ephraim to walk, taking them upon my arms, but they did not know that I healed them' (Hos. 11:3).
- G. "If the son begins to feel distress on account of the sun, his father stretches his cloak over him: 'He spread a cloud for a screen' (Ps. 105:39).
- H. "If he gets hungry, he feeds him: 'Behold, I will bring down as rain bread from heaven for you' (Ex. 16:4).
- I. "thirsty, he gives him something to drink: 'He brought streams out of the rock' (Ps. 78:16).
- J. "'streams' means living water: 'A fountain of gardens, a well of living water and flowing streams' (Song 4:15); 'Drink water out of your own cistern and running water out of your own well' (Prov. 5:15)."

Hosea portrays God tending to Ephraim as a father cares for a child.

Mekhilta Attributed to R. Ishmael XXIII:I.

- 8. A. "and the Lord drove the sea back by a strong east wind all night:"
- B. It was by the strongest wind of all. And what is that? It is the east wind.
- C. And so you find that the Omnipresent exacted punishment of the generation of the flood and of the men of Sodom only through an east wind:
- D. "By the breath of God they perish and by the blast of his anger they are consumed" (Job 4:9).
- E. "By the breath of God they perish:" this speaks of the generation of the flood.
- F. "and by the blast of his anger they are consumed:" this speaks of the men of Sodom.
- G. And so you find in the case of the men of the Tower that the Omnipresent exacted punishment from them only through an east wind:
- H. "And from there did the Lord scatter them abroad upon the face of all the earth" (Gen. 11:9),
- I. and "scattering abroad" is done only with the east wind: "With an east wind will I scatter them" (Jer. 18:17).
- J. And so you find that in the case of the Egyptians the Omnipresent exacted punishment of them only with the east wind:
- K. "And the Lord brought an east wind upon the land" (Ex. 10:13).
- L. And so you find that in the case of the tribes of Judah and Benjamin that the Omnipresent exacted punishment of them only with the east wind:

M. "For he will be fruitful among brothers, an east wind shall come" (Hos. 13:15).
N. And so you find that in the case of the ten tribes that the Omnipresent exacted punishment of them only with the east wind:
O. "With an east wind will I scatter them" (Jer. 18:17).
P. And so you find that in the case of Tyre that the Omnipresent exacted punishment of them only with the east wind:
Q. The east wind has broken you in the heart of the sea" (Ez. 27:26).
R. And so you find that in the case of this wanton empire that the Omnipresent in the time to come will exact punishment of them only with the east wind:

Hosea supplies proof that God exacts punishment through the east wind.

MEKHILTA ATTRIBUTED TO R. ISHMAEL XXIV:I.

2. A. R. Judah says, "When the Israelites stood at the sea, this one said, 'I am not going to go down first into the sea,' and that one said, 'I am not going to go down first into the sea,'
B. "for it is said, 'Ephraim surrounds me with lies, and the house of Israel with deceit' (Hos. 12:1).
C. "While they were standing and taking counsel, Nachshon b. Amminadab leaped forward first into the sea and fell into the waves of the ocean.
D. "In his connection Scripture says, 'Save me, O God, for the waters have come in even to the soul; I am sunk in deep mire, where there is no standing; I am come into deep waters, and the flood overwhelms me' (Ps. 69:2-3); 'Let not the water-flood overwhelm me, nor let the deep swallow me up; do not let the pit shut her mouth upon me' (Ps. 69:16).
E. "At that time Moses was standing and protracting a prayer before the Holy One, blessed be he.
F. "Said to him the Holy One, blessed be he, 'Moses, my friend is sinking into the water, and the sea shuts him off at the fore, and the enemy pursues from behind, and you stand her and protract your prayer before me!'
G. "He said before him, 'Lord of the world, and just what did you want me to do?'
H. "He said to him, 'Lift up your rod and stretch out your hand over the sea and divide it, that the people of Israel may go on dry ground through the sea.'
I. "What did the Israelites say at the sea?
J. "'The Lord will reign forever and ever' (Ex. 15:18).
K. "The Holy One, blessed be he, said, 'Him who made me king at the sea will I make king over Israel.'"

Hosea portrays Israel as deceitful at the Sea.

2. Hosea in Sifra, the Two Sifrés and the Mekhilta Attributed to R. Ishmael

MEKHILTA ATTRIBUTED TO R. ISHMAEL XXIV:I.

3. A. R. Tarfon and elders were in session in the shade of a dovecote in Yavneh, and this question was asked before them [as will be seen presently].
   B. [He said,] "'With their camels bearing spice and balm and laudanum' (Gen. 37:25).
   C. "This tells you the working of the merit of the righteous, showing how much it helps them.
   D. "For if this beloved friend had gone down with Arabs [to Egypt[, would they not have simply killed him with the stench of their camels and of the naphtha?
   E. "Accordingly, the Holy One, blessed be he, made arrangements for [them to be carrying] sacks of spices and sweet-smelling balms, so that he would not die from the stench of their camels and naphtha."
   F. [The disciples] said to him, "You have taught us, our master."
   G. They said to him, "Our master, teach us [the law on the following subject:]
   H. "'He who drinks water to quench his thirst — what blessing does he recite?'"
   I. He said to them, "'......who creates many sorts of souls and supplies the things they need.'"
   J. They said to him, "You have taught us, our master."
   K. They said to him, "Our master, teach us: on account of what merit did Judah inherit the monarchy?"
   L. He said to them, "You say."
   M. They said to him, "On account of the merit of having said to his brothers, 'What profit is it if we kill our brother?' (Gen. 37:26)."
   N. He said to them, "It suffices as a reward for the act of saving his life as atonement for the sin of his having sold the brother into slavery."
   O. "So on account of what merit did Judah inherit the monarchy?"
   P. [They said to him,] "It was on account of the merit of his having said, 'And Judah acknowledged then and said, "She is more righteous than I"' (Gen. 38:26)."
   Q. He said to them, "It suffices as a reward for the act of confessing the truth as atonement for the sin of his having had sexual relations with her anyhow."
   R. "If so, it was on account of the merit of his having said, 'Now therefore let your servant, I ask, stay here instead of the boy' (Gen. 44:33)."
   S. He said to them, "The one who guarantees a loan has to pay in the case of default. [He had no reward coming for simply carrying out his obligation; no merit accrues for that.]"
   T. They said to him, "Our master, teach us: on account of what merit did Judah inherit the monarchy?"

U. He said to them, "When the Israelites stood at the sea, this one said, 'I am not going to go down first into the sea,' and that one said, 'I am not going to go down first into the sea,'
V. "for it is said, 'Ephraim surrounds me with lies, and the house of Israel with deceit' (Hos. 12:1).
W. "While they were standing and taking counsel, Nachshon b. Amminadab and his tribe leaped forward first into the sea and fell into the waves of the ocean.
X. "Therefore he acquired the merit for the monarch to come from his tribe:
Y. "'When Israel came forth out of Egypt, the house of Jacob from a people of strange language, Judah became his sanctuary,' and therefore, 'Israel was his dominion' (Ps. 114:1-2)."

The same proposition is repeated in the same context.

MEKHILTA ATTRIBUTED TO R. ISHMAEL XXV:I.
30. A. So you find that the exiles are destined to be gathered together only as a reward for faith:
B. "Come with me from Lebanon, my bride, with me from Lebanon; look from the perspective of faith ["Hebrew: from the top of Amana," and the Hebrew letters of the word, Amana, can stand for 'faith']'" (Song 4:8).
C. "And I will betroth you to me forever...and I will betroth you to me because of faith" (Hos. 2:21-22).
D. Lo, great is faith before the One who spoke and brought the world into being.
E. For as a reward for the act of faith that the Israelites made in the Lord, the Holy Spirit rested upon them and they sang the song, as it is said, "and they believed in the Lord and in his servant Moses. Then Moses and the people of Israel sang this song [to the Lord, saying, 'I will sing to the Lord, for he has triumphed gloriously; the horse and his rider he has thrown into the sea].'"
F. So too: "Then they believed what he said, they sang his praises" (Ps. 106:12).

Hosea maintains that Israel's faith accounts for the enduring relationship of love that joins God to Israel.

MEKHILTA ATTRIBUTED TO R. ISHMAEL XVIII:II.
1. A. "this is my God and I will praise him:"
B. R. Eliezer says, "How on the basis of Scripture do you know that a slave-girl saw at the sea what neither Isaiah nor Ezekiel nor any of the other prophets saw?
C. "In their regard Scripture states, 'And by the ministry of the prophets I have used metaphors' (Hos. 12:11); 'The heavens were opened and I saw visions of God' (Ez. 1:1).

2. Hosea in Sifra, the Two Sifrés and the Mekhilta Attributed to R. Ishmael

    D. "The matter may be compared to a mortal king who came to town, with a retinue of guards surrounding him, and soldiers right and left, troops before and behind.
    E. "So everyone asked, 'Which one is the king,' because he was a mere mortal like them.
    F. "But when the Holy One, blessed be he, made his appearance at the sea, no one of them had to ask which one is the king.
    G. "But as soon as they saw him they knew him, and everyone opened their mouths and said, 'this is my God and I will praise him.'"

Hosea says that the prophets see God through metaphors, but, Eliezer notes, at the sea Israel saw God not through metaphors but as he truly was.

MEKHILTA ATTRIBUTED TO R. ISHMAEL XXIX:I.

  5. A. "The Lord is a man of war:"
    B. It is not possible to say so, for is it not stated: "Do I not fill heaven and earth, says the Lord" (Jer. 23:24); "And one called the other and said" (Is. 6:3); "And behold the glory of the God of Israel came" (Ez. 43:2).
    C. How then can Scripture say, "The Lord is a man of war"?
    D. "On account of the love that I bear for you, and on account of the sanctification that you bear, I shall sanctify my name through you."
    E. Thus Scripture says, "Though I am God and not man, still I, the Holy One, am in the midst of you" (Hos. 11:9),
    F. "I shall sanctify my name through you."

Hosea attests to God's presence within Israel, even though he fills heaven and earth.

MEKHILTA ATTRIBUTED TO R. ISHMAEL XXXII:I.

  1. A. "The enemy said, ['I will pursue, I will overtake, I will divide the spoil, my desire shall have its fill of them. I will draw my sword, my hand shall destroy them]:'"
    B. This [statement was made] at the outset of the sequence of events, and why then was it stated here?
    C. It is because considerations of temporal sequence play no role in the Torah.
  2. A. Along these same lines: "And it came to pass on the eighth day that Moses called" (Lev. 9:1).
    B. This [statement was made] at the outset of the sequence of events, and why then was it stated here?
    C. It is because considerations of temporal sequence play no role in the Torah.
  3. A. Along these same lines: ""In the year that king Uzziah died" (Is. 6:1).

- B. This [statement was made] at the outset of the sequence of events, and why then was it stated here?
- C. It is because considerations of temporal sequence play no role in the Torah.
4. A. Along these same lines: "Son of man, stand on your feet" (Ez. 2:1).
- B. Some say, "Son of man, put forth a riddle" (Ez. 17:2).
- C. This [statement was made] at the outset of the sequence of events, and why then was it stated here?
- D. It is because considerations of temporal sequence play no role in the Torah.
5. A. Along these same lines: "Go and cry in the ears of Jerusalem" (Jer. 2:2).
- B. This [statement was made] at the outset of the sequence of events, and why then was it stated here?
- C. It is because considerations of temporal sequence play no role in the Torah.
6. A. Along these same lines: "Israel was a luxuriant vine" (Hos. 10:1).
- B. This [statement was made] at the outset of the sequence of events, and why then was it stated here?
- C. It is because considerations of temporal sequence play no role in the Torah.

Hosea referred to the beginning of a sequence of events but spoke later on because considerations of temporal sequence do not pertain in Scripture.

MEKHILTA ATTRIBUTED TO R. ISHMAEL XLIII:I.

7. A. ["So they executed judgment upon Joash" (2 Chr. 24:24):] Do not read "judgment" but "sport."
- B. What sport did they make with him?
- C. They say that they set up harsh guards in charge of him, who had never in their lives known a woman, and they tortured him with pederasty,
- D. in line with this verse: "And restored the pride of Israel" (Hos. 5:5).
- E. And it is written, "And when they left him, for they left him in great diseases, his own servants conspired against him for the blood of the sons of Jehoiada the priest and killed him on his bed and he died" (2 Chr. 24:25).

Hosea refers to the torture of Joash.

MEKHILTA ATTRIBUTED TO R. ISHMAEL XLIX:I.

10. A. Another interpretation of the phrase, "in the sight of all the people:"
- B. This indicates that at that time they saw what Isaiah and Ezekiel never saw:

2. Hosea in Sifra, the Two Sifrés and the Mekhilta Attributed to R. Ishmael

    C.   "And through the hand of the prophets I have used similitudes" (Hos. 12:11)

As above.

Mekhilta Attributed to R. Ishmael LIV:III.
1. A. "How were the Ten Commandments set forth?
   B. "There were five on one tablet, five on the other.
   C. "On the one was written, 'I am the Lord your God.'
   D. "and opposite it: 'You shall not murder.
   E. "Scripture thus indicates that whoever sheds blood is regarded as though he had diminished the divine image.
   F. "The matter may be compared to the case of a mortal king who came into a town, and the people set up in his honor icons, and they made statues of him, and they minted coins in his honor.
   G. "After a while they overturned his icons, broke his statues, and invalidated his coins, so diminishing the image of the king.
   H. "Thus whoever sheds blood is regarded as though he had diminished the divine image, for it is said, 'Whoever sheds man's blood...for in the image of God he made man' (Gen. 9:6).
2. A. "One the one was written, 'You shall have no other god.'
   B. "and opposite it: 'You shall not commit adultery.'
   C. "Scripture thus indicates that whoever worships an idol is regarded as though he had committed adultery against the Omnipresent, for it is said, 'Your wife that commits adultery, that takes strangers instead of your husband' (Ez. 16:32); 'And the Lord said to me, Go yet, love a woman beloved of her friend and an adulteress' (Hos. 3:1).
3. A. "One the one was written, 'You shall not take the name of the Lord your God in vain.'
   B. "and opposite it: 'You shall not steal.'
   C. "Scripture thus indicates that whoever steals in the end will end up taking a false oath: 'Will you steal, murder, commit adultery, and swear falsely: (Jer. 7:9); 'Swearing and lying, killing and stealing, and committing adultery' (Hos. 4:2).

Serving a God other than the Lord is tantamount to committing adultery, so Hosea 3:1 in context, and stealing is in the end equivalent to a false oath, Hos. 4:2 proving that proposition.

3

Hosea in the Yerushalmi

YERUSHALMI PEAH 2:6 [TRANSLATED BY ROGER BROOKS]

[II. A] [The Talmud focuses on the difference between laws written at Sinai, and those transmitted orally. To this end, we consider several interpretations of Hos. 8:12]: R. Zeira in the name of R. Eleazar: "'The many teachings I wrote for him [have been treated as something alien]' (Hos. 8:12). Now do the Torah's many teachings consist of written laws? [No!] Rather, [the verse means that] those laws expounded on [the explicit authority of] written verses [i.e., those with prooftexts] are more numerous [and so more unfamiliar and alien] than those expounded on [the mere authority of] oral tradition [and without prooftexts]."

[B] And is this the proper [interpretation of Hos. 8:12]? [Are there really more laws expounded with prooftexts than without? No!] Rather, this verse means that those matters expounded on [the authority of] written sources are weightier than those expounded merely on [the authority of] oral tradition.

[C] [Offering a different interpretation of Hos. 8:12], R. Judah ben Pazzi says, " 'The many teachings I wrote for him...' (Hos. 8:12) — this refers to the curses [for not following the Torah's laws]. [This interpretation is consistent with the remainder of the verse, which states], and even if [I wrote the curses], 'have they not been treated as something alien?' [The point is that God's curses only rarely are invoked upon Israel, and hence are regarded as strange by the people.]"

[D] [Providing yet another interpretation of the verse], said R. Abin, "'Had I had written for you the bulk of my [orally transmitted] Torah, you would be considered like a foreigner.' [For] what [is the difference] between us and the gentiles? They bring forth their books, and we bring forth our books; they bring forth their national records, and we bring forth our national records." [The only difference between Israel and the gentile nations is that a portion of the Torah remains oral, and has a special claim upon the nation of Israel.]

Hos. 8:12 serves to validate the conception of an orally-formulated and orally-transmitted Torah.

YERUSHALMI SHEQALIM 5:4 II

A R. Hama bar Haninah and R. Hoshaia the Elder were strolling in the synagogues in Lud. Said R. Hama bar Haninah to R. Hoshaia, "How much money did my forefathers invest here [in building these synagogues]!"

[B] He said to him, "How many lives did your forefathers invest here! Were there not people who were laboring in Torah [who needed the money more]?"

[C] R. Abun made the gates of the great hall [of study]. R. Mana came to him. He said to him, "See what I have made!"

[D] He said to him, " 'For Israel has forgotten his Maker and built palaces'! (Hos. 8:14). Were there no people laboring in Torah [who needed the money more]?"

Building palaces instead of investing the money in Torah-students shows that Israel has forgotten their Maker. That judgment includes synagogues.

YERUSHALMI YOMA 7:3

[B] **"Tunic, underpants, head covering, and girdle [M. 7:3B]:**

[C] "The tunic effected atonement for those who wore linen and wool mixtures."

[D] There is he who wishes to say, It is for those who shed blood, as you say, "Then they took Joseph's robe, and killed a goat, and dipped the robe in the blood" (Gen. 37:21).

[E] "The underpants effected atonement for those who fornicate.

[F] "This is in line with the following verse: 'And you shall make for them linen breeches to cover their naked flesh; from the loins to the thighs they shall reach' (Exod. 28:42).

[G] "The head covering atoned for the proud.

[H] "This is in line with the following verse: 'And you shall set the turban on his head, and put the holy crown upon the turban' (Exod. 29:6).

[I] "The girdle atoned for thieves."

[J] And there is he who wishes to say, "It is for those who trick people."

[K] Said R. Levi, "It was thirty-two cubits, and he would twist it this way and that."

[L] The breastplate [M. 7:3C] atoned for whose who corrupt justice.

[M] This is in line with the following verse: "And you shall make a breast-piece of judgment, [in skilled work; like the work of the ephod you shall make it; of gold, blue and purple and scarlet stuff, and fine twined linen shall you make it]" (Exod. 28:15).

[N] The apron atoned for idolatry.

3. Hosea in the Yerushalmi

[O] This is in line with the following verse: "For the children of Israel shall dwell many days without king or prince, without sacrifice or pillar, without ephod or teraphim" (Hos. 3:4).

The clothing of the high priest atoned for various sins. The apron atoned for idolatry, proved by Hos. 3:4.

Yerushalmi Megillah 3:2

[I:4 A] **What is the law as to writing two or three words of a verse of Scripture [in a letter]? [Generally, to do so one must incise a line for that purpose. Is it necessary to observe the same restrictions in a letter?]**

[B] Mar Uqba sent a letter to the exilarch, who would lie down to sleep and get up in the morning to the sound of singing [in his palace]: "Rejoice not, O Israel! Exult not like the peoples; [for you have played the harlot, forsaking your God. You have loved a harlot's hire upon all threshing floors]" (Hos. 9:1). [The verse was cited with slight changes, so that it was not written in the letter precisely as it is written in Scripture.]

[C] R. Aha wrote, "The memory of the righteous is a blessing, [but the name of the wicked will rot]" (Prov. 10:7). [This verse was written precisely as it appears in Scripture, for Aha differs from Mar Uqba's view.]

[D] R. Zeirah wrote, "Thus Joash the king did not remember [the kindness which Jehoiada, Zechariah's father, had shown him, but killed his son]" (2 Chron. 24:22).

The citation of Hosea 9:1 in the letter Mar Uqba sent to the patriarch was not precise, showing that it is not necessary to cite the verse exactly as it is written in Scripture.

Yerushalmi Taanit 4:6

[L] **R. Isaac b. Eleazar, "When the ninth of Ab had ended, he made an announcement. and they opened the barber shops, and whoever wanted went and got a haircut."**

[M] It is written: "And I will put an end to all her mirth, her feasts, her new moons, her Sabbaths, and all her appointed feasts" (Hos. 2:11).

[N] The Southerners applied the prohibitions [of M. 4:6B] from the new moon of Ab onward.

[O] The Sepphoreans applied them for the entire month of Ab.

[P] The Tiberians applied them for the week [in which the ninth of Ab occurred].

[Q] The rabbis of Tiberias reverted and applied them as did the rabbis of Sepphoris.

In line with Hos. 2:11, various authorities extended the application of the restrictions of the 9th of Ab to the rest of the month.

YERUSHALMI HAGIGAH 1:8

[II:2A] R. Zeira in the name of R. Eleazar: "'Were I to write for him most of my laws, would they not be regarded as a strange thing?]' (Hos. 8:12). Now is the greater part of the Torah written down? [Surely not. The oral part is much greater.] But more abundant are the matters that are derived by exegesis from the written Torah than those derived by exegesis from the oral Torah."

[B] And is that so?

[C] But more cherished are those matters that rest upon the written Torah and those that rest upon the oral Torah.

[D] Said R. Judah bar Pazzi, "'Were I to write for him most of my laws' — this refers to the admonitions."

[E] "Even so, would they not be regarded as a strange thing?"

[F] Said R. Abun, "'Were I to write for him most of my laws, would they not be regarded as a strange thing?' What is the difference between them and [the sages of] the nations? These produce their books, and those produce theirs. These produce their documents, and those produce theirs." [Thus, the oral Torah serves to distinguish between Israel and the nations.]

Hos. 8:12 validates the oral Torah.

YERUSHALMI YEBAMOT 6:5

[I:2 A] Said R. Judah b. Pazzi, "It is written, 'Among the olive rows of the wicked they make oil' (Job 24:11). 'No treader turns toward their vineyards' (Job 24:18). It is because their act of sexual relations was not in order to procreate."

[B] Said R. Simon, "It is written, 'They shall eat but not be satisfied, they shall play the harlot, but not multiply' (Hos. 4:10), because their act of sexual relations was not in order to procreate."

[C] It is written, "And Lamech took two wives, the name of one was Adah, and the name of the other Zillah" (Gen. 4:19), Adah, because he took pleasure in her body, and Zillah, because she sat in the shade of her children.

Hos. 4:10 refers to the lack of sexual satisfaction deriving from sexual relations not for the sake of procreation.

YERUSHALMI YEBAMOT 8:3

[II:4A] Said R. Yohanan, "As to any family in which some invalidity has been submerged, they do not check too carefully about it."

3. Hosea in the Yerushalmi

[B] Said R. Simeon b. Laqish, "The Mishnah itself has made the same point: **The family of Beth Seripa was in the land beyond Jordan, and Ben Zion removed it afar by force, and yet another family was there, and Ben Zion brought it near by force [M. Ed. 8:7].**

[C] "But sages did not seek to reveal who they were.

[D] "But sages hand over the information to their sons and disciples two times every seven years."

[E] Said R. Yohanan, "By the Temple service! I know who they are, but what should we do? For the great men of the generation are mixed up with them."

[F] Said R. Joshua b. Levi, "Pashhur ben Immer had five thousand slaves and all of them were mixed up with the high priesthood, and they account for the arrogant among the priesthood."

[G] Said R. Eliezer, "The principal designation of the priests' usurpation is indicated in the following verse: '[Yet let no one contend, and let none accuse,] for with you is my contention, O priest' (Hos. 4:4)."

Hos. 4:4 speaks of the corruption of the priesthood.

YERUSHALMI KETUBOT 5:11

[I:2 A] She has no claim for wine, for the wives of the poor do not drink wine [T. Ket. 5:8E].

[B] And do the rich ones drink wine?

[C] [Indeed so.] For lo, it has been taught: There was the case of Marta, daughter of Boethus, for whom the sages decreed a portion of two seahs of wine every day.

[D] And does a court make provision for wine?

[E] [Surely not], for R. Hiyya b. Ada said, "It is on the count of the following verse: 'Wine and new wine take away the understanding'" (Hos. 4:11).

[F] Yet, lo, we have learned, **And if she was feeding a child, they take off the required weight of wool which she must spin as the fruit of her labor and they provide more food for her [M. 5:11F].**

[G] What do they add? R. Joshua b. Levi said, "Wine, for it makes one fatter."

[H] R. Hezekiah, R. Abbahu in the name of R. Yohanan, "Also as to cooked food for her have they made provision."

Hos. 4:11 condemns wine-drinking.

YERUSHALMI QIDDUSHIN 1:

[I:4 A] When Solomon came to kill Joab, [Joab] said to him, "Your father made five evil decrees against me [those at 2 Sam. 3: 29]. You accept them, and I shall accept the death penalty from you. Solomon accepted them, and all of them were fulfilled in the house of David."

[B] "One who has a discharge" applies to Rehoboam: "And King Rehoboam made haste to mount his chariot, to flee to Jerusalem" (l Kings 12 :18).
[C] There is he who says he had a discharge, and there is he who says he was spoiled.
[D] As to "a leper," this is Uzziah: 'And King Uzziah was a leper to the day of his death, [and being a leper dwelt in a separate house, for he was excluded from the house of the Lord]" (2 Chr. 26: 21).
[E] "One who holds a spindle" applies to Joash: "[Though the army of the Syrians had come with few men, the Lord delivered into their hand a very great army, because they had forsaken the Lord, the God of their fathers.] Thus they executed judgment on Joash" (2 Chr. 24: 24).
[F] R. Ishmael taught, "This teaches that they set up against him sadists, who had never known a woman in their lives, and they inflicted suffering on him as they inflict suffering on a woman."
[G] This is in line with what is written, "The pride of Israel testifies to his face; [Israel and Ephraim shall stumble in his guilt; Judah also shall stumble with them]" (Hos. 5: 5). [The meaning is,] they tormented the pride of Israel in his face.
[H] "One who is slain by the sword" refers to Josiah, in line with the following verse of Scripture: "And the archers shot King Josiah; [and the king said to his servants, 'Take me away, for I am badly wounded']" (2 Chr. 35: 23).
[I] R. Yohanan says, "This teaches that they made his body into a sieve."
[J] R. Ishmael taught, "Three hundred arrows did they shoot into the anointed of the Lord."
[K] "Who lacks bread" refers to Jehoiachin, as it is written, "[And every day of his life he dined regularly at the king's table;] and for his allowance, a regular allowance was given him [by the king, every day a portion, as long as he lived]" (2 Kings 25: 30).

Hos. 5:5 speaks of the sadism practiced on Joash.

Yerushalmi Qiddushin 4:1

[III:9 A] Said R. Yohanan, "As to any family in which some invalidity has been submerged, they do not check too carefully about it."
[B] Said R. Simeon b. Laqish, "The Mishnah itself has made the same point: **The family of Beth Seripa was in the land beyond Jordan, and Ben Zion removed it afar by force, and yet another family was here, and Ben Zion brought it near by force [M. Ed. 8: 7].** But sages did not seek to reveal who they were. But sages hand over the information to their sons and disciples two times every seven years. "

3. Hosea in the Yerushalmi

[C] Said R. Yohanan, "By the Temple service! I know who they are, but what should we do? For the great men of the generation are mixed up with them."

[D] Said R. Joshua b. Levi, "Pashhur ben Immer had five thousand slaves, and all of them were mixed up with the high priesthood, and they account for the arrogant among the priesthood."

[E] Said R. Eliezer, "The principal designation of the priests' usurpation is indicated in the following verse: '[Yet let no one contend, and let none accuse,] for with you is my contention, O priest'" (Hos. 4:4).

As above.

YERUSHALMI SOTAH 5:6

[I:1 A] When did Job live?

[F] R. Ishmael taught, "Job was one of the servants of Pharaoh. He was one of the great members of his retinue. That is in line with the following verse of Scripture: 'Then he who feared the word of the Lord among the servants of Pharaoh made his slaves and his cattle flee into the houses' (Exod. 9:20). And concerning him it is written, 'And the Lord said to Satan, Have you considered my servant Job, [that there is none like him on the earth,] a blameless and upright man, who fears God and turns away from evil?'" (Job 1:8).

[G] R. Yosé bar Judah says, "He was in the time in which the judges ruled Israel. That is indicated in the following verse of Scripture: 'Behold, all of you have seen it yourselves; why then have you become so vain?' (Job 27:12). You have seen the deeds of my generation. For they collected tithes at the threshing floors: '[Rejoice not, O Israel? Exult not like the peoples; for you have played the harlot, forsaking your God.] You have loved a harlot's hire upon all [20d] the threshing floors'" (Hos. 9:1).

Job lived at the time of the Judges, and Hos. 9:1 proves it.

YERUSHALMI ABODAH ZARAH 1:1

[I:1][U] Said R. Yudan, father of R. Matteniah, "The intention of [a verse of] Scripture [such as is cited below] was only to make mention of the evil traits of [39b] Israel. 'On the day of our king [when Jeroboam was made king] the princes became sick with the heat of wine; he stretched out his hand with mockers' (Hosea 7:5).

[V] "On the day on which Jeroboam began to reign over Israel, all Israel came to him at dusk, saying to him, 'Rise up and worship idolatry.'

[W] "He said to them, 'It is already dusk. I am partly drunk and partly sober, and the whole people is drunk. But if you want, go and come back in the morning.'

[X] "This is the meaning of the following Scripture, 'For like an oven their hearts burn with intrigue; all night their anger smolders; [in the morning it blazes like a flaming fire]' (Hosea 7:6)."

[Y] "'All night their anger smolders.'

[Z] "'In the morning it blazes like a flaming fire.'

[AA] "In the morning they came to him. Thus did he say to them, 'I know full well what you want, but I'm afraid of your sanhedrin, lest it come and kill me.'

[BB] "They said to him, 'We shall kill them.'

[CC] "That is the meaning of the following verse: 'All of them are hot as an oven. And they devour their rulers' (Hos. 7:7)."

[DD] [Concurring with this view,] R. Levi said, "They slew them. Thus do you read in Scripture [to prove that 'the princes became sick' (HHL) means 'the princes killed' (HLL)], 'If anyone is found slain [HLL] (Deut. 21:1).'"

Hos. 7:5-7 speak of the time at which Jeroboam was made king. Hos. 7:5 has the princes sick with excessive drinking. They want the king to worship an idol. He sends them away for the night, Hos. 7:6. In the morning they come back and threaten to kill the rulers who thwart their intentions, Hos. 7:7.

YERUSHALMI ABODAH ZARAH 1:1

[I:1][[PP] Said R. Yosé bar Jacob, "It was at the conclusion of a sabbatical year that Jeroboam began to rule over Israel. That is the meaning of the following verse: '[And Moses commanded them.] At the end of every seven years, at the set time of the year of release, at the feast of booths, when all Israel comes to appear before the Lord your God at the place which he will choose, you shall read this law before all Israel in their hearing' (Deut. 31:10-11).

[QQ] "[Jeroboam] said, 'I shall be called upon to read [the Torah, as Scripture requires]. If I get up and read first, they will say to me, 'The king of the place [in which the gathering takes place, namely, Jerusalem] comes first.' And if I read second, it is disrespectful to me. And if I do not read at all, it is a humiliation for me. And, finally, if I let the people go up, they will abandon me and go over to the side of Rehoboam the son of Solomon.'

[RR] "That is the meaning of the following verse of Scripture: '[And Jeroboam said in his heart, "Now the kingdom will turn back to the house of David;] if this people go up to offer sacrifices in the house of the Lord at Jerusalem, then the heart of this people will turn again to their Lord, to Rehoboam, king of Judah, and they will kill me and return to Rehoboam, king of Judah"' (1 Kings 12:27-28).

[SS] "What then did he do? 'He made two calves of gold' (1 Kings 12:28), and he inscribed on their heart, '. . . lest they kill you' [as counsel to his successors].

[TT] "He said, 'Let every king who succeeds me look upon them.'"
[UU] Said R. Huna, "'[The wicked go astray from the womb, they err from their birth speaking lies. They have venom like the venom of a serpent, like the deaf adder that stops its ear, so that it does not hear the voice of charmers] or of the cunning caster of spells' (Ps. 58:5). Over whoever was associated with him [Jeroboam] he [Jeroboam] cast a spell [in the sin of the bull-calves]."
[VV] Said R. Huna, "'[Hearken, O house of the king! For the judgment pertains to you; for you have been a snare at Mizpah, and a net spread upon Tabor.] And they have made deep the pit of Shittim[, but I will chastise all of them]' (Hos. 5:1-2). For [Jeroboam] deepened the sin. He said, 'Whoever explains [the meaning of what has been inscribed on the bull-calves] I shall kill.'"

Hos. 5:1-2 condemned the royal house for idolatry.

YERUSHALMI ABODAH ZARAH 5:10

[II:1 A] What is **a drop of wine** [of M. A.Z. 5:10E]?
[B] It is that in the dregs, as you read in Scripture, "tracked with blood" (Hos. 6:8).

Hosea clarifies the law.

YERUSHALMI SANHEDRIN 2:6

[VII:3 A] Yosé Meoni interpreted the following verse in the synagogue in Tiberias: "'Hear this, Priests' (Hos. 5:1) — why do you not labor in the Torah? Have not the twenty-four priestly gifts been given to you?"
[B] "They said to him, 'Nothing at all has been given to us.'"
[C] [20d] "'And give heed, O House of Israel!' (Hos. 5:1).
[D] "'Why do you not give the priests the twenty-four gifts concerning which you have been commanded at Sinai?'
[E] "They said to him, 'The king takes them all.'"
[F] "'Hearken, O house of the king! For the judgment pertains to you' (Hos. 5:1).
[G] "To you have I said, 'And this shall be the priests' due from the people, from those offering a sacrifice...: they shall give to the priest the shoulder, the two cheeks, and the stomach' (Deut. 18:3).
[H] "I am going to take my seat with them in court and to make a decision concerning them and blot them [the kings] out of the world. '
[I] R. Yudan the Patriarch heard [about this attack on the rulers] and was angry.
[J] [Yosé] feared and fled.
[K] R. Yohanan and R. Simeon b. Laqish went up to make peace with [the Patriarch].

[L] They said to him, "Rabbi, he is a great man."
[M] He said to them, "Is it possible that concerning everything which I ask of him, he will reply to me?"
[N] They said to him, "Yes." [So Yosé was called back.]
[O] [The Patriarch] said to [Yosé], "What is the meaning of that which is written: 'For their mother has played the harlot' (Hos. 2:5)?
[P] "Is it possible that our matriarch, Sarah, was a whore?"
[Q] He said to him, "As is the daughter, so is her mother.
[R] "As is the mother, so is the daughter.
[S] "As is the generation, so is the patriarch.
[T] "As is the patriarch, so is the generation.
[U] "As is the altar, so are its priests."
[V] Kahana said likewise: "As is the garden, so is the gardener."
[W] He said to them, "Is it not enough for him that he dishonors me one time not in my presence, but also in my presence he does so these three times!"
[X] He said to him, "What is the meaning of that which is written, 'Behold, everyone who uses proverbs will use this proverb about you, 'Like mother, like daughter' (Ez. 16:44).
[Y] "Now was our matriarch, Leah, a whore?
[Z] "As it is written, 'And Dinah went out' (Gen. 34:1) [like a whore, thus reflecting on her mother]"
[AA] He said to him, 'It is in accord with that which is written, 'And Leah went out to meet him' (Gen. 30:16).
[BB] "They compared one going out to the other [and Leah went out to meet her husband, and Dinah learned from this that it was all right to go out, so she went out to meet the daughters of the land, but got raped]." [This was an acceptable reply to Yudan.]

Hos. 5:1 yields the indictment of the priests for not laboring in the Torah, even though they are supported by the priestly rations. The Israelites are condemned for not giving the gifts to the priesthood, but they claim the king takes them all. The same verse condemns the monarch for doing so. The patriarch sees this interpretation as an attack on himself.

YERUSHALMI SANHEDRIN 7:7

[II:1 A] [With reference to M. 7:7C-D,] R. Ba bar Mamel raised the question: "Take note. If a man had sexual relations with a beast in a spell of inadvertence, lo, the beast is stoned on the man's account, but the man is exempt from stoning, [and this indicates that the principal consideration in this matter is M. 7:7D's reasoning, namely, avoiding unnecessary embarrassment to the man]."

[B] R. Simeon raised the question: "Take note. If a man ploughed with a beast on the Sabbath, lo, he is stoned to death on account of the beast, but the beast is exempt [in consequence of which the principal consideration in this matter is M. 7:7C's reasoning] ."

3. Hosea in the Yerushalmi

[C] [In fact, the principal consideration is disgrace to man, and] you have only the saying of R. Samuel bar R. Isaac: "'With their silver and gold they made idols, for his destruction' (Hos. 8:4). It is not written, '... for their destruction,' but '... for his destruction.'

[D] "This is exemplified in one's saying, 'May the bones of Mr. So-and-so be crushed, who has enticed his son to evil conduct.' [And this applies only in a case of deliberate misdeed. Here too we speak of deliberate misdeed, in which case the beast is stoned, and the matter of ploughing with the beast on the Sabbath is irrelevant, for there is no shame brought to man in that case by the deed of the beast.]"

Hos. 8:4 helps resolve the issue of identifying the principal consideration for the ruling.

YERUSHALMI SANHEDRIN 10:1

[I:5 A] Bar Qappara said, "Ahaz and all of the evil kings of Israel have no portion in the world to come."

[B] What is the Scriptural basis for this statement?

[C] "[All of them are hot as an oven, and they devour their rulers.] All their kings have fallen; and none of them calls upon me" (Hos. 7:7).

[D] They objected to him, "And lo, he is numbered in the era of the kings:

[E] "'[The vision of Isaiah the son of Amoz, which he saw concerning Judah and Jerusalem] in the days of Uzziah, Jotham, Ahaz and Hezekiah, kings of Judah'" (Is. 1:1).

[F] He said to them, "Because he was subject to shame."

Hos. 7:7 indicts Ahaz and the other wicked kings and denies them a portion in the world to come.

YERUSHALMI SANHEDRIN 10:1

[I:6 A] How long did the merit of the patriarchs endure [to protect Israel]?

[B] R. Tanhuma said in the name of R. Hiyya the Elder, Bar Nahman stated in the name of R. Berekiah, R. Helbo in the name of R. Ba bar Zabeda: "Down to Joahaz."

[C] "But the Lord was gracious to them and had compassion on them, [because of his covenant with Abraham, Isaac, and Jacob, and would not destroy them; nor has he cast them from his presence] until now" (2 Kings 13:23).

[D] "Up to that time the merit of the patriarchs endured."

[E] Samuel said, "Down to Hosea."

[F] "Now I will uncover her lewdness in the sight of her lovers, and no man shall rescue her out of my hand" (Hos. 2:12).

[G] "Now 'man' can refer only to Abraham, as you say, 'Now then restore the man's wife; for he is a prophet, [and he will pray for you, and you shall live. But if you do not restore her, know that you will surely die, you, and all that are yours]' (Gen. 20:7).

[H] "And 'man' can refer only to Isaac, as you say, '[Rebecca said to the servant,] "Who is the man yonder, walking in the field to meet us?" [The servant said, "It is my master." So she took her veil and covered herself' (Gen. 24:65).

[I] "And 'man' can refer only to Jacob, as you say, '[When the boys grew up, Esau was a skilful hunter, a man of the field,] while Jacob was a quiet man, [dwelling in tents]'" (Gen. 25:27).

[J] R. Joshua b. Levi said, "It was down to Elijah."

[K] "And at the time of the offering of the oblation, Elijah the prophet came near and said, 'O Lord, God of Abraham, Isaac, and Israel, let it be known this day that thou art God in Israel, and that I am thy servant, [and that I have done all these things at thy word]'" (1 Kings 18:36).

[L] R. Yudan said, "It was down to Hezekiah."

[M] "Of the increase of his government and of peace there will be no end, [upon the throne of David, and over his kingdom, to establish it, and to uphold it with justice and with righteousness from this time forth and for evermore. The zeal of the Lord of hosts will do this]" (Is. 9:6).

[N] Said R. Aha, "The merit of the patriarchs endures forever [to protect Israel]."

[O] "For the Lord your God is a merciful God; [he will not fail you or destroy you or forget the covenant with your fathers which he swore to them]" (Deut. 4:31).

[P] This teaches that the covenant is made with the tribes.

When Hos. 3:12 says, "No man shall rescue her out of my hand," he refers to the patriarchs and indicates that the merit of the patriarchs sufficed to save Israel, but no further merit beyond the patriarchs persisted.

YERUSHALMI SANHEDRIN 10:1

IV.2 [M] [When he came in, he found] there a flagon full of wine, Ammonite wine, which is very strong. And it serves as an aphrodisiac to incite the body to passion, and its scent was enticing. (Now up to this time the wine of gentiles had not been prohibited for Israelite use by reason of its being libation wine.) Now the ,girl would say to him, "Do you want to drink a cup of wine," and he would reply to her, "Yes." So she gave him a cup of wine, and he drank it. When he drank it, the wine would burn in him like the venom of a snake. Then he would say to her, "Surrender yourself to me."

[N] And she would say to him, "Separate yourself from the Torah of Moses, and I shall 'surrender' myself to you."

3. Hosea in the Yerushalmi

[O] That is in line with the following verse of Scripture: "[Like grapes in the wilderness, I found Israel. Like the first fruits on the fig tree, in its first season, I saw your fathers.] But they came to Baal Peor, and consecrated themselves to Baal, and became detestable like the thing they loved" (Hos. 9:10).

Hos. 9:10 refers to the idolatry and degradation of Israel at Baal Peor.

YERUSHALMI SANHEDRIN 10:5

[I:3 A] R. Yohanan said, "The party of Yohanan b. Korach has no portion in the world to come."

[B] What is the Scriptural basis for this view?

[C] "They have dealt faithlessly with the Lord; for they have borne alien children. Now the new moon shall devour them with their fields" (Hos. 5:7).

Hos. 5:7 refers to the party of Yohanan b. Korach.

YERUSHALMI SANHEDRIN 11:6

[I:2 A] [Read:] **He who prophesies to uproot something which is taught in the Torah is liable. R. Simeon says, "If he prophesied to nullify part and to keep part, he is exempt." But if he prophesied in the name of idolatry, even if he confirms it today and nullifies it tomorrow, he is liable [T. San.14:13].** Now with regard to idolatry, whether the prophet intended to uproot the whole principle or whether he did not intend to uproot the whole,

[B] in the view of R. Simeon, they strangle him to death.

[C] In the opinion of sages, they stone him.

[D] But with regard to [his preaching against] all the other commandments, if he did not intend to uproot the whole principle, in the view of sages, they stone him.

[E] In the view of R. Simeon, they exempt him.

[F] And as to the prophet who began to prophesy, if he gave a sign or did a wonder, they listen to him, and if he did not do so, they do not pay attention to him.

[G] As to two prophets who prophesied simultaneously,

[H] or two prophets who prophesied in the same town —

[I] R. Isaac and R. Hoshaiah —

[J] one said, "He has to give a sign or do a wonder."

[K] The other stated, "He does not have to give a sign or do a wonder."

[L] The one who said that he has to do so objected to the one who said he does not have to do so, "And lo, it is written, 'And Hezekiah said to Isaiah, What shall be the sign that the Lord will heal me, and that I shall go up to the house of the Lord on the third day?'" (2 Kings 20:8).

[M] He said to him, "That is a special case, because at issue was the resurrection of the dead.

[N] "'After two days he will revive us; on the third day he will raise us up, that we may live before him'" (Hos. 6:2).

Hos. 6:2 refers to resurrection of the dead on the third day after death.

4

Hosea in Genesis Rabbah, Leviticus Rabbah and Pesiqta deRab Kahana

GENESIS RABBAH

GENESIS RABBAH I:IV.

1. A.   ["In the beginning God created" (Gen. 1:1):] Six things came before the creation of the world, some created, some at least considered as candidates for creation.
   B.   The Torah and the throne of glory were created [before the creation of the world].
   C.   The Torah, as it is written, "The Lord made me as the beginning of his way, prior to his works of old" (Prov. 8:22).
   D.   The throne of glory, as it is written, "Your throne is established of old" (Ps. 93:2).
   E.   The patriarchs were considered as candidates for creation, as it is written, "I saw your fathers as the first-ripe in the fig tree at her first season" (Hos. 9:10).
   F.   Israel was considered [as a candidate for creation], as it is written, "Remember your congregation, which you got aforetime" (Ps. 74:2).
   G.   The Temple was considered as a candidate for creation], as it is written, "You, throne of glory, on high from the beginning, the place of our sanctuary" (Jer. 17:12).
   H.   The name of the Messiah was kept in mind, as it is written, "His name exists before the sun" (Ps. 72:17).

Hos. 9:10 refers to the patriarchs as the first fruits of creation.

Genesis Rabbah XVI:V.

1 A. "And the Lord God took the man [and put him in the garden of Eden to till it and keep it]" (Gen. 2:15):
B. R. Judah and R. Nehemiah:
C. R. Judah said, "He raised him up, in line with this verse [in which the use of the word 'take' bears the meaning of raise up]: 'And the peoples shall take them and bring them to their place' (Is. 14:2)."
D. R. Nehemiah said, "He enticed him [to enter the garden] in line with this verse: 'Take with you words and return to the Lord' (Hos. 14:3)."

Hos. 14:3 has God use words to entice Adam and Eve to enter the garden.

Genesis Rabbah XVI:VI.

1. A. "And the Lord God commanded the man, saying, 'You may freely eat of every tree of the garden, [but of the tree of the knowledge of good and evil you shall not eat, for in the day that you eat of it you shall die]'" (Gen. 2:16).
B. R. Levi said, "He made him responsible to keep six commandments.
C. "He commanded him against idolatry, in line with this verse: 'Because he willingly walked after idols' (Hos. 5:11).
D. "'The Lord' indicates a commandment against blasphemy, in line with this verse: 'And he who blasphemes the name of the Lord' (Lev. 24:16).
E. "'God' indicates a commandment concerning setting up courts [and a judiciary]: 'You shall not revile the judges' [in the verse at hand, 'God'] (Ex. 22:27).
F. "'...the man' refers to the prohibition of murder: 'Whoever sheds man's blood' (Gen. 9:6).
G. "'...saying' refers to the prohibition of fornication: 'Saying, "If a man put away his wife"'" (Jer. 3:1).
H. "'Of every tree you may eat' (Gen. 2:16) indicates that he commanded him concerning theft. [There are things one may take, and there are things one may not take.]"

Adam and Eve were subject to six commandments, including the prohibition of idolatry, Hos. 5:11.

Genesis Rabbah XIX:IX

2. A. R. Abbahu in the name of R. Yosé bar Haninah: "It is written, 'But they are like a man [Adam], they have transgressed the covenant' (Hos. 6:7).
B. "'They are like a man,' specifically, like the first man. [We shall now compare the story of the first man in Eden with the story of Israel in its land.]
C. "'In the case of the first man, I brought him into the garden of Eden, I commanded him, he violated my commandment, I judged

him to be sent away and driven out, but I mourned for him, saying "How...."' [which begins the book of Lamentations, hence stands for a lament, but which, as we just saw, also is written with the consonants that also yield, 'Where are you'].

D. "'I brought him into the garden of Eden,' as it is written, 'And the Lord God took the man and put him into the garden of Eden' (Gen. 2:15).

E. "'I commanded him,' as it is written, 'And the Lord God commanded...' (Gen. 2:16).

F. "'And he violated my commandment,' as it is written, 'Did you eat from the tree concerning which I commanded you' (Gen. 3:11).

G. "'I judged him to be sent away,' as it is written, "And the Lord God sent him from the garden of Eden' (Gen. 3:23).

H. "'And I judged him to be driven out.' 'And he drove out the man' (Gen. 3:24).

I. "'But I mourned for him, saying, "How...."' ' 'And he said to him, "Where are you"' (Gen. 3:9), and the word for 'where are you' is written, 'How....'

J. "'So too in the case of his descendants, [God continues to speak,] I brought them into the Land of Israel, I commanded them, they violated my commandment, I judged them to be sent out and driven away but I mourned for them, saying, "How...."'

K. "'I brought them into the Land of Israel.' 'And I brought you into the land of Carmel' (Jer. 2:7).

L. "'I commanded them.' 'And you, command the children of Israel' (Ex. 27:20). 'Command the children of Israel' (Lev. 24:2).

M. "'They violated my commandment.' 'And all Israel have violated your Torah' (Dan. 9:11).

N. "'I judged them to be sent out.' 'Send them away, out of my sight and let them go forth' (Jer 15:1).

O. "'....and driven away.' 'From my house I shall drive them' (Hos. 9:15).

P. "'But I mourned for them, saying, "How...."' 'How has the city sat solitary, that was full of people' (Lam. 1:1)."

Adam and Israel are compared with one another, Hos. 6:7.

GENESIS RABBAH XXVIII:VII.

1. A. ["Man and beast and creeping things and birds of the air" (Gen. 6:7):] Said R. Eleazar, "'Surely their wealth is cut off' (Job 22:20). First the Holy One, blessed be he, destroyed their capital [that is, the flocks and herds], so that they should not say, 'It is because he needs our capital [that he is destroying us].' [Perhaps the point is that people should not say God was jealous of the prosperity of the generation of the Flood.]

B. "'And their abundance the fire has consumed' (Job 22:20). For they furthermore saw their gold chains melted in fire."

2. A. Said R. Aqiba, "Every [prophet] railed against the silver and gold that came up from Egypt with them:
B. "'Your silver has become dross' (Is. 1:22). 'And multiplied unto her silver and gold which they used for Baal' (Hos. 2:10). 'Of their silver and their gold have they made them idols' (Hos. 8:4)."
3. A. R. Huna, R. Jeremiah in the name of R. Samuel b. R. Isaac, "It was so that they might be cut off' is not what is written (at Hos. 8:4), but rather, 'so that *he* may be cut off.' This is like a person who says, 'I shall wipe out the name of Mr. So and so, who led my son to bad ways.'"

Hosea was one of the prophets who condemned the gold and silver that the Israelites took from Egypt.

Genesis Rabbah XXIX:III.
1. A. "And Noah found grace" (Gen. 6:8):
B. Said R. Simon, "There were three acts of finding on the part of the Holy One, blessed be he:
C. "'And you found [Abraham's] heart faithful before you' (Neh. 9:8).
D. "'I have found David my servant' (Ps. 89:21).
E. "'I found Israel like grapes in the wilderness' (Hos. 9:10)."
F. His fellows said to R. Simon, "And is it not written, 'Noah found grace in the eyes of the Lord' (Gen. 6:8)?"
G. He said them, "He found it, but the Holy One, blessed be he, did not find it."
H. Said R. Simon, "'He found grace in the wilderness' (Jer. 31:1) on account of the merit of the generation of the Wilderness."

God found Israel in the wilderness, so Hos. 9:10.

Genesis Rabbah XXXVIII:VI.
6. A. Rabbi said, "Great is peace, for even if Israel should worship idols, if there is peace among them, said the Holy One, blessed be he, it is as if I shall not exercise dominion over them [and punish them], as it is said, 'Ephraim is united in idol worship, let him alone' (Hos. 4:17).
B. "But if they are torn by dissension, what is written concerning them? 'Their heart is divided, now shall they bear their guilt' (Hos. 10:23)."

If the Israelites are at peace with one another, God will forgive their idolatry, but if they exhibit dissension, they bear guilt.

Genesis Rabbah XLVI:I.
1. A. "When Abram was ninety-nine years old, [the Lord appeared to Abram and said to him, 'I am God Almighty. Walk before me and be blameless']" (Gen. 17:1).

4. Hosea in Genesis Rabbah, Leviticus Rabbah and Pesiqta deRab Kahana

- B. "I found Israel like grapes in the wilderness, I saw your fathers as the first-ripe in the fig-tree at her first season" (Hos. 9:10).
- C. R. Yudan said, "In the case of a fig-tree, to begin with the fruit is gathered one by one, then two by two, then three by three, until in the end people are able to gather whole basketsful and shovelsful. So too at the beginning there was only Abraham, then there were Abraham and Isaac, and then there were Abraham, Isaac, and Jacob, until: 'And the children of Israel were fruitful and increased abundantly and multiplied' (Ex. 1:7)."
- D. Said R. Yudan, "Just as in the case of a fig-tree, nothing goes to waste except for its stem, and when the stem is taken away the blemish is removed, so did the Holy One blessed be he say to Abraham, 'You have no refuse except for the foreskin. Remove it and the blemish will go away:' 'Walk before me and be blameless' (Gen. 17:1)."

Hos. 9:10 provides a metaphor for Israel, at first productive piece-meal, then in abundance.

GENESIS RABBAH XLVIII:VI.
1. A. "Sinners in Zion are afraid" (Is. 33:14):
   - B. Said R. Jeremiah b. Eleazar, "The matter may be compared to the case of two children who ran away from school. While the one was being thrashed, the other trembled."
   - C. Said R. Jonathan, "Whenever there is a reference in Scripture to faithlessness, the passage speaks of heretics. The generative case for all of them is in this verse: 'The sinners in Zion are afraid, trembling has seized the ungodly' (Is. 33:14)."
   - D. Said R. Judah bar Simon, "The matter may be compared to the case of a bandit chief who rebelled against the king. The king said, 'To whoever arrests him I shall give a bounty.' Someone went and arrested him. The king said, 'Hold the two of them over until morning.' The one was trembling about what sort of bounty the king would give to him, and the other was afraid about what sort of judgment the king would mete out to him.
   - E. "So in the age to come Israel will be afraid: 'And they shall come in fear to the Lord and to his goodness' (Hos. 3:5).

Hos. 3:5 indicates that in the age to come Israel will be afraid.

GENESIS RABBAH XLVIII:XIII.
1. A. "And Abraham ran to the herd [and took a calf, tender and good, and gave it to the servant, who hastened to prepare it]" (Gen. 18:7):
   - B. Said R. Levi, "He ran to get there before the nation of whom it is written, 'Ephraim is a heifer well broken, that loves to thresh' (Hos. 10:11)."

Hos. 10:11 speaks of Abraham in Gen. 18:7.

GENESIS RABBAH LIII:III.
1. A. "For though the fig tree does not blossom" (Hab. 3:17):
   B. This refers to Abraham, in line with the following verse: "I saw your fathers as the first ripe in the fig tree at her first season" (Hos. 9:10).
   C. "Neither is there fruit in the vines" (Hab. 32:17) speaks of Sarah, in line with this verse: "Your wife shall be as a fruitful vine" (Ps. 128:3).
   D. "The labor of the olive fails" (Hab. 3:17): the angels who brought the good news to Sarah made her face shine like an olive. Now did they tell lies?
   E. No, but "The fields yielded no food" (Hab. 3:17) indicates that "the withered breast" [a play on the fact that the word for "fields" and the word for "breasts" use the same consonants] yielded no food.
   F. "The flock is cut off from the fold" (Hab. 3:17) in line with this: "And you my flock, the flock of my pasture, are men" (Ez. 34:31).
   G. "There is no herd in the stalls" (Hab. 3:17). "And Ephraim is a heifer well broken, that loves to thresh" (Hos. 10:11).
   H. Now Sarah went and said, "Shall I then give up hoping in my creator? God forbid. I shall not give up hoping in my creator, 'For I will rejoice in the Lord, I will exalt in the God of my salvation' (Hab. 3:18)."
   I. Said to her the Holy One, blessed be he, "You did not give up hope in me. So I shall not give up hope in you."
   J. "The Lord remembered Sarah as he had said [and the Lord did to Sarah as he had promised]" (Gen. 21:1).

Hab. 3:17 intersects with Hos. 9:10, 10:11.

GENESIS RABBAH LVI:I.
1. A. "On the third day Abraham lifted up his eyes and saw the place afar off" (Gen. 22:4):
   B. "After two days he will revive us, on the third day he will raise us up, that we may live in his presence" (Hos.16:2).
   C. On the third day of the tribes: "And Joseph said to them on the third day, 'This do and live'" (Gen. 42:18).
   D. On the third day of the giving of the Torah: "And it came to pass on the third day when it was morning" (Ex. 19:16).
   E. On the third day of the spies: "And hide yourselves there for three days" (Josh 2:16).
   F. On the third day of Jonah: "And Jonah was in the belly of the fish three days and three nights" (Jonah 2:1).
   G. On the third day of the return from the Exile: "And we abode there three days" (Ezra 8:32).

H. On the third day of the resurrection of the dead: "After two days he will revive us, on the third day he will raise us up, that we may live in his presence" (Hos. 16:2).
I. On the third day of Esther: "Now it came to pass on the third day that Esther put on her royal apparel" (Est. 5:1).
J. She put on the monarchy of the house of her fathers.
K. On account of what sort of merit?
L. Rabbis say, "On account of the third day of the giving of the Torah."
M. R. Levi said, "It is on account of the merit of the third day of Abraham: 'On the third day Abraham lifted up his eyes and saw the place afar off' (Gen. 22:4)."

God will raise the dead on the third day, Hos. 16:2.

GENESIS RABBAH LVII:IV.

1. A. Another matter: Abraham was concerned about suffering [so, as stated above, "And it came to pass after these things" (Gen. 22:20) means that there were misgivings then. On whose part? On Abraham's.]
   B. Said the Holy One, blessed be he, "You do not have to worry. The one who is going to receive suffering has now been born, namely, 'Uz [who is Job], the first born and Buz his brother.'"
2. A. [Since Uz is the same as Job, a contemporary of Abraham, we proceed to discuss Job.] When did Job live?
   B. R. Simeon b. Laqish in the name of Bar Qappara: "He lived in the time of Abraham: 'Uz, the first born and Buz his brother' (Gen. 22:20). It is written, 'There was a man in the land of Uz. His name was Job' (Job 1:1)."
   C. R. Abba bar Kahana said, "Job lived in the time of Jacob."
   D. For R. Abba bar Kahana said, "Dinah was the wife of Job."
   E. R. Levi said, "Job lived in the time of the tribes [Reuben and Judah, who confessed their sins to Jacob (Freedman, p. 506, n. 2)], in line with this verse: 'Which wise man have told and have not hid it from their fathers' (Job 15:18).
   F. "And what reward did they receive on that account? 'Unto them alone the land was given' (Job 15:19)."
   G. R. Yosé bar Halputa said, "When the Israelites went down to Egypt he was born, and when they came up from Egypt, he died. You find that the period in which Job flourished was two hundred and ten years, and the Israelites spent two hundred and ten years in Egypt. What happened was that Satan came to condemn Israel, and God sicked him on Job."
   H. R. Hinena bar Aha and R. Hama bar Haninah:
   I. R. Hinena bar Aha said, "The matter may be compared to the case of a shepherd who was standing and watching his flock. A wolf came along and attacked him. He said, 'Throw him a he-goat on which to spend his wrath.'"

J. R. Hama bar Haninah said, "The matter may be compared to the case of a king who was sitting at a banquet and a dog came along and attacked him. He said, 'Give him a bone on which to spend his wrath.'"

K. [Reverting to G:] "That is in line with this verse: 'God delivers me to the ungodly and throws me into the hands of the wicked' (Job 16:11), and would that people were righteous, but they are indeed wicked."

L. R. Yosé bar Judah said, "He lived in the time that the judges ruled, in line with this verse: 'Behold, all you yourselves have seen it, why then are you altogether vain' (Job 27:12). That is to say, 'You have seen my deeds, you have seen the deeds of my contemporaries.' 'You have seen my deeds, which are the performance of religious duties and of good deeds.' 'You have seen the deeds of my contemporaries, who want to pay whores right out of the granaries, while righteous men do not pay whores right out of the granaries,' as it is said, 'You have loved a harlot's hire out of every grain-floor' (Hos. 9:1)."

M. R. Samuel bar Nahman said, "He lived in the time of the Chaldeans: 'The Chaldeans set themselves in three bands' (Job 1:17)."

N. R. Nathan said, "He lived in the time of the Queen of Sheba: 'And the Sabeans made a raid and took them away' (Job 1:15)."

O. R. Joshua said, "He lived in the days of Ahasuerus: 'Let there be sought for the king young virgins, fair to look on' (Est. 2:2), and it is written, 'And there were no women found so fair as the daughters of Job' (Job 42:15)."

Hos. 9:1 places Job in the time of the Judges.

Genesis Rabbah LIX:IX.

1. A. "The servant said to him, 'Perhaps [the woman may not be willing to follow me to this land; must I then take your son back to the land from which you came?]'" (Gen. 24:5):

B. That is in line with this verse: "Canaan, the balances of deceit are in his hand" (Hos. 12:8).

C. "Canaan" refers to Eliezer.

D. . " .. the balances of deceit are in his hand" (Hos. 12:8): For he sat and weighed the prospects of his own daughter, "Is she suitable or not suitable [to be married to Isaac]?"

E. "To rob the beloved one" (Hos. 12:8): to rob the one whom the world loves, Isaac.

F. He spoke to him in this way until he came to the word "perhaps," [which can be read, "to me." Thus he indicated that he had in mind a marriage between Isaac and his own family. Then his statement's sense was,] "Perhaps I may give him my daughter."

G. Abraham said to him, "You are cursed and my son is blessed, and a curse cannot cleave to a blessing."

Hos. 12:8 refers to Eliezer in his hope that his daughter might serve for a wife for Isaac.

GENESIS RABBAH LXX:XX.
   1. A. "[So Jacob did so and completed her work; then Laban gave him his daughter Rachel to wife]...So Jacob went in to Rachel also, and he loved Rachel more than Leah, and served Laban for another seven years" (Gen. 29:28-30):
      B. Said R. Judah bar Simon, "Under ordinary circumstances a worker works with a householder assiduously for two or three hours, but then he gets lazy at his work. But here just as the labor committed for the first years was complete, so the labor given in the latter seven years was hard and complete.
      C. "Just as the first years were worked out in good faith, so the last years were worked out in good faith."
   2. A. Said R. Yohanan, "It is written, 'And Jacob fled into the field of Aram, and Israel served for a wife, and for a wife he kept sheep' (Hos. 12:13).
      B. "He said to them, 'Your example is like Jacob. Just as Jacob was subjugated before he had married a wife and was also subjugated after he had married a wife, so you, before your redeemer was born, have been subjugated, and after your redeemer has been born you are still subjugated."

Hos. 12:13 speaks of Israel in the model of Jacob, subjugated before and after the redeemer was born.

GENESIS RABBAH LXXVIII:II.
   1. A. "Then he said, 'Let me go, for the day is breaking:'"
      B. [The angel said,] "For the time of giving praise has come."
      C. He said to him, "Let your fellow angels give praise."
      D. He said to him, "I cannot do that. Tomorrow I shall come to give praise, and people will say to me, 'Just as you did not give praise yesterday, so you will not give praise today [and I'll lose my position]."
      E. He said to him, "Stop the chatter, enough! 'I will not let you go unless you bless me' (Gen. 32:26)."
      F. Jacob further said to him, "Those angels who came to Abraham took their leave from him only by giving him a blessing."
      G. He said to him, "Those angels who came to Abraham were sent for that very purpose. I have not been sent for that purpose."
      H. He said to him, "Stop the chatter, enough! 'I will not let you go unless you bless me' (Gen. 32:26)."
      I. R. Levi in the name of R. Samuel b. Nahman said: "Because the ministering angels revealed the mystery of the Holy One, blessed

be he, [telling Lot what he was about to do], they were sent into exile from their appropriate dwelling for a hundred and thirty eight years." [This explains why the angel, for his part, cannot now do other than his assigned mission; it would be presumptuous.]

J. [The angel then continued,] "Shall I listen to you and be expelled from my proper station?"

K. He said to him, "Stop the chatter, enough! 'I will not let you go unless you bless me' (Gen. 32:26)."

L. Said R. Huna, "In the end he said, 'I shall reveal matters to you, and if the Holy One, blessed be he, should say to me, "Why did you reveal matters to him," I shall say to him, "Lord of all ages, your children make decrees, and you do not nullify their decrees, so do I have the power to nullify their decrees?"'

B. [Huna goes on,] "He said to him, 'He is destined to reveal himself to you in Beth El and to change your name, and I shall be standing there.'

C. [Huna concludes,] "That is why it is written, 'At Beth El he would find him, and there he would speak with *us* ' (Hos. 12:5). 'With you' is not what is written, but rather, 'with us' [that is, the angel and Jacob]."

Hos. 12:5 has God address Jacob and the angel.

Genesis Rabbah LXXX:I.

1. A. "And Dinah, daughter of Leah, whom she had borne to Jacob, went out [to visit the women of the land; and when Shechem, son of Hamor the Hivite, the prince of the land, saw her, he seized her and lay with her and humbled her]" (Gen. 34:1):

B. "Behold everyone that uses proverbs shall use this proverb against you, saying, 'As the mother, so her daughter'" (Ez. 16:44):

C. Yosé of Onayyah interpreted the verse that follows in the synagogue of Maon: "Hear this, O you priests, and attend, O house of Israel, and give ear, O house of the king, for to you pertains the judgment" (Hos. 5:1).

D. [As to "Hear this, O you priests,"] "He said, "The Holy One, blessed be he, is destined to call the priests to judgment, asking, 'Why did you not labor in study of the Torah? And did you not derive benefit from my children through the twenty-four priestly gifts [that were paid to you by them]?'

E. "They will say, 'They did not give us anything.'

F. "Then, as to '...and attend, O house of Israel:' 'Why did you not give them the twenty-four gifts to the priesthood of which I wrote in the Torah?'

G. "They will say, 'It was on account of the officers of the administration of the patriarch, who grabbed everything.'

H. "Then as to: '...give ear, O house of the king, for to you pertains the judgment,' 'Were the gifts yours, of which I said, "And this shall be the due of the priests from the people" (Deut. 18:3)?'
I. "'Therefore against you will the attribute of justice turn.'"
J. Rabbi [Judah the Patriarch] heard about this [subversive] speech and was outraged.
K. Toward evening R. Simeon b. Laqish came to pay his respects and to conciliate him. He said to him, "Rabbi, we have to be grateful to the nations of the world, who bring clowns into theaters and circuses and have a good time with them, so that they should not go into session and talk with one another [in a serious way]. But Yosé of Onayyah spoke words of Torah, and should you be angry with him?"
L. He said to him, "And does he know [the Torah]?"
M. He said to him, "Yes."
N. "And has he received proper instruction?"
O. He said to him, "Yes."
P. "And if I address a question to him, will he give a proper answer?"
Q. He said to him, "Yes."
R. He said to him, "Let him come."
S. When he had come up there, he said to him, "What is the meaning of the verse: 'Behold everyone that uses proverbs shall use this proverb against you, saying, "As the mother, so her daughter"' (Ez. 16:44)?"
T. He said to him, "Like daughter, like mother, like people, like leader, like altar, like priests."
U. Kahana said, "Like orchard, like gardener."
V. R. Simeon b. Laqish said to him, "Up to this point you have not completed the work of conciliating him for the first insult, and you produce another one? The main point of is this: what is the meaning of the verse, 'Behold everyone that uses proverbs shall use this proverb against you, saying, "As the mother, so her daughter"' (Ez. 16:44)?"
W. He said to him, "There is no cow that gores unless her calf kicks, there is no woman who turns into a whore unless her daughter commits an act of prostitution."
X. He said to him, "If that is the case, was our matriarch Leah a whore?"
Y. He said to them, "Indeed so, for it is written, 'And Leah went out to meet him' (Gen. 30:16). She went out all made up to meet him, just like a whore. That is why it is written, 'And Dinah, daughter of Leah, whom she had borne to Jacob, went out.'"

Hos. 5:1 condemns the priests for not studying the Torah even though the material means for doing so were available to them.

Genesis Rabbah LXXX:II.

1. A. "And as troops of robbers wait for a man [so the priests are banded together; they murder on the way to Shechem, yes, they commit whoredom; in the house of Israel I have seen a horrible thing, Ephraim's harlotry is there, Israel is defiled]" (Hos. 6:9):
   B. Just as highway men wait by the road and kill people and take their money, so is that which Simeon and Levi did in Shechem?
   C. Scripture states, "The priests are banded together."
   D. Just as priests form a company at the threshing floor to collect their share of the crop, so did Simeon and Levi do in Shechem:
   E. "they murder on the way to Shechem, yes, they commit whoredom."
   F. It was for good reason that Simeon and Levi committed murder in Shechem. For "they said, 'Will people treat our sister as a whore'" (Gen. 34:31)?
   G. They said, "Will these people treat us as if we were public property?"
   H. And what caused it all?
   I. "Now Dinah, the daughter of Leah...went out" (Gen. 34:1).

Hos. 6:9 compares the priests to troops of robbers.

Genesis Rabbah LXXXII:II.

5. A. "I am the Lord...who confirms the word of his servant and performs the counsel of his angels" (Is. 44:26ff.):
   B. R. Berekhiah in the name of R. Levi: "Since he confirms the word of his servant, do we not know that he also will perform the counsel of his angels?
   C. "But an angel appeared to Jacob and said to him, 'He is destined to reveal himself to you in Beth El and to change your name, and I shall be standing there.'
   D. "That is why it is written, 'At Beth El he would find him, and there he would speak with *us* ' (Hos. 12:5). 'With you' is not what is written, but rather, 'with us' [that is, the angel and Jacob].
   E. "So the Holy One, blessed be he, appeared to him in order to carry out the statements of that angel.
   F. "And as to Jerusalem, since all of the prophets prophesied about it, how much the more so [will God's words be confirmed]: 'God appeared to Jacob again, when he came from Paddan-aram, and blessed him.'"

As above.

Genesis Rabbah LXXXII:XI.

1. A. "While Israel dwelt in that land, [Reuben went and lay with Bilhah, his father's concubine, and Israel heard of it. Now the sons of Jacob were twelve. The sons of Leah: Reuben, Jacob's first born,

4. Hosea in Genesis Rabbah, Leviticus Rabbah and Pesiqta deRab Kahana 51

Simeon, Levi, Judah, Issachar, and Zebulun. The sons of Rachel: Joseph and Benjamin. The sons of Bilhah, Rachel's maid, Dan and Naphtali. The sons of Zilpah, Leah's maid, Gad and Asher. These were the sons of Jacob who were born to him in Paddan-aram]" (Gen. 35:22-26):

B. Said R. Simon, "It is difficult before the Holy One, blessed be he, to pull up a name from its proper place in the genealogical chain.

C. "'And the sons of Reuben, the first born of Israel' — for he was the firstborn, but, since he defiled his father's bed, his birthright was given to the sons of Joseph, the son of Israel, yet not so that he was to be reckoned in the genealogy as firstborn' (1 Chr. 5:1).

D. "What this indicates is that the birthright as to property was taken away from him, but not the birthright as to genealogy. [Thus we see, 'Reuben, Jacob's first born,' and that in the very context of the matter of Bilhah.]"

E. R. Levi and R. Simon:

F. One of them said, "It is not for Reuben to be reckoned in the genealogy [as the firstborn]."

G. The other of them said, "The genealogy lists not Joseph but Reuben as firstborn."

H. R. Haggai in the name of R. Isaac: "Even in the hour of his disgrace, the genealogy involving the firstborn is assigned only to Reuben.

I. "That is in line with this verse: 'While Israel dwelt in that land, Reuben went and lay with Bilhah, his father's concubine, and Israel heard of it. Now the sons of Jacob were twelve. The sons of Leah: Reuben, Jacob's first born...'"

J. R. Yudan in the name of R. Aha: "Reuben was firstborn as to conception, firstborn as to birth, firstborn as to the right of the firstborn, firstborn as to inheritance, firstborn as to transgression, firstborn as to repentance."

K. R. Azariah said, "Also firstborn as to prophecy: 'The Lord spoke first with Hosea [descended from Reuben]' (Hos. 1:2)."

Reuben was firstborn as to prophecy, because the Lord spoke first with his descendant, Hosea, Hos. 1:2.

GENESIS RABBAH LXXXIV:XIX.

1. A. ["When Reuben returned to the pit and saw that Joseph was not in the pit, he tore his clothes and returned to his brothers and said, 'The lad is gone, and I, where shall I go?' Then they took Joseph's robe and slaughtered a goat and dipped the robe in the blood, and they sent the long robe with sleeves and brought it to their father and said, 'This we have found; see now whether it is your son's robe or not'" (Gen. 37:29-34)]: "When Reuben returned to the pit:" Where had he been?

B. R. Eliezer said, "He had been occupied with his sackcloth and ashes [on account of his earlier sin with his father's concubine],

and when he had a free moment, he went and looked into the pit. That is in line with this verse: 'When Reuben returned to the pit.'"
C. R. Joshua said, "All of the management of the household was assigned to him. When he had a moment, he went and looked into the pit. That is in line with this verse: 'When Reuben returned to the pit.'"
D. Said the Holy One, blessed be he, to him, "No person ever sinned and then repented before me, but you have begun the practice of repentance. By your life, your son's son will stand and open the way to repentance first of all.
E. "And who is this? It is Hosea: 'Return, O Israel, to the Lord your God' (Hos. 14:2)."

Reuben's heir, Hosea, realized the value of repentance first of all, so Hos. 14:2.

Genesis Rabbah LXXXVI:I.
1. A. "Now Joseph was taken down to Egypt, [and Potiphar, an officer of Pharaoh, the captain of the guard, an Egyptian, bought him from the Ishmaelites who had brought him down there] (Gen. 39:1):
B. "I drew them with cords of a man, [with bands of love. Yet I was to them as those who lift up a yoke, on account of their jaws. I reached out food to them]" (Hos. 11:4):
C. "I drew them with cords of a man:" this refers to Israel: "Draw me, we will run after you" (Song 1:4).
D. "With bands of love" (Hos. 11:4): "I have loved you, says the Lord" (Mal. 1:2).
E. "Yet I was to them as those who lift up a yoke:" "For I raised their enemies over them." Why so?
F. "On account of their jaws:" On account of something that they issued from their jaws, saying to the golden calf, "These are your Gods, Israel" (Ex. 32:8).
G. And at the end: "I reached out food to them:" [God says,] "I provided much food for them. 'May he be as a rich grain field in the land' (Ps. 72:16)."

Hos. 11:4 refers to Israel, drawn by God with bands of love; God still raised their enemies over them because of their praise of the golden calf but in the end provided them with food.

Genesis Rabbah XCI:VII.
7. A. "On the third day Joseph said to them, 'Do this and you will live'" (Gen. 42:18):
B. That is in line with this verse: "After two days he will revive us, on the third day he will raise us up, that we may live in his presence" (Hos. 6:2).

4. Hosea in Genesis Rabbah, Leviticus Rabbah and Pesiqta deRab Kahana

    C.   That is, on the third day as in the case of the tribal fathers.

On the third day God raised up the dead, Hos. 6:2.

LEVITICUS RABBAH

LEVITICUS RABBAH I:II

1. A.   R. Abbahu opened [discourse by citing the following verse]: "'They shall return and dwell beneath his shadow, they shall grow grain, they shall blossom as a vine, their fragrance shall be like the wine of Lebanon' (Hos. 14:7).
    B.   "'They shall return and dwell beneath his shadow' — these are proselytes who come and take refuge in the shadow of the Holy One, blessed be he.
    C.   "'They shall grow grain' — they are turned into part of] the root, just as [any other] Israelite.
    D.   "That is in line with the following verse: 'Grain will make the young men flourish, and wine the women' (Zech. 9:17).
    E.   "'They shall blossom as a vine' — like [any other] Israelite.
    F.   "That is in line with the following verse: 'A vine did you pluck up out of Egypt, you did drive out the nations and plant it'" (Ps. 80:9).

Hos. 14:7 speaks of proselytes.

LEVITICUS RABBAH I:XIV

1. A.   What is the difference between Moses and all the other [Israelite] prophets?
    B.   R. Judah b. R. Ilai and rabbis:
    C.   R. Judah said, "All the other prophets saw [their visions] through nine lenses [darkly], in line with the following verse of Scripture: 'And the appearance of the vision which I saw was like the vision that I saw when I came to destroy the city; and the visions were like the vision that I saw by the River Chebar, and I fell on my face' (Ex. 43:3) [with the root RH occurring once in the plural, hence two, and seven other times in the singular, nine in all].
    D.   "But Moses saw [his vision] through a single lense: 'in [one vision] and not in dark speeches'" (Num. 12:8).
    E.   Rabbis said, "All other [Israelite] prophets saw [their visions] through a dirty lense. That is in line with the following verse of Scripture: 'And I have multiplied visions, and by the ministry of the angels I have used similitudes' (Hos. 12:11)
    F.   "But Moses saw [his vision] through a polished lense: 'And the image of God does he behold'" (Num. 12:8).

Hos. 12:11 speaks of the other prophets, besides Moses, who had a clouded vision; Moses's vision was clear.

LEVITICUS RABBAH VI:I

2. A. Said R. Aha, "The following [passage represents] the Holy One, blessed be he, making excuses in defense of this party and of that party too. [How so?] It addresses Israel: 'Be not a witness against your neighbor [God] without cause' (Prov. 24:28).

B. "And it says to the Holy One, blessed be he: 'Do not say, "I will do to him as he has done to me; I will pay the man back for what he has done"'" (Prov. 24:29).

C. Said R. Phineas, "It is written, 'But like a man they transgressed the covenant,' [which applies to Israel].

D. "But here [in regard to God]: '[I will not execute my fierce anger, I will not again destroy Ephraim,] for I am God and not man'" (Hos. 11:9).

Hos. 11:9 has God promise not to destroy Ephraim, making excuses in defense of sinners.

LEVITICUS RABBAH VI:V

6. A. When the Israelites transgressed the agreement of Sinai, the Holy One, blessed be he, said to them, "I too shall do the same to you" (Lev. 26:16). ["But if you will not hearken to me . . . but break my covenant, I will do this to you . . . " (Lev. 26:14ff.)].

B. Said R. Phineas, "It is written, 'And they, being men, have transgressed the covenant' [Hos. 6:7].

C. "But as to the other: 'For I am God and not man'" (Hos. 11:9).

As above.

LEVITICUS RABBAH VI:VI

1. A. [With reference to Is. 8:18-19: "Behold, I and the children whom the Lord has given me are signs and portents in Israel from the Lord of hosts, who dwells on Mount Zion. And when they say to you, 'Consult the mediums and the wizards who chirp and mutter,' should not a people consult their God? Should they consult the dead on behalf of the living?"] said R. Simeon, "Two verses [only] did Beeri [father of Hosea, Hos. 1:1] prophesy, and they were not enough to fill a scroll, so they are attached to the book of Isaiah.

B. "And these are they: 'And when they say to you, Consult the mediums and the wizards' (Is. 8:19) and the neighboring verse" (8:20).

Hosea's father was a prophet.

LEVITICUS RABBAH VII:III

3. A. R. Huna made two statements.

4. Hosea in Genesis Rabbah, Leviticus Rabbah and Pesiqta deRab Kahana

B. R. Huna said, "All of the communities of exiles will be gathered back into the land only on account of the merit of the passages of the Mishnah [that they have memorized].

C. "That is in line with the following verse of Scripture: 'Especially when they repeat [Mishnah-traditions and memorize them] among the gentiles, then will I gather them back'" (Hos. 8:10).

Studying the Torah will bring about the ingathering of the exiles.

LEVITICUS RABBAH X:VI

1. A. "[The Lord said to Moses, 'Take Aaron and his sons with him,] and the garments [and the anointing oil and the bull of the sin offering, the two rams, and the basket of unleavened bread, and assemble all the congregation at the door of the tent of meeting]'" (Lev. 8:1-3).

B. R. Simon said, "Just as the sacrifices effect atonement, so [wearing of the] garments effects atonement.

C. "This is in accord with the following teaching, which we have learned in the Mishnah [M. Yoma 7:5]: 'The high priest serves in eight garments, and an ordinary priest in four: tunic, underpants, head-covering, and girdle. The high priest in addition wears the breastplate, apron, upper garment, and frontlet.'

D. "The tunic serves to effect atonement for those who wear garments made up of mixed fabrics [deriving from both vegetable matter and animal matter, such as linen and wool].

E. "That is in line with the following verse of Scripture: 'And he made from him a tunic of many colors' (Gen. 37:3).

F. "Underpants serve to effect atonement for licentiousness.

G. "That is in line with the following verse of Scripture: 'And you shall make linen underpants for them to cover the flesh of nakedness' (Ex. 28:42).

N. "The apron serves to effect atonement for idolatry.

O. "This is in line with the following verse of Scripture: '[For the children of Israel shall dwell many days without king or prince without sacrifice or pillar,] without apron or teraphim. [Afterward the children of Israel shall return and seek the Lord]'" (Hos. 3:4).

P. The upper garment: R. Simon in the name of R. Nathan said, "For two matters there is no possibility of atonement, yet the Torah has [still] assigned a mode of atonement to them, and these are they: gossip and unintentional manslaughter.

Hos. 3:4 indicates that the apron of the high priest atones for idolatry.

LEVITICUS RABBAH XII:V

3. A. Now Solomon slept to the fourth hour of the day, with the keys of the house of the sanctuary kept under his head.

- B. That is in line with that which we have learned in the Mishnah (M. Ed. 6:1): "The morning burnt offering is offered at the fourth hour."
- C. Lo, what did [Pharaoh's daughter] do for him? She made a kind of canopy and set stars and planets in it and spread it over his bed. When he wanted to get up, he saw it and supposed that it was still night, so he slept until the fourth hour.
- D. His mother then came in and rebuked him.
- E. And there is he who says that it was Jeroboam b. Nabat who came in and rebuked him.
- F. And could [Jeroboam] have done any such thing?
- G. R. Haggai in the name of R. Isaac: "He went and gathered eighty thousand men of his tribe [Ephraim] and went in and rebuked him.
- H. "That is in line with the following verse of Scripture: 'When Ephraim spoke, people trembled. He was exalted in Israel. But he incurred guilt through Baal and died'" (Hos. 13:1).
- I. "When Ephraim spoke, people trembled" — when Jeroboam spoke of the incontinence of Solomon, the Holy One, blessed be he, said to him, "Why do you rebuke him?"
- J. [God continues:] "'He was exalted in Israel' — he is a prince in Israel.
- K. "By your life, I shall give you a taste of the kind of authority that he wields, and you will not be able to endure it."
- L. When [Jeroboam] entered his dominion, forthwith: "He incurred guilt through Baal and died" (Hos. 13:1).
- M. Rabbis say, "It was most certainly his mother who went in and rebuked him.
- N. "She took her slipper and slapped him this way and that, saying to him, 'What my child'" (Prov. 31:2).

Hos. 13:1 speaks of Jeroboam.

LEVITICUS RABBAH XIX:II

- 7. A. It is written, "Hear, Israel, the Lord, our God, is one (HD) Lord" (Deut. 6:4).
- B. "If you turn the D into an R (HR) [in the Hebrew word one], you will destroy the whole world, [since you will not read, 'is one, but is <u>another</u> Lord']."
- C. It is written, "You shall not bow down to any other (HR) god" (Ex. 32 34:13).
- D. If you turn the R [of the word other] into a D (HD), you will destroy the entire world [by reading, "You will not bow down to one God"].
- E. It is written, "You will not profane (THLLW) my Holy name" (Lev. 22:32).
- F. If you turn the H of the word of profane into an H, you will destroy the entire world [by reading, "You will not praise (THLLW) my holy name"].

4. Hosea in Genesis Rabbah, Leviticus Rabbah and Pesiqta deRab Kahana

G. It is written, "Every soul will praise (THLL) the Lord" (Ps. 103:6).
H. If you turn the H into an H, you will destroy the entire world [by reading, "Every soul will profane (THLL) the Lord"].
I. It is written, "They have acted deceptively against (B) the Lord" (Jer. 5:12).
J. If you turn the B into a K, you will destroy the entire world [by reading, "They have acted deceptively, like (K) the Lord"].
K. It is written, "Against (B) the Lord they have acted treacherously" (Hos. 5:7).
L. If you turn the B into a K, you will destroy the world [by reading, "The have acted treacherously, like (K) the Lord"].

Changing a single letter at Hos. 5:7 will produce blasphemy.

LEVITICUS RABBAH XXIII:VI

6. A. Another interpretation of "Like a rose among thorns:"
B. Just as a rose wilts so long as the hot spell persists, but [when the hot spell passes] and dew [TL for SL] falls on it, the rose thrives again, so for Israel, so long as the shadow of Esau falls across the world, as it were Israel wilts.
C. But when the shadow of Esau passes from the world, Israel will once more thrive.
D. That is in line with the following verse of Scripture: "I shall be like the dew for Israel. It will blossom like a rose" (Hos. 14:6).

When Rome goes its way, Israel will prosper, so Hos. 14:6.

LEVITICUS RABBAH XXIV:I

1. A. "You shall be holy [for I the Lord your God am Holy]" (Lev. 19:2).
B. "But the Lord of hosts is exalted in justice, [and the holy God shows himself holy in righteousness]" (Is. 5:16).
C. It has been taught: Said R. Simeon b. Yohai, "When is the name of the Holy One, blessed be he, magnified in his world?
D. "When he applies the attribute of justice to the wicked.
E. "And there are many verses of Scripture [that prove that point]:
F. "'Thus I shall magnify myself and sanctify myself and make myself known [in the eyes of many nations]' (Ez. 38:23).
G. "'The Lord has made himself known, he has executed judgment' (Ps. 9:7).
H. "'I will make myself known among them when I judge you' (Ez. 35:11).
I. "'And it shall be known that the hand of the Lord is with his servants, [and his indignation is against his enemies]' (Is. 66:14)
J. "'This time I shall make them know [my hand and my might]' (Jer. 16:21).
K. "'That you may know the hand of the Lord' (Hos. 4:24).

L. "And this verse: 'But the Lord of hosts is exalted in justice'" (Is. 5:16).

God is magnified when he does justice, Hos. 4:24.

LEVITICUS RABBAH XXVII:VI

1. A. "O my people, what have I done to you, in what have I wearied you? Testify against me" (Mic. 6:3).
   B. Said R. Aha, "'Testify against me' and receive a reward, but 'Do not bear false witness' [Ex. 20:13] and face a settlement of accounts in the age to come."
2. A. Said R. Samuel b. R. Nahman, "On three occasions the Holy One, blessed be he, came to engage in argument with Israel, and the nations of the world rejoiced, saying, 'Can these ever [dare] engage in an argument with their creator? Now he will wipe them out of the world.'
   B. "One was when he said to them, 'Come, and let us reason together, says the Lord' (Is. 1:18). When the Holy One, blessed be he, saw that the nations of the world were rejoicing, he turned the matter to [Israel's] advantage: 'If your sins are as scarlet, they shall be white as snow' (Is. 1:18).
   C. "Then the nations of the world were astonished, and said, 'This is repentance, and this is rebuke? He has planned only to amuse himself with his children.'
   D. "[A second time was] when he said to them, 'Hear, you mountains, the controversy of the Lord' (Mic. 6:2), the nations of the world rejoiced, saying, 'How can these ever [dare] engage in an argument with their creator? Now he will wipe them out of the world.'
   E. "When the Holy One, blessed be he, saw that the nations of the world were rejoicing, he turned the matter to [Israel's] advantage: 'O my people, what have I done to you? In what have I wearied you? Testify against me' [Mic. 6:3]. 'Remember what Balak king of Moab devised' (Mic. 6:5).
   F. "Then the nations of the world were astonished, saying, 'This is repentance, and this is rebuke, one following the other? He has planned only to amuse himself with his children.'
   G. "[A third time was] when he said to them, 'The Lord has an indictment against Judah, and will punish Jacob according to his ways' (Hos. 12:2), the nations of the world rejoiced, saying, 'How can these ever [dare] engage in an argument with their creator? Now he will wipe them out of the world.'
   H. "When the Holy One, blessed be he, saw that the nations of the world were rejoicing, he turned the matter to [Israel's] advantage. That is in line with the following verse of Scripture: 'In the womb he [Jacob = Israel] took his brother [Esau = other nations] by the heel [and in his manhood he strove with God. He strove with the

angel and prevailed, he wept and sought his favor]'" (Hos. 12:3-4).

Hos. 12:3-4 speaks of an occasion on which the nations wanted to take advantage of Israel's insolence toward God.

Leviticus Rabbah XXVII:VIII

1. A. "By their wickedness they make the king glad, [and the princes by their adultery]" (Hos. 7:3).
   B. Now why was the bull recognized as the first of all of the offerings ["bull, sheep, goat"] (Lev. 22:27)?
   C. Said R. Levi, "The matter may be compared to the case of a highborn lady who got a bad name on account of [alleged adultery with] one of the lords of the state.
   D. "The king looked into the matter and found nothing. What did the king do? He made a banquet and sat the [accused] man at the head of the guests.
   E. "Why so? To show that the king had looked into the matter and found nothing.
   F. "So the nations of the world taunt Israel and say to them, 'You made the golden calf!'
   G. "The Holy One, blessed be he, looked into the matter and found nothing. Accordingly, the bull was made the first among all the offerings: 'Bull, sheep, goat'" (Lev. 22:27).
2. A. R. Huna, R. Idi in the name of R. Samuel b. R. Nahman: "The [true] Israelites were saved from that act. For if the Israelites had themselves made the calf, they ought to have said, 'These are our gods, O Israel.' It was the proselytes who came up with Israel from Egypt [who made the calf]: 'And also a mixed multitude came up with them' (Ex. 12:38).
   B. "They are the ones who made the calf. They taunted them, saying to them, 'These are your gods, O Israel'" (Ex. 32:8).
3. A. Said R. Judah b. R. Simon, "It is written, 'An ox knows its owner, and an ass its master's crib, but Israel does not know' (Is. 1:3).
   B. "Did they really not know? Rather, they trampled under heel [God's commandments]. [They did not pay adequate attention and sinned by inadvertence.]"
   C. Along these same lines: "For my people is foolish. Me they have not known'" (Jer. 4:22). Did they not know? Rather, they trampled under heel.
   D. Along these same lines: "And she did not know that it was I who gave her the grain, wine, and oil" (Hos. 2:8). Did she not know? Rather, she trampled under heel.

Hos. 2:8 speaks of Israel's inadvertent sin against God.

Leviticus Rabbah XXVII:XI

1. A. "And whether the mother is a cow or a ewe, [you shall not kill both her and her young in one day]" (Lev. 22:28).
   B. R. Berekhiah in the name of R. Levi: "It is written, 'A righteous man has regard for the life of his beast, but the mercy of the wicked is cruel' [Prov. 12:10].
   C. "'A righteous man has regard' refers to the Holy One, blessed be he, in whose Torah it is written, 'You will not take the dam with the young' [Deut. 22:6].
   D. "'But the mercy of the wicked is cruel' refers to Sennacherib, the wicked one, concerning him it is written, 'The mother was dashed into pieces with her children'" (Hos. 10:14).

Hos. 10:14 speaks of Sennacherib's cruelty to Israel.

Leviticus Rabbah XXXII:IV

1. A. "Whose father was an Egyptian" (Lev. 24:10).
   B. Rabbis and R. Levi:
   C. Rabbis say, "Even though there were no *mamzerim* [children born in violation of the law of appropriate unions] at that time [since Israelite women did not engage in sexual relations with Egyptian men], he was in the status of a *mamzer*."
   D. R. Levi said, "He was in fact a *mamzer*."
   E. How so? The taskmasters were Egyptians and the officers were Israelites. A taskmaster oversaw ten officers, and an officer oversaw ten ordinary people. It turned out that a taskmaster oversaw a hundred and ten men.
   F. One time a taskmaster came early in the morning to an officer and said to him, "Go and call together your group of ten." When he went into his house, his wife smiled at [the taskmaster].
   G. The taskmaster said, "That woman belongs to that man [me]." He went out and hid behind the ladder. When the woman's husband had gone out, he went in and made sport with her.
   H. [The husband] turned around and saw [the taskmaster] leaving his house. When [the taskmaster] realized that he had seen him going forth from his house, he beat him all day long and said, "Harder! harder!" He was planning to kill him [in that way].
   I. At that moment the Holy Spirit aroused Moses. That is the meaning of the statement, "He looked this way and that" (Ex. 2:12).
   J. What is the meaning of, "He looked this way and that"?
   K. He perceived what [the taskmaster] had done to him in the house and what he was going to do to him in the field. He said, "It is not enough for him that he made sport with his wife, but now he wants to kill him!"
   L. Forthwith: "He saw that there was no man" (Ex. 2:12).
   M. What did he see? R. Judah, R. Nehemiah, and rabbis:

N. R. Judah said, "He saw that there was no one else who would rise up and act zealously for the sake of the Holy One, blessed be he, by killing him, so he went and acted zealously for the sake of the Holy One, blessed be he, and killed him."

O. R. Nehemiah said, "He saw that there was no one who would rise up and make mention in his regard of the name [of God] and kill him, so he went and made mention of the name of God and killed him."

P. Rabbis say, "He saw that nothing of value would ever come forth from that man, from his children, or from his descendants for all generations."

Q. Forthwith: "He smote the Egyptian" (Ex. 2:12).

R. With what did he kill him?

S. R. Isaac said, "He killed him with his fist. That is in line with the following verse of Scripture: 'And to smite with the fist of wickedness'" (Is. 58:4).

T. R. Levi said, "He smote him with the Mystery of Israel [by stating the Ineffable Name]."

U. [Supply: That is in line with the following verse of Scripture: "'Is it to kill me that you intend?' And he hid him in the sand" (Ex. 2:12). He hid him on account of Israel, who are compared to sand.] That is in line with the following verse of Scripture: "And the number of the people of Israel will be like the number of grains of sand on the seashore" (Hos. 2:2).

Hos. 2:2 compares Israel in numbers to the sand at the sea.

LEVITICUS RABBAH XXXIII:VI

1. A. R. Samuel bar Nahman made two statements. R. Samuel bar Nahman said, "[Nebuchadnezzar] said to them, 'Was your idol not made out of silver and gold? For it is said, "With their silver and gold they made themselves idols" (Hos. 8:4). But my idol is entire made of gold, pure gold, for it is written, "Nebuchadnezzar the king made an idol out of gold" (Dan. 3:1). And now have you come here to turn my idol into desolation?'"

B. R. Samuel bar Nahman made yet a second statement. "[Nebuchadnezzar] said to them, 'Did not Moses write for you as follows in the Torah: "And there you served gods that were the work of man"'? [Deut. 4:28]

C. "They said to him, 'My lord, O king, This service did not involve worship but rather labor in taxes, fines, head taxes, and *arnonae.*'"

D. Said R. Samuel bar Nahman, "There [in Babylonia] they call the kings gods.

E. "[A. Samuel concludes, 'Nebuchadnezzar said,] "And now have you come to turn my idol into desolation?"'"

Hos. 8:4 proves that the Israelites made idols of silver and gold.

Leviticus Rabbah XXXVI:III

1. A. "Be assured, an evil man will not go unpunished, [but those who are righteous will be delivered]" (Prov. 11:21).
   B. Bar Qappara said, "Ahaz and all the evil kings of Israel will have no share in the world to come.
   C. "What is the proof text? 'All their kings are fallen, there is none among them who calls to me'" (Hos. 7:7).
   D. Yet surely [Ahaz] is counted in the chronology of kings: "In the time of Uzziah, Jotham, Ahaz, and Hezekiah, kings of Judah" (Is. 1:1).
   E. R. Aha in the name of R. Eleazar, R. Yosé in the name of R. Joshua b. Levi said, "It was because he was capable of shame [that he was enumerated, despite his not getting a portion of the world to come].
   F. "How so? When the prophet came to rebuke him, he would go out to an unclean place and turn his face to an unclean place, as if to say that the Presence of God [resting upon the prophet] will not come to rest in an unclean place.
   G. "That is in line with the following verse of Scripture: 'And the Lord said to Isaiah, "Go forth to meet Ahaz, [you and Shearjashub, your son, at the end of the conduit of the upper pool] on the highway to the Fuller's Field"' [Is. 7:3]. Do not read 'fuller' (KWBS) but rather 'cast down' (KWBS), teaching that he cast his face down [to the earth in shame]."

Hos. 7:7 proves that Ahaz and the other evil Israelite kings have no share in the world to come.

Leviticus Rabbah XXXVI:VI

1. A. [Returning to] the body [of the matter:] How long does the merit of the patriarchs endure?
   B. R. Tanhuma made this statement, Rab in the name of R. Hiyya the Elder, R. Menehama said it, R. Berekhiah and R. Helbo in the name of R. Abba bar Zabeda: "Down to Jehoahaz. 'But the lord was gracious to them and had compassion on them [and he turned toward them, because of his covenant with Abraham, Isaac, and Jacob, and would not destroy them; nor has he cast them from his presence until now]' (2 Kgs. 13:23).
   C. "Until now [the time of Jehoahaz, 2 Kgs. 13:22] the merit of the patriarchs has endured."
   D. R. Joshua b. Levi said, "Until the time of Elijah: 'And it came to pass at the time of the evening offering, that Elijah the prophet came near and said, "O Lord, [the God of Abraham, Isaac, and Israel, this day let it be known that you are God"' (1 Kgs. 18:36). Thus, to this day the merit endured, but not afterward.]"
   E. Samuel said, "Down to the time of Hosea: 'Now will I uncover her shame in the sight of her lovers, and no man will [ever again] deliver her out of my hand' (Hos. 2:12).

4. *Hosea in Genesis Rabbah, Leviticus Rabbah and Pesiqta deRab Kahana*

F. "'Man' refers then to Abraham, as it is said in Scripture: 'And now, return the wife of the man' (Gen. 20:7)

G. "'Man' refers only to Isaac, as it is said, 'Who is this man?' (Gen. 24:65).

H. "'Man' refers only to Jacob, as it is said, 'Jacob, a quiet man, dwelling in tents'" (Gen. 28:27).

I. R. Yudan said, "Down to the time of Hezekiah: 'That the government may be increased [and of peace there be no end ... the zeal of the Lord of hosts [thus: not the merit of the patriarchs] does this'" (Is. 9:6).

J. R. Yudan bar Hanan in the name of R. Berekiah said, "If you see that the merit of the patriarchs is slipping away, and the merit of the matriarchs is trembling, then go and cleave to the performance of deeds of loving kindness.

K. "That is in line with the following verse of Scripture: 'For the mountains will melt (YMWSW), and the hills will tremble, [but my love will not depart from you]' [(Is. 54:10).

L. "'Mountains' refers to the patriarchs, and 'hills' to the matriarchs.

M. "Henceforward: 'But my love will not (YMWS) depart from you'" (Is. 54:10).

N. Said R. Aha, "The merit of the patriarchs endures forever. Forever do people call it to mind, saying, 'For the Lord your God is a merciful God. He will not fail you nor destroy you nor forget the covenant he made with your fathers'" (Deut. 4:31).

Hosea marked the end of the merit of the patriarchs, so Hos. 2:12.

PESIQTA DERAB KAHANA

PESIQTA DERAB KAHANA I:VIII.

7. A. ["...came forward and brought their offering before the Lord, six] covered [wagons and twelve oxen, one wagon from every two chiefs and from each one an ox]" (Num. 7:2):] How long did they live?

B. R. Yudan in the name of R. Samuel bar Nahman, R. Hunia in the name of Bar Qappara, "In Gilgal they sacrificed the oxen" (Hos. 12:12)."

C. And where did they offer them up?

D. R. Abba bar Kahana said, "In Nob they offered them up."

E. R. Abbahu said, "In Gibeon they offered them up."

F. R. Hama bar Hanina said, "In the eternal house [of Jerusalem] they offered them up."

Hos. 12:12 indicates the disposition of the chief's offering.

PESIQTA DERAB KAHANA II:II

1. A. R. Jacob bar Judah in the name of R. Jonathan of Bet Gubrin opened [discourse by citing the following intersecting-verse:] "The way

of a sluggard is overgrown with thorns, but the path of the upright is a level highway" (Prov. 15:19):

B. "The way of a sluggard refers to the wicked Esau.

C. ." ..is overgrown with thorns: for he is comparable to a hedge. If you take away [thorns] from one side, it pricks from the other. So too the wicked Esau [Rome] turns this way and that: 'Produce your poll tax, produce your share of the crop.' If one does not have the money, [the government then] imposes fines and penalties on him.

D. "...but the path of the upright is a level highway – this refers to the Holy One, blessed be He, concerning whom it is written, 'The ways of the Lord are straight, and the righteous will walk in them' (Hos. 14:10).

E. "So he used appropriate language in telling Moses, 'When you take the census of the people of Israel, then each shall give a ransom for himself to the Lord when you number them, that there be no plague among them when you number them (Ex. 30:12).'"

Hos. 14:10 says that "the path of the upright" refers to God.

PESIQTA DERAB KAHANA II:VIII

1. A. [The Lord spoke to Moses and said, "When you number the Israelites] according to their number" (Ex. 30:12):

B. Said R. Joshua bar Nehemiah, "Said the Holy One, blessed be He, to Moses, 'Moses, Go, count Israel.'

C. "Moses said before the Holy One, blessed be He, 'Lord of all ages, it is written, 'And your seed will be like the dust of the earth' (Gen. 28:14),'And I shall multiply your seed like the stars of the heaven' (Gen. 26:4), 'And the number of the children of Israel will be like the sand of the sea' (Hos. 2:1), and yet you say to me, 'Go, count Israel'"!

D. "He said to him, 'Moses, it is not as you are thinking. But if you want to master the exact number of the Israelites, take the first letters of the tribes' names, and you will know their count. The R in the name of Reuben stands for two hundred thousand, the S of Simeon, three hundred thousand, the N of Naftali, fifty thousand, the Y [in the Hebrew] of Judah, Joseph, and Issachar, thirty thousand, the Z of Zebulun, seven thousand, the D of Dan, four thousand, the G of Gad, three thousand, the B of Benjamin, two thousand, the A of Asher, one thousand. So you come up with five hundred ninety-seven thousand.'

E. "As to the other three thousand [of the anticipated 600,000]?

F. "They are those who fell in the time of the golden calf: 'And the children of Levite acted in accord with the word of Moses, and of the people on that day three thousand men fell' (Ex. 32:28)."

4. *Hosea in Genesis Rabbah, Leviticus Rabbah and Pesiqta deRab Kahana* 65

Hos. 2:1 shows that the Israelites are beyond counting.

PESIQTA DERAB KAHANA IV:X
1. A. Another matter: ." ..a heifer: this refers to Israel: For like a stubborn heifer Israel was stubborn" (Hos. 4:16).
   B. ...red: this refers to Israel:" ...were redder than rubies" (Lam. 4:7).
   C. ...without defect: this refers to Israel: "My dove, my perfect one, is unique" (Song 6:9).
   D. ...in which there is no blemish: this refers to Israel: " You were all fair, my love, and there was no blemish in you" (Song 4:7).
   E. ...and upon which a yoke has never come: this refers to Israel. in the generation of Jeremiah, which did not accept the yoke of the Holy One, blessed be He.
   F. You shall give it to Eleazar the priest: this refers to Jeremiah, "one of the priests of Anatoth" (Jer. 1:1).
   G. ." ..and it shall be taken outside the camp:" "Nebuchadnezzar ...carried the people away to Babylonia" (Ezra 5:12).
   H. ..."and slaughtered to the east of it:" "And the sons of Zedekiah he slaughtered before him" (2 Kgs. 25:7).

Israel is compared to a heifer, Hos. 4:16.

PESIQTA DERAB KAHANA V:VII
1. A. "Hark! My beloved! Here he comes, bounding over the mountains, leaping over the hills. [My beloved is like a gazelle, or a young wild goat: there he stands outside our wall, peeking in at the windows, glancing through the lattice. My beloved answered, he said to me, Rise up, my darling; my fairest, come away. For now the winter is past, the rains are over and gone; the flowers appear in the countryside; the time is coming when the birds will sing, and the turtle-dove's cooing will be heard in our land; when the green figs will ripen on the fig-trees and the vines give forth their fragrance. Rise up my darling, my fairest, come away]" (Song 2:8-10):
2. A. R. Nehemiah says, "Hark! My beloved! Here he comes refers to Moses.
   B. "When Moses came and said to Israel, 'In this month you will be redeemed,' they said to him, 'Moses, our lord, how are we going to be redeemed? And the land of Egypt is filled with the filth of idolatry that belongs to us.'
   C. "He said to them, 'Since he wants to redeem you, he does not pay attention to your idolatry. But he goes bounding over the mountains, leaping over the hills, and hills refers to idolatry, in line with this verse: "On the tops of mountains they make sacrifices and in hills they offer incense" (Hos. 4:12).'"

God over looked the Israelites' idolatry in Egypt, despite the evidence alluded to at Hos. 4:12.

PESIQTA DERAB KAHANA V:VIII

14. A. R. Berekhiah in the name of R. Levi, "Like the first redeemer, so will the final redeemer be:
B. "Just as the first redeemer appeared to them and then went and disappeared from them, so the final redeemer will appear to them and then go and disappear from them."
C. And how long will he disappear from them?
D. R. Tanhuma in the name of R. Hama bar Hoshaia, R. Menahema in the name of R. Hama bar Hanina: "Forty-five days, in line with this verse of Scripture: From the time when the regular offering is abolished and 'the abomination of desolation' is set up, there shall be an interval of one thousand two hundred and ninety days. Happy the man who waits and lives to see the completion of one thousand three hundred and thirty-five days [a difference of forty-five days] (Dan. 12:11-12)."
E. "As to the forty-five days that remain over the figure given in the earlier verse, what are they? They are the forty-five days on which the Messiah, having appeared to them, will go and disappear from them."
F. Where will he lead them?'
G. Some say, "To the wilderness of Judea," and some, "To the wilderness of Sihon and Og."
H. That is in line with this verse of Scripture: Therefore I will seduce Israel and bring her into the wilderness (Hos. 2:16).
I. He who believes in him will eat saltwort and the roots of the broom and live, for in the wilderness they pick saltwort with wormwood and the roots of the broom are their food (Job 30:4).
J. And he who does not believe in him will go to the nations of the world, who will kill him.
K. Said R. Isaac bar Marian, "At the end of forty-five days the Holy One, blessed be He, will appear to them and bring down manna.
L. "Why? For there is nothing new under the sun (Qoh. 1:9).
M. "What is the pertinent scriptural verse? 'I am the Lord your God from the land of Egypt; I will make you dwell in tents again as in the days of the festival' (Hos. 12:10)."

Hos. 2:16 has the redeemer disappear into the wilderness, and the process of redemption will replicate the original liberation from Egypt, dwelling in tents in particular.

PESIQTA DERAB KAHANA V:X

1. A. R. Jonah opened discourse by citing this verse of Scripture: "So I got her back for fifteen pieces of silver, a homer of barley, [and a

4. *Hosea in Genesis Rabbah, Leviticus Rabbah and Pesiqta deRab Kahana*

measure of wine; and I said to her, Many a long day you shall live in my house and not play the wanton and have no intercourse with a man, nor I with you. For the Israelites shall live many a long day without king or prince, without sacrifice or sacred pillar, without image or household gods, but after that they will again seek the Lord their God and David their king and turn anxiously to the Lord for his bounty in days to come]" (Hos. 3:2-5).

B. Said R. Yohanan, "'So I got her back for me, for fifteen pieces of silver,' lo, fifteen; and for a homer of barley, lo, thirty, and a half-homer of barley, lo, sixty.

C. "This refers to the sixty religious duties that Moses inscribed for us in the Torah."

D. For R. Yohanan said in the name of R. Simeon b. Yohai, "There were three passages that Moses wrote for us in the Torah, in each one of which there are sixty religious duties, and these are they:

E. "the passage concerning the Passover offering, that concerning torts, and that concerning Holy Things."

F. R. Levi in the name of R. Shilah of Kefar Tamratah, "There are seventy in each."

G. Said R. Tanhuma, "They really do not differ. One who treats the passage concerning the Passover-offering as containing seventy religious duties treats it as encompassing the passage on the phylacteries. One who treats the passage on torts as containing seventy religious duties maintains that it encompasses the passage covering the year of release. One who treats the passage of Holy Things as including seventy religious duties encompasses with it the passage on orlah-fruit."

Hos. 3:2-5 refers to the religious duties that Moses put into the Torah.

Pesiqta deRab Kahana VI:III

3. A. R. Huna made two statements.

B. R. Huna said, "All of the exiles will be gathered together only on account of the study of Mishnah-teachings.

C. "What verse of Scripture makes that point? 'Even when they recount [Mishnah-teachings] among the gentiles, then I shall gather them together' (Hos. 8:10)."

D. R. Huna made a second statement.

E. R. Huna said, "From the rising of the sun even to the setting of the sun my name is great among the nations, and in every place offerings are presented to my name, even pure-offerings (Malachi 1:11). Now is it the case that a pure-offering is made in Babylonia?

F. "Said the Holy One, blessed be He, 'Since you engage in the study of the matter, it is as if you offered it up.'"

Hos. 8:10 means that the exiles are redeemed only on the merit of oral traditions.

PESIQTA DERAB KAHANA **IX:V**

2. A. Said R. Samuel b. R. Nahman, "On three occasions the Holy One, blessed be He, came to engage in argument with Israel, and the nations of the world rejoiced, saying, 'Can these ever [dare] engage in an argument with their creator? Now he will wipe them out of the world.'

B. "One was when he said to them, 'Come, and let us reason together,' says the Lord (Is. 1:18). When the Holy One, blessed be He, saw that the nations of the world were rejoicing, he turned the matter to [Israel's] advantage: 'If your sins are as scarlet, they shall be white as snow' (Is. 1:18).

C. "Then the nations of the world were astonished, and said, 'This is repentance, and this is rebuke? He has planned only to amuse himself with his children.'

D. "[A second time was] when he said to them, Hear, you mountains, the controversy of the Lord (Mic. 6:2), so the nations of the world rejoiced, saying, 'How can these ever [dare] engage in an argument with their creator? Now he will wipe them out of the world.'

E. "When the Holy One, blessed be He, saw that the nations of the world were rejoicing, he turned the matter to [Israel's] advantage: O my people, what have I done to you? In what have I wearied you? Testify against me (Mic. 6:3). Remember what Balak king of Moab devised (Mic. 6:5).

F. [Leviticus Rabbah adds:] "Then the nations of the world were astonished, saying, 'This is repentance, and this is rebuke, one following the other? He has planned only to amuse himself with his children.'

G. "[A third time was] when he said to them, 'The Lord has an indictment against Judah, and will punish Jacob according to his ways' (Hos. 12:2), the nations of the world rejoiced, saying, 'How can these ever [dare] engage in an argument with their creator? Now he will wipe them out of the world.'

H. "When the Holy One, blessed be He, saw that the nations of the world were rejoicing, he turned the matter to [Israel's] advantage. That is in line with the following verse of Scripture: ' In the womb he [Jacob = Israel] took his brother [Esau = other nations] by the heel [and in his manhood he strove with God. He strove with the angel and prevailed, he wept and sought his favor]' (Hos. 12:3-4)."

When God indicted Judah, Hos. 12:1, the nations thought that they could take advantage of the situation, but were wrong. Hos. 12:3-4 shows the favorable outcome for Israel.

PESIQTA DERAB KAHANA **IX:VII**

1. A. "By their wickedness they make the king glad, and the princes by their adultery" (Hos. 7:3).

B. Now why was the bull recognized to be designated as the first of all of the offerings [bull, sheep, goat (Lev. 22:27)]?
C. Said R. Levi, "The matter may be compared to the case of a highborn lady who got a bad name on account of [alleged adultery with] one of the lords of the state.
D. "The king looked into the matter and found nothing. What did the king do? He made a banquet and sat the [accused] man at the head of the guests.
E. "Why so? To show that the king had looked into the matter and found nothing.
F. "So the nations of the world taunt Israel and say to them, 'You made the golden calf!'
G. "The Holy One, blessed be He, looked into the matter and found nothing. Accordingly, the bull was made the first among all the offerings: 'Bull, sheep, goat' (Lev. 22:27)."

Hos. 7:3 speaks of the nations rejoicing at Israel's sinfulness, but God rejected the charge and signaled his favorable attitude toward Israel by adopting the bull as the principal offering.

PESIQTA DERAB KAHANA IX:VIII
2. A. Said R. Judah b. R. Simon, "It is written, 'An ox knows its owner, and an ass its master's crib, [but Israel does not know]' (Is. 1:3).
B. "Did they really not know? Rather, they trampled under heel [God's commandments].
C. "Along these same lines: 'For my people is foolish. Me they have not known' (Jer. 4:22). Did they not know? Rather, they trampled under heel.
D. "Along these same lines: 'And she did not know that it was I who gave her the grain, [wine, and oil]' (Hos. 2:8). Did she not know? Rather, she trampled under heel."

Hos. 2:8 treats Israel's churlishness: she knew exactly what she was doing.

PESIQTA DERAB KAHANA IX:XI
1. A. "And whether the mother is a cow or a ewe, [you shall not kill] both her and her young [in one day]" (Lev. 22:28).
B. R. Berekhiah in the name of R. Levi: "It is written, 'A righteous man has regard for the life of his beast, [but the mercy of the wicked is cruel]' (Prov. 12:10).
C. "A righteous man has regard for the life of his beast refers to the Holy One, blessed be He, in whose Torah it is written, 'You will not take the mother with the young' (Deut. 22:6).
D. "But the mercy of the wicked is cruel refers to Sennacherib, the wicked one, concerning whom it is written,' The mother was dashed into pieces with her children' (Hos. 10:14)."

Hos. 10:14 speaks of the cruelty of Sennacherib.

Pesiqta deRab Kahana X:X
6. A. "[Year by year you shall set aside a tithe of all the produce of your seed, of everything that grows on the land.] You shall eat it in the presence of the Lord your God [in the place which he will choose as a dwelling for his name – the tithe of your corn and new wine and oil, and the firstborn of your cattle and sheep, so that for all time you may learn to fear the Lord your God] " (Deut. 14:22):
   B. If [by tithing] you attain merit, it is your grain, and if not, [the grain not having been tithed,] it is my grain.
   C. That is in line with this verse: "And I shall take my grain in its due season" (Hos. 2:11).

Hos. 2:11 speaks of the share of the crop that belongs to God.

Pesiqta deRab Kahana X:IX
7. A. [Year by year you shall set aside a tithe of all the produce of your seed, of everything that grows on the land. You shall eat it in the presence of the Lord your God in the place which he will choose as a dwelling for his name] – the tithe of your corn [and new wine and oil, and the firstborn of your cattle and sheep, so that for all time you may learn to fear the Lord your God] (Deut. 14:22):
   B. If [by tithing] you attain merit, it is your new wine, and if not, it is mine.
   C. That is in line with this verse: "And my new wine in its due time" (Hos. 2:11).

As above.

Pesiqta deRab Kahana XII:I
1. A. R. Judah bar Simon commenced discourse by citing the following verse: "Many daughters show how capable they are, but you excel them all. [Charm is a delusion and beauty fleeting; it is the God-fearing woman who is honored. Extol her for the fruit of her toil and let her labors bring her honor in the city gate]' (Prov. 31:29-31):
   B. "The first man was assigned six religious duties, and they are: not worshipping idols, not blaspheming, setting up courts of justice, not murdering, not practicing fornication, not stealing.
   C. "And all of them derive from a single verse of Scripture: And the Lord God commanded the man, saying, 'You may freely eat of every tree of the garden, [but of the tree of the knowledge of good and evil you shall not eat, for in the day that you eat of it you shall die]' (Gen. 2:16).

4. Hosea in Genesis Rabbah, Leviticus Rabbah and Pesiqta deRab Kahana

- D. "And the Lord God commanded the man, saying: this refers to idolatry, as it is said, For Ephraim was happy to walk after the command (Hos. 5:11).
- E. "The Lord: this refers to blasphemy, as it is said, Whoever curses the name of the Lord will surely die (Lev. 24:16).
- F. "God: this refers to setting up courts of justice, as it is said, God [in context, the judges] you shall not curse (Ex. 22:27).

Hos. 5:11 speaks of the prohibition of idolatry.

PESIQTA DERAB KAHANA XII:IV

1. A. R. Yohanan opened his discourse by citing this verse of Scripture: "So I got her back for fifteen pieces of silver, [a homer of barley, and a measure of barley; and I said to her, 'Many a long day you shall live in my house and not play the wanton and have no intercourse with a man, nor I with you. For the Israelites shall live many a long day without king or prince, without sacrifice or sacred pillar, without image or household gods, but after that they will again seek the Lord their God and David their king and turn anxiously to the Lord for his bounty in days to come'] "(Hos. 3:2-5).
   B. Said R. Yohanan, "'So I got her back for me, for fifteen pieces of silver:' this refers to the fifteenth day of Nisan [Passover].
   C. ."..and for a homer of barley, lo, thirty.
   D. ."..and a measure of barley, lo, forty-five.
   E. "And where are the other five [to reach the number of fifty days after Passover, on which Pentecost, celebrating the giving of the Torah, is reached]?
   F. "and I said to her, 'Many a long day you shall live in my house.'"
2. A. [As to the verse, "and I said to her, 'Many a long day you shall live in my house']", it was taught on Tannaite authority by R. Hiyya, "Many refers to two days, long to three – lo, the fifty days of the counting of the sheaf of first grain.
   B. "From that point we refer to the Ten Commandments."
3. A. ."..and not play the wanton:"
   B. "You will not make for yourself graven images" (Lev. 26:1).
   C. ...and have no intercourse with a man:
   D. "You will have no other gods" (Ex. 20:3).
   E. And if you have done so, nor I with you.
   F. When? In the third month [after Israel had left Egypt, they came to the wilderness of Sinai. They set out from Rephidim and entered the wilderness of Sinai, where they encamped, pitching their tent opposite the Mountain. Moses went up the mountain of God, and the Lord called to him from the mountain and said, 'Speak thus to the house of Jacob and tell this to the sons of Israel: You have seen with your own eyes what I did to Egypt and how I have carried you on eagles' wings and brought you here to me. If only you will

now listen to me and keep my covenant, then out of all peoples you shall become my special possession; for the whole earth is mine. You shall be my kingdom of priests, my holy nation'] (Exodus 19:1-6).

Hos. 3:2-5 speaks of the counting of the omer, leading to Pentecost.

Pesiqta deRab Kahana XIII:IV

2. A. Said R. Abba bar Kahana, "It is written, 'Yet you were not like a harlot, because you scorned hire' (Ez. 16:31).
   B. "Let the son of the women who was in a state of utter disarray but corrected her ways and rebuke the son of the one who was in order and who then corrupted her ways.
   C. "You find that whatever is written with respect to Israel in a negative spirit is written as a matter of praise for Rahab.
   D. "In regard to Rahab it is written, 'And now, take an oath, I ask, to me, by the Lord, that I have done mercy with you' (Joshua 2:12). And in respect to Israel: 'Therefore they take an oath in vain' (Jer. 5:2).
   E. "In regard to Rahab it is written, 'And you will keep alive my father and my mother' (Joshua 2:13). And in respect to Israel: 'In you have they ridiculed father and mother' (Ez. 22:7).
   F. "In regard to Rahab it is written, 'And she brought them up to the roof' (Joshua 2:6). And in connection with Israel:' Those who bow down on the roofs to the host of the heaven' (Zeph. 1:5).
   G. "In regard to Rahab it is written, 'And she hid them in the stalks of flax' (Josh. 2:6). And in connection with Israel: 'Who say to a piece of wood, You are my father' (Jer. 2:27).
   H. "In regard to Rahab it is written, 'And she said, Go to the mountain' (Josh. 2:16). And in connection with Israel: 'They sacrifice on the tops of the mountains' (Hos. 4:13).
   I. "In regard to Rahab it is written, 'You will give me a true token' (Josh. 2:13). And in connection with Israel: 'Truth they will not speak' (Jer. 9:4).
   J. "Thus whatever is written with respect to Israel in a negative spirit is written as a matter of praise for Rahab."

Rahab saved the spies by sending them to the mountain, but Israel practiced idolatry on the mountain, Hos. 4:12, so illustrating the generalization: Let the son of the women who was in a state of utter disarray but corrected her ways and rebuke the son of the one who was in order and who then corrupted her ways.

Pesiqta deRab Kahana XIII:VII

1. A. R. Tanhuma said it, R. Eleazar in the name of R. Meir, R. Menahama, and R. Bibi:

4. Hosea in Genesis Rabbah, Leviticus Rabbah and Pesiqta deRab Kahana

    B.   R. Eleazar in the name of R. Meir: "Every passage in which it is said, the words, words of, or words – the intent is to deliver curses, and rebukes.

    C.   "It is written, 'These are the words which Moses spoke to all Israel' (Deut. 1:1), and what, further, is written there? 'The wasting of hunger and the devouring of the fiery bolt' (Deut. 32:24).

    D.   "It is written, 'The word of the Lord that come to Hosea the son of Beeri' (Hos. 1:1), and what further is written there? 'You are not my people' (Hos. 1:9).

    E.   "It is written, 'The words of Jeremiah' (Jer. 1:1-3), and what further is written there? 'Such as are for death to death, [and such as are for captivity to captivity'] (Jer. 32:11)."

"The words of...," signifies a curse and a rebuke, Hos. 1:1 1:9 illustrating that generalization.

Pesiqta deRab Kahana XIII:XI

3. A.   **Said R. Jonathan, "For three and a half years the Presence of God stayed on the Mount of Olives, declaring three times a day, saying, 'Return, wandering children, I shall heal your backslidings' (Jer. 3:22).**

    D.   "But when they did not repent, the Presence of God began to fly in the air, reciting this verse of Scripture: 'I will go and return to my place until they confess their guilt and seek my face, in their trouble they will seek me earnestly' (Hos. 5:15)."

Hos. 5:15 speaks of God's abandoning Jerusalem and returning to his place in heaven.

Pesiqta deRab Kahana XV:I

1. A.   R. Abbahu in the name of R. Yosé bar Haninah commenced discourse by citing this verse: "But they are like a man, they have transgressed the covenant. There they dealt treacherously against me" (Hos. 6:7).

    B.   "They are like a man, specifically, like the first man [Adam]. [We shall now compare the story of the first man in Eden with the story of Israel in its land.]

    C.   "Said the Holy One, blessed be He, 'In the case of the first man, I brought him into the garden of Eden, I commanded him, he violated my commandment, I judged him to be sent away and driven out, but I mourned for him, saying "How..."'[which begins the book of Lamentations, hence stands for a lament, but which also is written with the consonants that also yield, Where are you].

    J.   "'So too in the case of his descendants, [God continues to speak,] I brought them into the Land of Israel, I commanded them, they violated my commandment, I judged them to be sent out and driven away but I mourned for them, saying, How....'

Hos. 6:7 compares Israel and Adam.

Pesiqta deRab Kahana XV:IV
1. A. "Thus says the Lord of hosts: 'Consider, and call for the mourning women to come. [Send for the skilful women to come; let them make haste and raise a wailing over us, that our eyes may run down with tears, and our eyelids gush with water. For a sound of wailing is heard from Zion: 'How we are ruined, we are utterly shamed, because we have left the land, because they have cast down our dwellings]' (Jer. 9:17-19):"
   B. R. Yohanan, R. Simeon b. Laqish, and rabbis:
   C. R. Yohanan said, "The matter may be compared to the case of a king who had two sons. He got mad at the first and took a staff and beat him and sent him away.
   D. "He said, 'Woe is this one! From how abundant a life he has been driven out.'
   E. "He got mad at the second and took a staff and beat him and sent him away. He said, 'I am the one whose way of bringing up sons is all wrong.'
   F. "So the Ten Tribes went into exile, and the Holy One, blessed be He, thereupon recited in their regard this verse: 'Woe is them, for they have strayed from me' (Hos. 7:13).
   G. "But when the tribes of Judah and Benjamin went into exile, it is as if the Holy One, blessed be He, said, 'Woe is me on account of my hurt' (Jer. 10:19)."

Hos. 7:13 speaks of God's blaming the Ten Tribes for their exile, but blaming himself for the exile of Judah and Benjamin.

Pesiqta deRab Kahana XV:V
9. A. Said R. Judah bar Pazzi, "'Israel has cast off that which is good, the enemy shall pursue him' (Hos. 8:3).
   B. "The word good refers only to words of Torah, in line with this verse: I have given you a good doctrine, my Torah, do not forsake it (Prov. 4:2).
   C. "And so Scripture says, 'As the stubble devours the tongue of fire [Hebrew text: As the tongue of fire devours stubble]' (Is. 5:24). Now does the stubble consume the fire? Is it not the way of fire to consume stubble, and yet you say, As the stubble devours the tongue of fire!
   D. "But in this case, the word stubble refers to the house of Esau, which is compared to stubble, as it is said, 'The house of Esau is

4. Hosea in Genesis Rabbah, Leviticus Rabbah and Pesiqta deRab Kahana

          for stubble' (Ob. 1:18).
- E. "And the tongue of fire refers to the house of Jacob, which is compared to fire, as it is said, 'The tongue the House of Jacob shall be a fire' (Ob. 1:18).
- F. "'And the house of Joseph shall be a flame' (Ob. 1:18):
- G. "And as the chaff is consumed in the flame (Is. 5:24) refers to the house of Joseph, which is compared to a flame in the following verse: And the house of Joseph shall be a flame (Ob. 1:18).
- H. "'Their root shall be as rottenness' (Is. 5:24) refers to the patriarchs, who are the root of Israel.
- I. "'And their blossom shall go up as dust' (Is. 5:24) refers to the tribes, who are the blossoms of Israel.
- J. "On what account? 'Because they have rejected the Torah of the Lord of hosts' (Is. 5:24)."

Israel has cast off good (Hos. 8:3) refers to the Torah.

PESIQTA DERAB KAHANA XV:VII

7. A. Seven transgressions did the Israelites commit on that day: they murdered [1] a priest, [2] prophet, [3] judge, [4] they spilled innocent blood, [5] they blasphemed the divine name, [6] they imparted uncleanness to the courtyard, and it was, furthermore, [7] a Day of Atonement that coincided with the Sabbath.
- B. When Nebuzaradan came in, the blood began to drip. He said to them, "What sort of blood is this dripping blood?"
- C. They said to him, "It is the blood of oxen, rams, and sheep that we offered on the altar."
- D. He forthwith sent and brought oxen, rams, and sheep and slaughtered them in his presence, but the blood continued to drip.
- E. Since they did not confess the truth, he took them and put them in prison.
- F. They said, "Clearly, the Holy One, blessed be He, wishes now to exact vengeance from us for this blood, the blood of a priest, prophet, and judge, who prophesied against us concerning all the very deeds which you are now doing to us, for we rose against him and killed him."
- G. Forthwith he took eighty thousand young priests and killed them on his account, until the blood lapped the grave of Zechariah.
- H. What verse of Scripture indicates it? "[Oaths are imposed and broken, they kill and rob, there is nothing but adultery] and license, one deed of blood after another" (Hos. 4:2).
- I. Still the blood seethed.
- J. At that moment he grew wroth at [the blood], saying to it, "What do you think? What do you want? Should we destroy your entire nation on your account?"
- K. At that moment the Holy One, blessed be He, was filled with mercy and he said, "Now if this one, who is mortal and fierce, who is

here today and gone tomorrow, is filled with mercy for my children, I, concerning whom it is written, A merciful God, the Lord your God will not fail you nor destroy you (Deut. 4:31) all the more so [should show mercy]."

L. At that moment the Holy One, blessed be He, gave a signal to the blood and it was swallowed up in its place.

Hos. 4:2 refers to the murder of young priests to pacify the blood dripping in the Temple.

Pesiqta deRab Kahana XVI:VIII

1. A. "How will you comfort me through vanity, and as for your answers, there remains only faithlessness" (Job 21:34):
   B. Said R. Abba bar Kahana [on the meaning of the word translated as faithlessness], "Your words [of comfort and consolation, that Job's friends had provided him] require clarification."
   C. Rabbis say, "Your words contain contradictions." [We shall now have a long series of examples of how God's messages to the prophets contradict themselves.]
2. A. The Holy One said to the prophets, "Go and comfort Jerusalem."
   B. Hosea went to give comfort. He said to her [the city], "The Holy One, blessed be He, has sent me to you to bring you comfort."
   C. She said to him, "What do you have in hand."
   D. He said to her, "'I will be as the dew to Israel' (Hos. 14:6).
   E. She said to him, "Yesterday, you said to me, Ephraim is smitten, their root is dried up, they shall bear no fruit (Hos. 9:16), and now you say this to me? Which shall we believe, the first statement or the second?"
3. A. Joel went to give comfort. He said to the city, "The Holy One, blessed be He, has sent me to you to bring you comfort."
   B. She said to him, "What do you have in hand."
   C. He said to her, "It shall come to pass in that day that the mountains shall drop down sweet wine and the hills shall flow with milk" (Joel 4:18).
   D. She said to him, "Yesterday, you said to me, 'Awake you drunkards and weep, wail, you who drink wine, because of the sweet wine, for it is cut off from your mouth' (Joel 1:5), and now you say this to me? Which shall we believe, the first statement or the second?"
4. A. Amos went to give comfort. He said to the city, "The Holy One, blessed be He, has sent me to you to bring you comfort."
   B. She said to him, "What do you have in hand."
   C. He said to her, "On that day I will raise up the fallen tabernacle of David" (Amos 9:11).
   D. She said to him, "Yesterday, you said to me, 'The virgin of Israel is fallen, she shall no more rise' (Amos 5:2), and now you say this to

me? Which shall we believe, the first statement or the second?"
5. A. Micah went to give comfort. He said to the city, "The Holy One, blessed be He, has sent me to you to bring you comfort."
B. She said to him, "What do you have in hand."
C. He said to her, "Who is like God to you who pardons iniquity and passes by transgression" (Mic. 7:18).
D. She said to him, "Yesterday, you said to me, 'For the transgression of Jacob is all this and for the sins of the house of Israel' (Mic. 1:56), and now you say this to me? Which shall we believe, the first statement or the second?"
6. A. Nahum went to give comfort. He said to the city, "The Holy One, blessed be He, has sent me to you to bring you comfort."
B. She said to him, "What do you have in hand."
C. He said to her, "The wicked one shall no more pass through you, he is utterly cut off" (Nahum 2:1).
D. She said to him, "Yesterday, you said to me, 'Out of you came he forth who devises evil against the Lord, who counsels wickedness' (Nah. 1:11), and now you say this to me? Which shall we believe, the first statement or the second?"
7. A. Habakkuk went to give comfort. He said to the city, "The Holy One, blessed be He, has sent me to you to bring you comfort."
B. She said to him, "What do you have in hand."
C. He said to her, "You have come forth for the deliverance of your people, for the deliverance of your anointed" (Hab. 3:13).
D. She said to him, "Yesterday, you said to me, 'How long, O Lord, shall I cry and you will not hear, I cry to you of violence' (Hab. 1:22), and now you say this to me? Which shall we believe, the first statement or the second?"
8. A. Zephaniah went to give comfort. He said to the city, "The Holy One, blessed be He, has sent me to you to bring you comfort."
B. She said to him, "What do you have in hand."
C. He said to her, "It shall come to pass at that time that I will search Jerusalem with the lamps" (Zeph. 1:12).
D. She said to him, "Yesterday, you said to me, 'A day of darkness and gloominess a day of clouds and thick darkness' (Zeph. 1:15), and now you say this to me? Which shall we believe, the first statement or the second?"
9. A. Haggai went to give comfort. He said to the city, "The Holy One, blessed be He, has sent me to you to bring you comfort."
B. She said to him, "What do you have in hand."
C. He said to her, "Shall the seed ever again remain in the barn? Shall the vine, the fig tree, the pomegranate, and the olive tree ever again bear no fruit? Indeed not, from this day I will bless you" (Hag. 2:19).
D. She said to him, "Yesterday, you said to me, 'You sow much and bring in little' (Hag. 1:6), and now you say this to me? Which shall we believe, the first statement or the second?"

10. A. Zechariah went to give comfort. He said to the city, "The Holy One, blessed be He, has sent me to you to bring you comfort."
    B. She said to him, "What do you have in hand."
    C. He said to her, "I am very angry with the nations that are at ease" (Zech. 1:15).
    D. She said to him, "Yesterday, you said to me, 'The Lord was very angry with your fathers' (Zech. 1:2), and now you say this to me? Which shall we believe, the first statement or the second?"
11. A. Malachi went to give comfort. He said to the city, "The Holy One, blessed be He, has sent me to you to bring you comfort."
    B. She said to him, "What do you have in hand."
    C. He said to her, "All the nations shall call you happy, for you shall be a happy land" (Mal. 3:12).
    D. She said to him, "Yesterday, you said to me, 'I have no pleasure in you says the Lord of hosts' (Mal. 1:10), and now you say this to me? Which shall we believe, the first statement or the second?"
12. A. The prophets went to the Holy One, blessed be He, saying to him, "Lord of the ages, Jerusalem has not accepted the comfort [that we brought her]."
    B. Said to them the Holy One, blessed be He, "You and I together shall go and comfort her."
    C. Thus we say: "Comfort, comfort my people" but read the letters for my people as with me.
    D. Let the creatures of the upper world comfort her, let the creatures of the lower world comfort her.
    E. Let the living comfort her, let the dead comfort her.
    F. Comfort her in this world, comfort her in the world to come.
    G. Comfort her on account of the Ten Tribes, comfort her on account of the tribe of Judah and Benjamin.
    H. [Thus we must understand the statement, "Comfort, comfort my people, says your God. Speak tenderly to the heart of Jerusalem and cry to her that her warfare is ended, that her iniquity is pardoned, that she has received from the Lord's hand double for all her sins" (Is. 40:1-2) in this way:] Comfort, comfort my people but read the letters for my people as with me.

God's messages to the prophets contradict themselves, as at Hos. 14:6, 9:16.

Pesiqta deRab Kahana XVII:VIII

1. A. Said R. Abbahu, "There were two things that Israel asked before the Holy One, blessed be He, and the prophets said to them, 'You have not asked properly.'
   B. "The Israelites asked, 'Let him come to us as the rain, as the latter rain that waters the earth' (Hos. 6:3).
   C. "The prophets said to them, 'You have not asked properly. As to

4. Hosea in Genesis Rabbah, Leviticus Rabbah and Pesiqta deRab Kahana

rain, wayfarers are bothered by it, roof-plasterers are bothered by it, wine-pressers and grain-threshers are bothered by it.
D. "'But if you wish to ask, say it this way: 'I shall be as dew to Israel, and she will blossom like a rose' (Hos. 14:6).'
E. "The Israelites further asked, 'Set me as a seal on your heart' (Song 8:6).
F. "The prophets said to them, 'You have not asked properly. As to the heart, sometimes it is open, sometimes it is hidden.
G. "'But if you wish to ask, say it this way: '[To be] a crown of beauty in the hand of the Lord and a royal diadem in the open hand of your God' (Is. 42:3).'"
H. R. Simon bar Ba in the name of R. Yohanan: "Said to them the Holy One, blessed be He, 'Neither you nor your prophets have asked in the proper way.
I. "'But if you wish to ask, say it this way: 'Behold I have graven you on the palms of my hands; your walls are continually before me'. (Is. 49:16). Just as it is not possible for a person to forget the palms of his hands, so also 'Even these may forget, yet I will not forget you' (Isaiah 49:14-16)."

The improper mode of asking, illustrates at Hos. 6:3, was corrected by Hosea at Hos. 4:6: dew, not rain.

Pesiqta deRab Kahana XXIV:IX

1. A. "A man shall have his fill of good by the fruit of his mouth" (Prov. 12:14):
B. It is written, "When Reuben returned to the pit [and saw that Joseph was not in the pit, he tore his clothes and returned to his brothers and said, 'The lad is gone, and I, where shall I go?' Then they took Joseph's robe and slaughtered a goat and dipped the robe in the blood, and they sent the long robe with sleeves and brought it to their father and said, 'This we have found; see now whether it is your son's robe or not']" (Gen. 37:29-34)]:
C. R. Eliezer, R. Joshua, and Rabbis: [Where had he been?]
D. R. Eliezer says, "He had been occupied with his sackcloth and ashes [on account of his earlier sin with his father's concubine (Gen. 35:22)], and when he had a free moment from his sack cloth and ashes, he went and looked into the pit. That is in line with this verse: And behold Joseph was not in the pit."
E. R. Joshua said, "All of the management of the household was assigned to him. When he had a moment free of the cares of management of the household, he went and looked into the pit. That is in line with this verse: And behold Joseph was not in the pit."
D. And rabbis said, "Said the Holy One, blessed be He, to him, 'You sought to restore the beloved son to his father. By your life, your son's son will restore Israel to their father in heaven. And who is

that? It is Hosea.' The word of the Lord which came to Hosea ben Beeri (Hos. 1:1), and it is written, his son Beerah' (I Chron 5:6)."

2. A. Why is he called Beeri? Because he is the well (Beerah) of the Torah.
   B. And why did Beerah die in exile? So that the ten tribes should return on account of his merit.
   C. And why did Moses die in the wilderness? So that the generation of the wilderness should return on account of his merit.
3. A. R. Berekhiah said, "Said the Holy One, blessed be He, to him, 'You have opened the way to repentance first of all. By your life, the son of your son will come and open the way to repentance first of all:
   B. "'Return O Israel [to the Lord your God, for you have stumbled because of your iniquity. Take with you words and return to the Lord and say to him, Take away all iniquity; accept that which is good, and we will render the fruit of our lips. Assyria shall not save us, we will not ride upon horses; and we will say no more, Our God to the work of our hands. In you the orphan finds mercy]' (Hosea 14:1-3)."

God rewarded Beeri with Hosea, his grandson, who opened the way to Israel to repent.

Pesiqta deRab Kahana XXIV:X

1. A. "For my thoughts are not your thoughts, [and your ways are not my ways This is the very word of the Lord. For as the heavens are higher than the earth, so are my ways higher than your ways and my thoughts than your thoughts]" (Is. 55:8-9):
   B. The matter may be compared to the case of a thug on trial before a magistrate.
   C. First he reads the charge, then he beats him, then he puts a bit in his mouth [so that he cannot retract his confession], then he lays down the verdict, then he goes forth to be put to death.
   D. But the Holy One, blessed be He, is not that way. First he announces the charge against the tribes: "Now they sin more and more and have made molten images of their silver" (Hos. 13:2).
   E. Then he beats them: "Ephraim is beaten, their root is dried up" (Hos. 9:16).
   F. Then he puts a bit in their mouth: "The iniquity of Ephraim is bound up, his sin is stored up" (Hos. 13:12).
   G. Then he announces the verdict: "Samaria shall bear her guilt for she has rebelled against her God" (Hos. 14:1).
   H. And then he draws them back in repentance: "Return O Israel to the Lord your God, for you have stumbled because of your iniquity. Take with you words and return to the Lord and say to him, Take away all iniquity; accept that which is good, and we will render the fruit of our lips. Assyria shall not save us, we will not ride

upon horses; and we will say no more, Our God to the work of our hands. In you the orphan finds mercy" (Hosea 14:1-3).

First God reads the charge, then he beats them, then prevents them from retracting their confession, then announces the verdict, and finally he leads them to repentance, Hos. 13:2, 9:16, 14:1-3.

Pesiqta deRab Kahana XXIV:XI

1. A. What is written prior to [the base-verse, Hos. 14:2]? It is the following: "Samaria shall bear her guilt [for she has rebelled against her God]" (Hos. 14:1).
   B. And thereafter: "Return O Israel [to the Lord your God, for you have stumbled because of your iniquity. Take with you words and return to the Lord and say to him, Take away all iniquity; accept that which is good, and we will render the fruit of our lips. Assyria shall not save us, we will not ride upon horses; and we will say no more, Our God to the work of our hands. In you the orphan finds mercy"] (Hosea 14:1-3).
   C. R. Eleazar in the name of R. Samuel bar Nahman: "The matter may be compared to the case of a town that rebelled against the king, who sent against it a general of the army to destroy it. The general was skilled and cool.
   D. "He said to them, 'Take time for yourselves, so that the king not do to you what he did to such-and-such a town and its environs, and to such and such a district and its area.'
   E. "So said Hosea to Israel, 'My children, repent, so that the Holy One, blessed be He, will not do to you what he did to Samaria and its environs.'
   F. "Said Israel before the Holy One, blessed be He, 'Lord of the ages, if we repent, will you accept us?'
   G. "He said to them, 'The repentance of Cain I accepted, will I not accept yours?'
   H. "'For a harsh decree was issued against him.'"

Hosea warned Israel to repent so as not to suffer the fate of Samaria and promised Israel that God would accept their repentance.

Pesiqta deRab Kahana XXIV:XVI

1. A. R. Levi and R. Isaac:
   B. R. Levi said, "Said the Holy One, blessed be He, to Jeremiah, 'Go, say to Israel, Repent.' He went and said it to them.
   C. "They said to him, 'Our lord, Jeremiah, how shall we repent? How shall we have the impudence to come before the Omnipresent? Have we not angered him, and have we not made him jealous? Those mountains and hills on which we served idols — do they not yet endure [to testify against us]? 'They sacrifice on the tops

of mountains [and make offerings on the hills]' (Hos. 4:13). 'Let us lie down in our shame and let our confusion cover us' (Jer. 3:25).'
- D. "He went before the Holy One, blessed be He, and repeated this. He said to him, 'Go, tell them, 'Did I not write for you in my Torah, '[The one who consults ghosts and familiar spirits to go astray after them –] I will set my face against that person and cast him off from among his people' (Lev. 20:6)? Have I ever done so to you? Rather: 'I will not frown on you, for I am merciful, says the Lord. I will not bear a grudge forever (Jer. 3:12).'"
2. A. R. Isaac said, "Said the Holy One, blessed be He, to Jeremiah, 'Go, say to Israel, Repent.' He went and said it to them.
- B. "They said to him, 'Our lord, Jeremiah, how shall we repent? How shall we have the impudence to come before the Omnipresent? Have we not angered him, and have we not made him jealous? Those mountains and hills on which we served idols – do they not yet endure [to testify against us]? 'They sacrifice on the tops of mountains [and make offerings on the hills]' (Hos. 4:13). 'Let us lie down in our shame [and let our confusion cover us]' (Jer. 3:25).'
- C. "He went before the Holy One, blessed be He, and repeated this. He said to him, 'Go, tell them, 'If you come, is it not to your father who is in heaven that you are coming? '[For so I have been a father for Israel, and Ephraim has been my first born]' (Jer. 31:8).'"

Hos. 4:13 indicates that the Israelites worshipped idolatry on the mountains.

PESIQTA DERAB KAHANA XXIV:XVII
1. A. ." ..for you have stumbled because of your iniquity" (Hosea 14:2):
- B. Said R. Simon, "The matter may be compared to a tall rock, which was standing at a crossroads. People would stumble on it. Said the king to them, 'Cut it down little by little, so that when the time comes, I can remove it from the world.'
- C. "So said the Holy One, blessed be He, to Israel, 'My children, the impulse to do evil is a great obstacle in the world. But cut it down little by little, so that when the time comes I shall remove it from the world.'
- D. "That is in line with this verse: 'And I shall remove the stony heart from your flesh' (Ez. 36:26)."
2. A. Said R. Isaac, "As matters go in the world, if someone stumbles in transgression and he becomes liable for the death penalty at the hands of heaven, his ox may expire, his chicken perish, his flask break, he may stub his toe, for part of the soul is tantamount to the whole of it."

Hos. 14:2 speaks of Israel stumbling because of iniquity, but God advises to cut it down little by little and he will remove the stumbling block from the world.

PESIQTA DERAB KAHANA **XXIV:XVIII**
1. A. "[Return O Israel to the Lord your God, for you have stumbled because of your iniquity.] Take with you words (Hosea 14:1) [and return to the Lord and say to him, Take away all iniquity; accept that which is good, and we will render the fruit of our lips. Assyria shall not save us, we will not ride upon horses; and we will say no more, Our God to the work of our hands. In you the orphan finds mercy" (Hosea 14:1-3)]...Take with you words:
B. R. Judah and R. Nehemiah:
C. R. Judah said, "Was it not with words that you seduced him at Sinai: ;They seduced him with their mouth and lied to him with their tongue; (Ps. 78:36). [So too now you can seduce me with mere words.]"
D. R. Nehemiah said, "Take with you words. Let people who are good with words come, people who do well in proclaiming the words of Scripture, people who do well in expounding it,
E. "for example, Levi b. Sisi and his colleagues."

Hos. 14:1 speaks of conciliating God with words.

5

Hosea in Esther Rabbah I, Ruth Rabbah, Song of Songs Rabbah, Lamentations Rabbah and The Fathers According to Rabbi Nathan

ESTHER RABBAH I

I find no reference to Hosea.

RUTH RABBAH

RUTH RABBAH III:I
1. A. "**And it came to pass in the days when the judges ruled, there was a famine in the land:**"
   B. "The way of the guilty man is crooked and strange, but the conduct of the pure is right" (Prov. 21:8):
4. A. R. Aha said, "'the way...is crooked' refers to the Israelites: 'For they are a crooked generation' (Dt. 32:20).
   B. "'man: 'Now the men of Israel had sworn' (Judges 21:1).
   C. "'strange: they alienated themselves from the Holy One, blessed be He: 'They have dealt treacherously against the Lord for they have produced strange children' (Hos. 5:7).
   D. "'...but the conduct of the pure is right: this speaks of the Holy One, blessed be He, who behaves toward him in a fair measure in this world, but gives them the full reward that is coming to them in the world to come,
   E. "like a worker who in good faith carries out work for a householder.
   F. "At that time said the Holy One, blessed be He, 'My children are rebellion. But as to exterminating them, that is not possible, and to bring them back to Egypt is not possible, and to trade them for some other nation is something I cannot do. But this shall I do for them: lo, I shall torment them with suffering and afflict them with famine in the days when the judges judge.'

G. "That is in line with this verse: 'And it came to pass in the days when the judges ruled, there was a famine in the land.'"

Hos. 5:7 says that the Israelites alienated themselves from God by producing strange offspring.

RUTH RABBAH V:I
3. A. **Rabbi asked R. Besallel, "What is the meaning of this verse of Scripture: 'For their mother has played the harlot' (Hos. 2:7)?**
   B. "Is it possible that our matriarch, Sarah, was a whore?!"
   C. He said to him, "God forbid! When are the words of Torah despised before the ordinary folk? It is when those who have mastered them despise them."
   D. Came R. Jacob bar Abdimi and [Rabinowitz:] made an exposition of it: "When are words of the Torah made like whores before the ordinary people? It is when those who have mastered them despise them."

Hos. 2:7 does not mean Sarah was a whore, but refers to the case when masters of the Torah despise the words of the Torah.

RUTH RABBAH XL:I
1. A. **"And at mealtime Boaz said to her, 'Come here and eat some bread, and dip your morsel in the wine.' So she sat beside the reapers, and he passed to her parched grain; and she ate until she was satisfied, and she had some left over:"**
   B. R. Yohanan interested the phrase "come here" in six ways:
5. A. "The fifth interpretation refers to the Messiah: 'Come here: means, to the throne.
   B. "'...and eat some bread: this is the bread of the throne.
   C. "'...and dip your morsel in vinegar: this refers to suffering: 'But he was wounded because of our transgressions' (Is. 53:5).
   D. "'So she sat beside the reapers: for the throne is destined to be taken from him for a time: For I will gather all nations against Jerusalem to battle and the city shall be taken' (Zech. 14:2).
   E. "'...and he passed to her parched grain: for he will be restored to the throne: 'And he shall smite the land with the rod of his mouth' (Is. 11:4)."
   F. R. Berekhiah in the name of R. Levi: "As was the first redeemer, so is the last redeemer:
   G. "Just as the first redeemer was revealed and then hidden from them—"
   H. And how long was a hidden? Three months: "And they met Moses and Aaron" (Ex. 5:20),
   I. [reverting to G:] "so the last redeemer will be revealed to them and then hidden from them."

J. How long will he be hidden?
K. R. Tanhuma in the name of rabbis: "Forty-five days: 'And from the time that the continual burnt offering shall be taken away...there shall be a thousand two hundred and ninety days. Happy is the one who waits and comes to the thousand three hundred and thirty-five days' (Dan. 12:11-12)."
L. What are the extra days?
M. R. Isaac b. Qaseratah in the name of R. Jonah: "These are the forty-five days in which the Israelites will harvest saltwort and eat it: 'They pluck saltwort with wormwood' (Job 30:45)."
N. Where will he lead them?
O. From the [holy] land to the wilderness of Judah: "Behold, I will entice her and bring her into the wilderness" (Hos. 2:16).
P. Some say, "To the wilderness of Sihon and Og: 'I will yet again make you dwell in tents as in the days of the appointed season' (Hos. 12:10)."
Q. And whoever believes in him will live.
R. But whoever does not believe in him will go to the nations of idolatry, who will kill him.
S. [Supply: "and she ate and was satisfied and left some over:"] Said R. Isaac b. R. Merion, "In the end the Holy One, blessed be He, will be revealed upon them and bring down manna for them: 'And there is nothing new under the sun' (Qoh. 1:9)."
T. "'...and she ate and was satisfied and left some over':

Hos. 2:16, 12:10 refer to the Messiah's enticing the Israelites to the wilderness.

RUTH RABBAH LVI:I
5. A. "...he went to lie down at the end of the heap of grain:"
   B. R. Judah the Patriarch raised the question before R. Phineas b. R. Hama: "Boaz was a leading figure in his generation, and you say, 'at the end of the heap of grain'!"
   C. He said to him, "It is because that generation was drunk with fornication, and they were paying wages of whores from the threshing floors: 'Do not rejoice, O Israel, like the peoples...you have loved a harlot's hire on every threshing floor' (Hos. 9:1).
   D. "But the righteous do not act in that way.
   E. "Not only so, but the righteous are far from thievery, so their capital is valuable to them" [since they do not want it used for immoral purposes].

The Israelites turned the threshing floors into houses of ill-repute, so Hos. 9:1.

Song of Songs Rabbah

Song of Songs Rabbah II.ii

15. A. ["And the Lord God commanded the man, saying, 'You may freely eat of every tree of the garden, [but of the tree of the knowledge of good and evil you shall not eat, for in the day that you eat of it you shall die]'" (Gen. 2:16).]
B. [Gen. R. XVI:VI.1B adds:] R. Levi said, "He made him responsible to keep six commandments.
C. "He commanded him against idolatry, in line with this verse: 'Because he willingly walked after idols' (Hos. 5:11).
D. "'The Lord' indicates a commandment against blasphemy, in line with this verse: 'And he who blasphemes the name of the Lord' (Lev. 24:16).

Hos. 5:11 signifies that God commanded Adam not to worship idols and condemned him for doing so.

Song of Songs Rabbah II:viii

1. A. Another explanation of the verse, "For your love is better than wine:"
B. Words of the Torah are compared to water, wine, oil, honey, and milk.
2. P. Said R. Hanina of Caesarea, "Just as water is drawn not only for gardens and orchards, but also for baths and privies, shall I say that that is so also for words of the Torah?
Q. "Scripture says, 'For the ways of the Lord are right' (Hos. 14:10)."
R. Said R. Hama b. Uqba, "Just as water makes plants grow, so words of the Torah make everyone who works in them sufficiently grow.

Hos. 14:10 means words of the Torah sustain those that are engaged by them.

Song of Songs Rabbah IV:i

1. A. "Draw me after you, let us make haste. The king has brought me into his chambers. We will exult and rejoice in you; we will extol your love more than wine; rightly do they love you:"
B. Said R. Meir, "When the Israelites stood before Mount Sinai to receive the Torah, said to them the Holy One, blessed be He, 'Shall I really give you the Torah? Bring me good sureties [Simon: guarantors] that you will keep it, and then I shall give it to you.'
C. "They said to him, 'Lord of the ages, our fathers are our sureties for us.'...
P. "They said to him, 'Lord of the world, our prophets will be our sureties.

5. Hosea in Esther Rabbah I, Ruth Rabbah, Song of Songs Rabbah...

Q. "He said to them, 'I have my complaints against them: 'And the shepherds transgressed against me' (Jer. 2:8); 'Your prophets have been like foxes in ruins' (Ez. 13:4).

R. "'Bring me good sureties, and then I shall give it to you.'

S. "They said to him, 'Lo, our children will be our sureties for us.'

T. "Said to them the Holy One, blessed be He, 'Lo, these are certainly good sureties. On their account I shall give it to you.'

U. "That is in line with the following verse of Scripture: 'Out of the mouth of babes and sucklings you have founded strength' (Ps. 8:3).

V. "'Strength' bears the sole meaning of Torah: 'The Lord will give strength to his people' (Ps. 29:11).

W. "Now when the debtor has to pay up and cannot pay, who is seized? Is it not the surety? That is in line with this verse: 'Seeing that you have forgotten the Torah of your God, I also will forget your children' (Hos. 4:6)."

The Israelites' children were the surety for the Israelites' devotion to the Torah and when the Israelites forgot the Torah, God forgot their children, Hos. 4:6.

Song of Songs Rabbah XV:I

1. A. **"Behold, you are beautiful, my love; behold, you are beautiful; [your eyes are doves]:"**

3. A. "Doves:"

B. Just as a dove is innocent, so the Israelites are [Simon supplies: innocent; just as the dove is beautiful in its movement, so Israel are] beautiful in their movement, when they go up for the pilgrim festivals.

C. Just as a dove is distinguished, so the Israelites are distinguished: not shaving, in circumcision, in show-fringes.

D. Just as the dove is modest, so the Israelites are modest.

E. Just as the dove puts forth its neck for slaughter, so the Israelites: "For your sake are we killed all day long" (Ps. 44:23).

F. Just as the dove atones for sin, so the Israelites atone for other nations.

G. For all those seventy bullocks that they offer on the Festival of Tabernacles correspond to the nations of the world, so that the world should not become desolate on their account: "In return for my love they are my adversaries, but I am all prayer" (Ps. 109:4).

H. Just as the dove, once it recognizes its mate, never again changes him for another, so the Israelites, once they recognized the Holy One, blessed be He, never exchanged him for another.

I. Just as the dove, when it enters its nest, recognizes its nest and young, fledglings and apertures, so the three rows of the disciples of the sages, when they take their seats before them, knows each one his place.

J. Just as the dove, even though you take its fledglings from under it, does not ever abandon its cote, so the Israelites, even though the house of the sanctuary was destroyed, never nullified the three annual pilgrim festivals.
K. Just as the dove renews its brood month by month, so the Israelites every month renew Torah and good deeds.
L. Just as the dove goes far afield but returns to her cote, so do the Israelites: "They shall come trembling as a bird out of Egypt" (Hos. 11:11), this speaks of the generation of the wilderness; "and as a dove out of the land of Assyria" (Hos. 11:11), this speaks of the Ten Tribes.
M. And in both cases: "And I will make them dwell in their houses, says the Lord" (Hos. 11:11).

Hos. 11:11 speaks of the return of the Israelites to their houses.

Song of Songs Rabbah XVII.I
3. A. ." ..our rafters are pine:"
   B. Said R. Yohanan, "No one can derive any use of pine. Why? Because it bends."
   C. So too is the view of R. Yohanan, for R. Yohanan said, "'I am like a leafy cypress tree' (Hos. 14:9): 'I am the one who bowed down so as to uproot the desire to serve idolatry.'
   D. "'Ephraim shall say, what have I to do with idols' (Hos. 14:9): 'What have I to do with the impulse to worship idols?'
   E. "'As for me I respond' (Hos. 14:9): 'I raise up my voice to him.'
   F. "'And look on him' (Hos. 14:9): 'did I not sing a song to you?'
   G. "Thus: 'I am the one who bowed down so as to uproot the desire to serve idolatry.'"

Hos. 14:9 compares God to a cypress tree, bowing down so as to uproot the Israelites' desire for idolatry, and the Israelites overcome their impulse to worship idols.

Song of Songs Rabbah XIX:I
1. A. "As a lily among brambles, [so is my love among maidens]:"
10. A. R. Abun said, "Just as a lily wilts so long as the hot spell persists, but when the dew falls on it, the lily thrives again,
    B. "so Israel, so long as the shadow of Esau falls across the world, Israel wilts,
    C. "but when the shadow of Esau passes from the world, Israel will once more thrive:
    D. "'I shall be like the dew for Israel. It will blossom as the lily' (Hos. 14:6)."

When Esau/Rome passes from the world, Israel blossoms (Hos. 14:6).

Song of Songs Rabbah XXV:I

1. A. **"The voice of my beloved! Behold he comes [leaping upon the mountains, bounding over the hills]:"**
   B. R. Judah and R. Nehemiah and Rabbis:
   C. R. Judah says, "'The voice of my beloved! Behold he comes: this refers to Moses.
2. A. R. Nehemiah says, "'The voice of my beloved! Behold he comes: this refers to Moses.
3. A. Rabbis say, "'The voice of my beloved! Behold he comes: this refers to Moses.
   B. "When he came and said to the Israelites, 'In this month you will be redeemed,' they said to him, 'Our lord, Moses, how are we going to be redeemed? And the whole of Egypt is made filthy by our own worship of idols!'
   C. "He said to them, 'Since he wants to redeem you, he is not going to pay attention to your worship of idols.
   D. "'Rather, "leaping upon the mountains, bounding over the hills:" mountains and hills refer only to idolatry, in line with this usage: "They sacrifice on the tops of the mountains and offer upon the hills" (Hos. 4:13).
   E. "'And in this month you are to be redeemed: "This month is the beginning of months" (Ex. 12:1).'"

Hos. 4:13 refers to idolatry, and the Israelites worshipped idols on the hills.

Song of Songs Rabbah XLII:I

1. A. **"King Solomon made himself a palanquin, [from the wood of Lebanon]:"**
   B. R. Azariah in the name of R. Judah b. R. Simon interpreted the verse to speak of the tabernacle:
   C. "'palanquin' refers to the tabernacle.
2. A. Said R. Judah b. R. Ilai, "The matter may be compared to the case of a king who had a little daughter. Before she reached maturity and produced the signs of puberty, he would see her in the marketplace and speak with her quite publicly, whether in an alleyway or in a courtyard.
   B. "After she grew up and produced the signs of puberty, the king said, 'It is not becoming for my daughter that I should speak with her in public. So make her a pavilion, and when I have to speak with her, I shall speak with her in the pavilion.'
   C. "So: 'When Israel was a child, then I loved him' (Hos. 11:1).
   D. "In Egypt they saw him in public: 'For the Lord will pass through to smite the Egyptians' (Ex. 12:23).
   E. "At the Sea they saw him in public: 'And Israel saw the great work' (Ex. 14:31).

F. ." ..and the children pointed at him with their finger, saying, 'This is my God and I will glorify him' (Ex. 15:2).
G. "At Sinai they saw him face to face: 'And he said, the Lord came from Sinai' (Dt. 33:2).
H. "When the Israelites stood at Mount Sinai and received the Torah and said, 'All that the Lord has spoken we shall do and obey' (Dt. 24:7), so becoming for him a nation complete in all ways,
I. "then said the Holy One, blessed be He, 'It is not becoming for my children for me to speak with them in public. Make me a tabernacle, and when I have to speak with them, I shall speak with them from within the tabernacle: 'But when Moses went in before the Lord that he might speak with him' (Ex. 34:34).''

Hos. 11:1 speaks of Israel as a child, with whom God speaks in private.

SONG OF SONGS RABBAH XLV:I
3. A. "doves:"
   B. Just as a dove is innocent, so the Israelites are [Simon supplies: innocent; just as the dove is beautiful in its movement, so Israel are] beautiful in their movement, when they go up for the pilgrim festivals.
   C. Just as a dove is distinguished, so the Israelites are distinguished: not shaving, in circumcision, in show-fringes.
   D. Just as the dove is modest, so the Israelites are modest.
   E. Just as the dove puts forth its neck for slaughter, so the Israelites: "For your sake are we killed all day long" (Ps. 44:23).
   F. Just as the dove atones for sin, so the Israelites atone for other nations.
   G. For all those seventy bullocks that they offer on the Festival of Tabernacles correspond to the nations of the world, so that the world should not become desolate on their account: "In return for my love they are my adversaries, but I am all prayer" (Ps. 109:4).
   H. Just as the dove, once it recognizes its mate, never again changes him for another, so the Israelites, once they recognized the Holy One, blessed be He, never exchanged him for another.
   I. Just as the dove, when it enters its nest, recognizes its nest and young, fledglings and apertures, so the three rows of the disciples of the sages, when they take their seats before them, knows each one his place.
   J. Just as the dove, even though you take its fledglings from under it, does not ever abandon its cote, so the Israelites, even though the house of the sanctuary was destroyed, never nullified the three annual pilgrim festivals.
   K. Just as the dove renews its brood month by month, so the Israelites every month renew Torah and good deeds.
   L. Just as the dove goes far afield but returns to her cote, so do the Israelites: "They shall come trembling as a bird out of Egypt" (Hos.

11:11), this speaks of the generation of the wilderness; "and as a dove out of the land of Assyria" (Hos. 11:11), this speaks of the Ten Tribes.
- M. And in both cases: "And I will make them dwell in their houses, says the Lord" (Hos. 11:11).

Hos. 11:11 means that both the Ten Tribes and the generation of the wilderness will return to their homeland.

Song of Songs Rabbah XLVIII:v
4. A. **For we have learned in the Mishnah:**
   - B. **The high priest serves in eight garments, and an ordinary priest in four:**
   - C. **tunic, underpants, head-covering, and girdle.**
   - D. **The high priest in addition wears the breastplate, apron, upper garment, and frontlet [M. Yoma 7:5A-C].**
   - E. The tunic would atone for bloodshed: "And they dipped the coat in the blood" (Gen. 37:31).
   - F. Some say, "It atoned for those who wear mixed varieties: 'And he made him a coat of many colors' (Gen. 37:3)."
   - G. The underpants atone for fornication: "And you shall make them linen underpants to cover the flesh of their nakedness" (Ex. 27:42).
   - H. The head-covering atones for arrogance: "And he set the head-covering on his head" (Lev. 8:9).
   - I. For what did the girdle atone?
   - J. For the double-dealers.
   - K. Others say, "For thieves."
   - L. The one who says that it was for thieves maintains that view because the garment was hollow, standing for thieves, who work in hiding.
   - M. The one who says that it was for the double-dealers is in accord with that which R. Levi said, "It was thirty-two cubits long, and he would twist it on either side."
   - N. The breastplate would atone for those who pervert justice: "And you shall put in the breastplate of judgment the Urim and the Thummim" (Ex. 28:30).
   - O. The apron [ephod] would atone for idolatry: "And without ephod or teraphim" (Hos. 3:4).
   - P. The upper garment [robe] would atone for slander.

Hos. 3:4 means that the ephod/apron of the high priest atones for idolatry.

Song of Songs Rabbah XLVIII:ix
1. A. **Another interpretation of the verse, "Your lips are like a scarlet thread:"**
2. A. [Supply: "Your lips are like a scarlet thread:"]
   - B. On this verse R. Abbahu said, "'So shall we render for bullocks the offering of our lips' (Hos. 14:3):

C. "What shall we pay instead of the bullocks and the goat that is sent away?
　　　D. "Our lips."

Hos. 14:3 refers to the offering of the lips.

SONG OF SONGS RABBAH XLVIII:VIII
　　1. A. Another interpretation of the verse, "Your hair is like a flock of goats:"
　　11. A. One verse of Scripture says, "And my eyes and heart will be there perpetually" (1 Kgs. 9:3), and another says, "I will go and return to my place" (Hos. 5:15):
　　　B. How are the two to be harmonized?
　　　C. His face is above, but his heart is below.
　　　D. For so it has been taught: [And if he cannot turn his face,] he should direct his heart toward the Chamber of the Holy of Holies [M. Ber. 4:5C].
　　　E. R. Hiyya the Elder and R. Simeon b. Halafta:
　　　F. R. Hiyya the Elder said, "Toward the Holy of Holies that is above."

Hos. 5:15 refers to God's face above but his heart on earth.

SONG OF SONGS RABBAH XLIX:I
　　5. A. R. Abbah in the name of R. Simeon: "A mortal cannot put on the poultice before seeing the wound.
　　　B. "But the One who spoke and thereby brought the world into being is not that way. But rather he puts on the poultice and only afterward inflicts the wound.
　　　C. "'Behold I will bring it healing and cure and I will cure them' (Jer. 33:6); 'When I would heal Israel' (Hos. 7:1).
　　　D. "Said the Holy One, blessed be He, 'I have come to heal the transgressions of Israel, and 'Then is the iniquity of Ephraim uncovered and the wickedness of Samaria' (Hos. 7:1).
　　　E. "But as to the nations of the world, he smites them and then heals them: 'And the Lord will smite Egypt, smiting and healing' (Isa. 19:22),
　　　F. "smiting through Aaron, healing through Moses."

Hos. 7:1 refers first to the healing, then to the infliction of the wound.

SONG OF SONGS RABBAH LXXI:I
　　15. A. "Hear O Israel, the Lord our God, the Lord is one" (Dt. 6:4):
　　　B. If you turn the D of "one" into an R, you get "another," so you will destroy the world.
　　　C. "You shall not bow down to any other god" (Ex. 34:14):
　　　D. If you turn the R of other into a D [yielding, one], you will destroy the world.

5. *Hosea in Esther Rabbah I, Ruth Rabbah, Song of Songs Rabbah...*

E. You will not profane my holy name" (Lev. 22:32);
F. If you turn the H of the word profane into an H, you will destroy the entire world [by reading, You will not praise my holy name"].
G. "Every soul will praise the Lord" (Ps. 103:6).
H. If you turn the H into a different H, you will destroy the entire world [by reading, "Every soul will profane the Lord"].
I. "They have acted deceptively against the Lord" (Jer. 5:12).
J. If you turn the B into a K, you will destroy the entire world [by reading, "They have acted deceptively like the Lord"].
K. "Against the Lord they have acted treacherously" (Hos. 5:7).
L. If you turn the B into a K, you will destroy the entire world [by reading, "They have acted treacherously like the Lord"].
M. "There is none holy like the Lord" (1 Sam. 2:2).
N. If you turn the B into a K, you will destroy the entire world [by reading, "There is nothing holy in the Lord"].
O. "For there is none beside you" (1 Sam. 2:2):
P. For R. Abba b. R. Kahana said, "Everything wears out, but you do not wear out.
Q. "'For there is none beside you' – for there is none that wears you out' [no one can outlive you or supersede you]."

Hos. 5:7 supplies an example of how changing a single letter drastically revises the meaning of a statement.

SONG OF SONGS RABBAH LXXVI:I

3. A. **[Leviticus Rabbah XXVII:VI.2ff.:] Said R. Samuel b. R. Nahman, "On three occasions the Holy One, blessed be He, came to engage in argument with Israel, and the nations of the world rejoiced, saying, 'Can these ever [dare] engage in an argument with their creator? Now he will wipe them out of the world.'**
  B. "One was when he said to them, 'Come, and let us reason together, says the Lord' (Isa. 1:18). When the Holy One, blessed be He, saw that the nations of the world were rejoicing, he turned the matter to [Israel's] advantage: 'If your sins are as scarlet, they shall be white as snow' (Isa. 1:18).
  C. "Then the nations of the world were astonished, and said, 'This is repentance, and this is rebuke? He has planned only to amuse himself with his children.'
  D. "[A second time was] when he said to them, 'Hear, you mountains, the controversy of the Lord' (Mic. 6:2) the nations of the world rejoiced, saying, 'How can these ever [dare] engage in an argument with their creator? Now he will wipe them out of the world.'
  E. "When the Holy One, blessed be He, saw that the nations of the world were rejoicing, he turned the matter to [Israel's] advantage: 'O my people, what have I done to you? In what have I wearied

you? Testify against me' (Mic. 6:3). 'Remember what Balak king of Moab devised' (Mic. 6:5)

F. "Then the nations of the world were astonished, saying, 'This is repentance, and this is rebuke, one following the other? He has planned only to amuse himself with his children.'

G. "[A third time was] when he said to them, 'The Lord has an indictment against Judah, and will punish Jacob according to his ways' (Hos. 12:2), the nations of the world rejoiced, saying, 'How can these ever [dare] engage in an argument with their creator? Now he will wipe them out of the world.'

H. "When the Holy One, blessed be He, saw that the nations of the world were rejoicing, he turned the matter to [Israel's] advantage. That is in line with the following verse of Scripture: 'In the womb he [Jacob = Israel] took his brother [Esau = other nations] by the heel [and in his manhood he strove with God. He strove with the angel and prevailed, he wept and sought his favor]'" (Hos. 12:3-4).

When Hos. 12:2 was stated, the nations rejoiced because they thought God would wipe Israel off the face of the world. But Hos. 12:3-4 show that God still favored Israel.

SONG OF SONGS RABBAH LXXX:II

17. A. [Supply: "The Lord spoke to Moses, saying, Take it from them, that they may be to do the service" (Num. 7:4):]

B. The sense is that they should live and endure for ages to come.

C. How long did they endure?

D. R. Yudan and R. Huna in the name of Bar Qappara: "To Gilgal: 'In Gilgal they sacrificed bullocks, yes, their altars were as heaps in the furrows of the field' (Hos. 12:12)."

E. Where did they offer them?

F. R. Abun said, "In Nob they offered them."

G. R. Abba said, "In Gibeon they offered them."

H. Levi said, "In Shiloh they offered them."

I. And rabbis said, "In the eternal house they offered them."

J. R. Hama said, "The verse of Scripture supporting the view of rabbis is as follows: 'And king Solomon offered the sacrifice of oxen' (2 Chr. 7:5).

K. "What Scripture says is not, 'a sacrifice of oxen,' but, 'the sacrifice of oxen.' And which one is that? One must say, it is 'the two wagons and four oxen' (Num. 7:7), and further, 'the four wagons and eight oxen' (Num. 7:8)."

Sacrifices persisted until Gilgal, so Hos. 12:12.

5. *Hosea in Esther Rabbah I, Ruth Rabbah, Song of Songs Rabbah...*

SONG OF SONGS RABBAH XCI:I
13. A. R. Nehemiah in the name of R. Abun says, "The nations of the world have no planting, nor sowing, nor root.
    B. "The three matters derive from a single verse of Scripture: 'They are scarcely planted, scarcely sown, scarcely has their stock taken root in the earth' (Is. 40:24).
    C. "But the Israelites have a planting: 'And I will plant them in this land' (Jer. 32:41); they have a sowing: 'And I will sow her to me in the land' (Hos. 2:25); they have a root: 'In days to come Jacob shall take root' (Isa. 27:6).

Hos. 2:12 proves that Israel has a sowing in the Land.

SONG OF SONGS RABBAH XCVI:I
2. A. When was the impulse to worship idols eliminated?
    B. R. Benaiah said, "In the time of Mordecai and Esther."
    C. Rabbis said, "It was in the time of Hananiah, Mishael, and Azariah."
    D. Rabbis objected to the view of R. Benaiah, "And was it eliminated by the efforts of an individual?"
    E. Objected R. Benaiah to rabbis, "And were Mordecai and Esther mere individuals?"
    F. The following sustains the position of R. Benaiah:
    G. Said R. Tanhuma, R. Miasha, and R. Jeremiah in the name of R. Samuel b. R. Kahana, "'Many lay in sackcloth and ashes' (Est. 4:3) – [so] the great majority of that generation were righteous."
    H. The following sustains the position of rabbis:
    I. R. Phineas and R. Hilqiah in the name of R. Samuel: "'And those of you who escape shall remember me among the nations where they were carried captives, how I broke their straying heart, which has departed from me' (Ex. 6:9).
    J. "'And those of you who escape:' this refers to Hananiah, Mishael, and Azariah, who were refugees from the fiery furnace.
    K. "What is written is not 'among the nations who carried captive there,' but 'among the nations where they were carried captive.'
    L. "Said the Holy One, blessed be He, to Israel, "'Ephraim shall say, What have I to do any more with idols" (Hos. 14:9). What have I to do any more with the inclination to worship idols. "As for me, I respond" (Hos. 14:9) – I lift up my voice to him. "And look on him" – have we not sung hymns before you?'
    M. "[God continues,] 'If so, you must conclude that I was the one who subdued the impulse to worship idols.'"

Hos. 14:9 proves that idolatry came to an end in Israel by the time of Mordecai and Esther.

Song of Songs Rabbah CVIII:I

11. A. Said R. Aibu, "Two matters did the Israelites ask from the Holy One, blessed be He, but they did not ask properly, so the prophets went and corrected them in their behalf.
    B. "The Israelites said, 'And he shall come to us as the rain' (Hos. 6:3).
    C. "Said the prophets to them, 'You did not ask properly. For rains may well be a mark of inconvenience for the world. Travelers are bothered by them, seafarers are bothered by them, roofers are bothered by them, vintners are bothered by them, porters at the threshing floor are bothered by them, someone who has a full cistern or a full vat is bothered by them, and yet you say, "he shall come to us as the rain" (Hos. 6:3)?'
    D. "The prophets went and corrected what they had said in their behalf: 'I will be as the dew to Israel' (Hos. 14:6)."
    E. "Furthermore, the Israelites said before the Holy One, blessed be He, 'Set me as a seal upon your heart, as a seal upon your arm.'"
    F. "Said the prophets to them, 'You did not ask properly. For at times the heart is visible, and at times it is not visible, so then the seal will not be visible.'
    G. "What then would be the proper way? "You shall also be a crown of beauty in the hand of the Lord'" (Isa. 62:3).
    H. R. Simon b. Quzit said in the name of R. Levi, "Said to them the Holy One, blessed be He, 'Neither you nor your prophets have asked in a right and appropriate manner.
    G. "'For, after all, a mortal king can go along and have the crown fall off his head, with the royal diadem upon it! What, then, would be the proper way? "Behold, I have graven you upon the palms of my hands, your walls are continually before me" (Isa. 49:16). Just as a man cannot forget the palms of his hands, so "These may forget, but I will not forget you" (Isa. 49:15).'"

Hosea 6:3 shows the Israelites asking God for rain in an improper manner, and Hos. 14:6 shows Hosea correcting matters.

Song of Songs Rabbah CXI:III

13. A. When R. Simeon b. Laqish saw them [Babylonians] swarming in the marketplace [in the Land of Israel], he would say to them, "Scatter yourselves."
    B. He would say to them, "When you went up, you did not come up as a wall [of people], now have you come to form a wall [of people]?"
14. A. When R. Yohanan would see them, he would rebuke them, saying, "If a prophet can rebuke them, 'My God will cast them away, because they did not listen to him' (Hos. 9:17),
    B. "can I not rebuke them?"

5. *Hosea in Esther Rabbah I, Ruth Rabbah, Song of Songs Rabbah...*

Hos. 9:17 shows the prophet rebuking Israelites, and Yohanan follows his model.

LAMENTATIONS RABBAH

LAMENTATIONS RABBAH II:I.

9. A. Said R. Judah b. Pazzi, "'Israel has cast off that which is good, the enemy pursues' (Hos. 8:3):
   B. "'good' refers only to Torah: 'For I give you good doctrine' (Prov. 4:2)."

Hosea's reference to Israel's casting off that which is good speaks of the Torah in particular.

LAMENTATIONS RABBAH II.II.

1. A. "Thus says the Lord of hosts: 'Summon the dirge-singers, let them come; send for the skilled women, let them come.' [Let them quickly start a wailing for us, that our eyes may run with tears, our pupils flow with water. For the sound of wailing is heard from Zion, How are we despoiled! How greatly are we shamed!]" (Jer. 9:16-18).
   B. R. Yohanan and R. Simeon b. Laqish and rabbis [comment on the cited verse in different ways].
2. A. R. Yohanan said, "The matter may be compared to the case of a king who had two sons. He lost his temper with the first, took a stick and beat him and threw him out of the house.
   B. "He said, 'Woe for this one! From what luxury he has been thrown out!'
   C. "He lost his temper with the second, took a stick and beat him and threw him out of the house.
   D. "He said, 'I am the one [who is at fault], for my way of bringing them up is no good.'
   E. "So when the Ten Tribes went into exile, the Holy One, blessed be He, began to recite for them the following verse: 'Woe is they, for they have strayed from me' (Hos. 7:13).
   F. "But when Judah and Benjamin went into exile, it is as though the Holy One, blessed be He, said, 'Woe is me for my hurt' (Jer. 10:19)."

Hosea blamed the ten tribes for their exile, but Jeremiah had God blame himself for the exile of Judah and Benjamin.

LAMENTATIONS RABBAH IV.I.

1. A. R. Abbahu in the name of R. Yosé bar Haninah commenced [discourse by citing this verse]: "'But they are like a man, they have transgressed the covenant. There they dealt treacherously against me "(Hos. 6:7).

B. "They are like a man, specifically, this refers to the first man [Adam]. [We shall now compare the story of the first man in Eden with the story of Israel in its land.]

C. "Said the Holy One, blessed be He, 'In the case of the first man, I brought him into the garden of Eden, I commanded him, he violated my commandment, I judged him to be sent away and driven out, but I mourned for him, saying "How..."'[which begins the book of Lamentations, hence stands for a lament, but which also is written with the consonants that also yield, Where are you].

J. "'So too in the case of his descendants, [God continues to speak,] I brought them into the Land of Israel, I commanded them, they violated my commandment, I judged them to be sent out and driven away but I mourned for them, saying, How....'

P. "'But I mourned for them, saying, How...:' How lonely sits the city [that was full of people! How like a widow has she become, she that was great among the nations! She that was a princess among the cities has become a vassal. She weeps bitterly in the night, tears on her cheeks, among all her lovers she has none to comfort her; all her friends have dealt treacherously with her, they have become her enemies] (Lamentations 1:1-2)."

Hos. 6:7 compares Israel to a man, namely Adam, and that yields the systematic contrast of Israel's fate and Adam's.

LAMENTATIONS RABBAH VI.I.

1. A. **R. Abbah in the name of R. Yosé bar Hanina commenced [by citing the following verse of Scripture]: "'Ephraim shall become a desolation [in the day of punishment among the tribes of Israel I declare what is sure. The princes of Judah have become like those who remove the landmark; upon them I will pour out my wrath like water]' (Hos. 5:9-10).**

B. "When will this come about?

C. "'in the day of punishment.'

D. "This is the day on which the Holy One, blessed be He, is destined to enter into litigation with them in court.

E. "You find that when the Ten Tribes went into exile, the tribes of Judah and Benjamin did not, so the Ten Tribes were saying, 'How come he has sent us into exile but them he has not sent into exile? It is because they belong to his court. So maybe there's some sort of favoritism in play here!'

F. "[He replied to them,] 'God forbid! There is no favoritism, but they have not yet sinned.'

G. "When they did sin, he sent them into exile.

H. "Said the Ten Tribes, 'Lo, our God! lo, our God! Lo, the mighty one! lo, the mighty one! Lo, the truthful one! lo, the truthful one!

I. "'For even to those who belong to his court he did not give preference.'"

2. A. When they sinned, they went into exile,
    B. and when they went into exile, Jeremiah began to lament for them: "Alas! Lonely sits the city once great with people!" (Lam. 1:1).

Hos. 5:9-10 indicates that God will punish the Judeans just as he punished the northern Israelites, no favoritism was shown to the southern tribes over the Ten Tribes of the north.

LAMENTATIONS RABBAH XXI.I.
 2. A. Said R. Yosé b. Halapta, "Whoever knows how many years the Israelites worshipped idolatry knows also when the son of David will come."
    B. "And we have three verses of Scripture that support this position.
    C. "'And I will visit upon her the days of the Baalim, wherein she offered to them' (Hos. 2:15).
    D. "The second: 'And it came to pass that, as he called and they would not hear, so they shall call and I will not hear' (Zech. 7:13).
    E. "The third: 'And when they ask, Because of what did the Lord our God do all these things? you shall answer them, Because you forsook me and served alien gods on your own land, you will have to serve foreigners in a land not your own' (Jer. 5:19)."

Hos. 2:15 forms part of the proof of the proposition that the son of David will come only after the years in which Israel worshipped idols are matched by the years in which they are exiled.

LAMENTATIONS RABBAH XXII I.
 1. A. R. Joshua of Sikhnin in the name of R. Levi commenced [by citing the following verse of Scripture]: "'Ah! those who add house to house [and join field to field, till there is room for none but you to dwell in the land! In my hearing said the Lord of Hosts: Surely, great houses shall lie forlorn, spacious and splendid ones without occupants]' (Isa. 5:8-9)."
 3. A. "...till there is room [for none but you to dwell in the land]:"
    B. What is it that caused the place to be destroyed? It is because they left no place in which they had not worshipped idolatry.
    C. In the beginning they would worship it in secret: "Then he said to them, 'Have you seen what the elders of the house of Israel do in the dark?'"(Ezek. 8:12).
    D. And since [the leaders] did not stop them, they went and did it behind a door: "And behind the door and the posts you have set up your symbol" (Isa. 57:8).
    E. And since they did not stop them, they went and did it on the roofs: "And them that worship the host of heaven upon the housetops" (Zeph. 1:5).

F. And since they did not stop them, they went and did it in gardens, "That sacrifice in gardens" (Isa. 65:3).
G. And since they did not stop them, they went and did it on mountain tops: "They sacrifice on the tops of mountains and offer on the hills" (Hos. 4:13).
H. And since they did not stop them, they went and did it in the fields: "Yes, their altars shall be as heaps in the furrows of the field" (Hos. 12:12).

Hos. 4:13 proves the Israelites committed idolatry on mountain tops, and Hos. 12:12, in fields.

LAMENTATIONS RABBAH XXIII.I.
23. A. Seven transgressions did the Israelites commit on that day: they murdered [1] a priest, [2] prophet, [3] judge, [4] they spilled innocent blood, [5] they blasphemed the divine name, [6] they imparted uncleanness to the courtyard, and it was, furthermore, [7] a Day of Atonement that coincided with the Sabbath.
B. When Nebuzaradan came in, the blood began to drip. He said to them, "What sort of blood is this dripping blood?"
C. They said to him, "It is the blood of oxen, rams, and sheep that we offered on the altar."
D. He forthwith sent and brought oxen, rams, and sheep and slaughtered them in his presence, but the blood continued to drip.
E. He said to them, "If you tell the truth, well and good, but if not, I shall comb your flesh with iron combs."
F. They said to him, "What shall we tell you? He was a prophet who rebuked us. We conspired against him and killed him. And lo, years have passed, but his blood has not stopped seething."
G. He said to them, "I shall appease it."
H. He brought before him the great sanhedrin and the lesser sanhedrin and killed them, until their blood mingled with that of Zechariah: "Oaths are imposed and broken, they kill and rob, there is nothing but adultery and license, one deed of blood after another" (Hos. 4:2).

Hos. 4:2 attests to the wickedness of the Jerusalemites.

LAMENTATIONS RABBAH XXIV.II.
1. A. **Another interpretation of the passage, "My Lord God of Hosts summoned on that day to weeping and lamenting, to tonsuring and girding with sackcloth:"**
B. When the Holy One, blessed be He, considered destroying the house of the sanctuary, he said, "So long as I am within it, the nations of the world cannot lay a hand on it.
C. "I shall close my eyes to it and take an oath that I shall not become engaged with it until the time of the end."

5. Hosea in Esther Rabbah I, Ruth Rabbah, Song of Songs Rabbah...

D. Then the enemies came and destroyed it.
E. Forthwith the Holy One, blessed be He, took an oath by his right hand and put it behind him: "He has drawn back his right hand from before the enemy" (Lam. 2:3).
F. At that moment the enemies entered the sanctuary and burned it up.
G. When it had burned, the Holy One, blessed be He, said, "I do not have any dwelling on earth any more. I shall take up my presence from there and go up to my earlier dwelling."
H. That is in line with this verse: "I will go and return to my place, until they acknowledge their guilt and seek my face" (Hos. 5:15).
I. At that moment the Holy One, blessed be He, wept, saying, "Woe is me! What have I done! I have brought my Presence to dwell below on account of the Israelites, and now that they have sinned, I have gone back to my earlier dwelling. Heaven forfend that I now become a joke to the nations and a source of ridicule among people."
J. At that moment Metatron came, prostrated himself, and said before him, "Lord of the world, let me weep, but don't you weep!"
K. He said to him, "If you do not let me weep now, I shall retreat to a place in which you have no right to enter, and there I shall weep."
L. That is in line with this verse: "But if you will not hear it, my soul shall weep in secret for pride" (Jer. 13:17).

When the Temple was burned, God returned to his place n heaven, so Hos. 5:15.

LAMENTATIONS RABBAH XXV.i.

3. A. In ten upward stages the Presence of God departed: from the cherub to the cherub, from the cherub to the threshold of the temple-building; from the threshold of the temple to the two cherubim; from the two cherubim to the eastern gate of the sanctuary; from the eastern gate of the sanctuary to the [wall of the] temple court; from the [wall of the] temple court to the altar; from the altar to the roof; from the roof to the city wall, from the city wall to the city, from the city to the Mount of Olives.

4. A. Said R. Jonathan, "For three and a half years the Presence of God stayed on the Mount of Olives, thinking that the Israelites might repent, but they did not do so.
B. "And an echo would go forth, proclaiming, 'Return, wandering children, I shall heal your backslidings' (Jer. 3:22).
C. "But when they did not repent, the Presence of God began to fly in the air, reciting this verse of Scripture: 'I will go and return to my place until they confess their guilt and seek my face, in their trouble they will seek me earnestly' (Hos. 5:15)."
D. It is in connection with that moment that [Jeremiah] says, "Give glory to the Lord your God before he brings darkness, [before

your feet stumble on the twilight mountains, and while you look for light, he turns it into gloom and makes it deep darkness. But if you will not listen, my soul will weep in secret for your pride; my eyes will weep bitterly and run down with tears, because the Lord's flock has been taken captive]" (Jer. 13:16-17).

The same proposition is expressed in other language.

LAMENTATIONS RABBAH XXV:VI.
1. A. "How like a widow has she become:"
   B. Said R. Abba bar Kahana, "They did not fully explore the limits of the measure of justice, so the measure of justice did not go to extremes against them.
   C. "They did not fully explore the limits of the measure of justice: 'And the people were like murmurers' (Num. 11:1).
   D. "What is written is not 'murmurers,' but only, 'like murmurers.'"
   E. "'The princes of Judah are like those who remove the landmark' (Hos. 5:10).
   F. "What is written is not 'remove,' but 'like those who remove.'
   G. "'For Israel is like a stubborn heifer' (Hos. 4:16).
   H. "What is written is not 'a stubborn heifer,' but 'like a stubborn heifer.'
   I. "What is written here is not 'a widow' but 'like a widow.'
   J. "She is like a woman waiting for her husband, who has left her and gone on a distant journey.
   K. "'He has bent his bow like an enemy' (Lam. 2:4).
   L. "What is written here is not 'an enemy' but 'like an enemy.'"

Hosea's formulation at Hos. 4:16 places limits on the condemnation of Israel: not the thing but like the thing.

LAMENTATIONS RABBAH XLIII.I.
3. A. ["The proud have dug pits for me, which is not according to your Torah" (Ps. 119:85).] R. Judah b. R. Simon said, "[Cohen: In two matters the enemy transgressed the Torah.] 'Whether it be cow or ewe, you shall not kill it and its young both in one day' (Lev. 22:28), but here the child was killed together with its mother on one day: 'The mother was dashed in pieces with her children' (Hos. 10:14), which is contrary to your Torah.
   B. "The other instance: 'And whatsoever man there be of the children of Israel, or of the strangers who live among them, who takes in hunting any beast or fowl that may be eaten, he shall pour out the blood thereof and cover it with dust' (Lev. 17:13). But here: 'They have shed their blood like water around Jerusalem, with none to bury them' (Ps. 79:3), which is contrary to the Torah."

Hos. 10:14 shows that the enemy violated the Torah in one of two aspects.

LAMENTATIONS RABBAH XLIII:II.
2. A. **["The proud have dug pits for me, which is not according to your Torah" (Ps. 119:85).]**
   B. "['"The proud have dug pits for me, which is not according to your Torah" (Ps. 119:85).] R. Abba b. Kahana said, "[Cohen: In two matters the enemy transgressed the Torah.] 'You shall not take the dam with the young' (Dt. 22:6). But here: 'The mother was dashed in pieces with her children' (Hos. 10:14), which is contrary to your Torah.
   H. "The other instance: 'To cut off the children from the street' (Jer. 9:20), but not from the synagogues, 'and the young men from the broad places' (Jer. 9:20), but not from the houses of study. But here: 'When the anger of God went up against them and killed the most vigorous among them and smote down the young men of Israel' (Ps. 88:31), contrary to your Torah."

As above.

LAMENTATIONS RABBAH L.I.
2. A. "For these things I weep:"
   B. Hadrian – may his bones be pulverized – set up three guards, one in Emmaus, one in Kefar Leqatia, and the third in Bethel in Judah.
   C. He thought, "Whoever escapes the one will be caught by the other."
   D. He sent forth a proclamation, saying, "Wherever a Jew is located, let him come out, because the king wants to assure him."
   E. The heralds made this announcement and caught Jews, in line with this verse: "And Ephraim is become like a silly dove, without understanding" (Hos. 7:11).
   F. [The Jews who were caught were taunted:] "Instead of asking that the dead be resurrected, pray that those alive will not be caught" [following Cohen, p. 126].
   G. Those who understood did not come out of hiding, but those who did not gathered in the valley of Bet Rimmon.
   H. [Hadrian] said to his general, "Before I am done eating this piece of cake and chicken leg, I want to be able to look for a single one of these yet alive and not find him."
   I. He surrounded them with the legions and slaughtered them, so the blood streams as far as Cyprus.

Hos. 7:11 declares that Israel acted in a silly manner, falling for the ruse of the conqueror.

LAMENTATIONS RABBAH L.II.
4. A. ["For these things I weep; my eyes flow with tears:"] "These things I remember and pour out my soul within me" (Ps. 42:5):
   B. The Community of Israel said to the Holy One, blessed be He, "In the past I went up to Jerusalem on well-maintained roads, now through thorny hedges: 'Therefore behold I will hedge up your way with thorns' (Hos. 2:8)."

Israel remembers better days, when the pilgrimage for the festival took place over well-maintained roads, but God has scattered thorns on the road now.

LAMENTATIONS RABBAH L.II.
6. A. There was the case of Miriam [Buber: Martha], daughter of Boethus, that she was betrothed to Joshua b. Gamla, and the king appointed him high priest.
   B. He married her.
   C. One time she said, "I shall go and see how he reads in the Torah on the Day of Atonement."
   D. What did they do for her? They brought out carpets from the door of her house to the door of the house of the sanctuary, so that her feet should not be exposed. Nonetheless, her feet were exposed.
   E. When her husband died, sages decreed for her [a settlement of her marriage contract involving] two seahs of wine a day.
   F. But it has been taught, "They do not allot wine for a woman by the act of a court"? And why not? R. Hiyya b. Abba said, "It is a precaution against wantonness: 'Harlotry, wine, and new wine take away the heart' (Hos. 4:11)."

Wine corrupts, so Hos. 4:11.

LAMENTATIONS RABBAH LVII:III.
1. A. "How the Lord in his anger has set the daughter of Zion under a cloud!"
2. A. "He has cast down from heaven to earth the splendor of Israel:"
   B. R. Huna bar Aha in the name of R. Hanina b. R. Abbahu: "The matter may be compared to the case of a king who had a son.
   C. "The son cried, so he put him on his knees. He cried some more, so he held him in his arms. He cried some more, so he put him up on his shoulders. The boy dirtied the father, so he threw him to the ground, and he was not thrown down in the way that he was lifted up. The lifting up was step by step, but the throwing down was in a single angry gesture.
   D. "So it is said, 'And I, I taught Ephraim to walk, taking them by their arms' (Hos. 11:3). Then: 'I will make Ephraim ride, Judah shall plow, Jacob shall break his clods' (Hos. 10:11). And finally: 'He has cast down from heaven to earth the splendor of Israel.'"

5. Hosea in Esther Rabbah I, Ruth Rabbah, Song of Songs Rabbah...   *107*

When Israel was taken up by God, God did the act gently and in a kind way, Hos. 11:3, but when he rejected Israel, it was with a violent gesture, Hos. 10:11.

LAMENTATIONS RABBAH LVIII.I.
1. C. Until what time did the [penalty because of] the sin of the golden calf last?
   D. Said R. Berekhiah, and some say, R. Nehemiah b. Eleazar, "To the time of the calves made by Jeroboam, son of Nebat: 'When I would heal Israel, then is the iniquity of Ephraim uncovered and the wickedness of Samaria' (Hos. 7:1).
   E. "Said the Holy One, blessed be He, 'I came to heal Israel from the sin that it committed through the calf, but now is the iniquity of Ephraim uncovered.'"
   F. R. Ishmael b. Nahmani in the name of R. Yohanan said, "It was up to the destruction of the house of the sanctuary: 'Cause the visitations of the city to draw near, every man with his destroying weapon in his hand' (Ezek. 9:1). 'Nevertheless in the day when I visit, I will visit their sin upon them' (Ex. 32:34)."

The penalty for the golden calf persisted to the time of Jeroboam, so Hos. 7:1.

LAMENTATIONS RABBAH LVIII:II.
27. **A. Seven transgressions did the Israelites commit on that day: they murdered [1] a priest, [2] prophet, [3] judge, [4] they spilled innocent blood, [5] they blasphemed the divine name, [6] they imparted uncleanness to the courtyard, and it was, furthermore, [7] a Day of Atonement that coincided with the Sabbath.**
   B. When Nebuzaradan came in, the blood began to drip. He said to them, "What sort of blood is this dripping blood?"
   C. They said to him, "It is the blood of oxen, rams, and sheep that we offered on the altar."
   D. He forthwith sent and brought oxen, rams, and sheep and slaughtered them in his presence, but the blood continued to drip. [Cohen, p. 164: the blood did not behave similarly]. He had all kinds of animals brought, but the blood did not behave similarly.
   E. He said to them, "If you tell the truth, well and good, but if not, I shall comb your flesh with iron combs."
   F. They said to him, "What shall we tell you? He was a prophet-priest who rebuked us in the name of Heaven: 'Submit, but we did not submit.' We conspired against him and killed him. And lo, years have passed, but his blood has not stopped seething."
   G. He said to them, "I shall appease it."
   H. He brought before him the great sanhedrin and the lesser sanhedrin and killed them, [until their blood mingled with that of Zechariah:

"Oaths are imposed and broken, they kill and rob, there is nothing but adultery and license, one deed of blood after another (Hos. 4:2).] He had the young priests brought and killed them by it, but it did not stop.

As above.

LAMENTATIONS RABBAH LX.I.

1. A. **"He has bent his bow like an enemy, with his right hand set like a foe:"**
   B. Said R. Aibu, "They did not fully explore the limits of the measure of justice, so the measure of justice did not go to extremes against them.
   C. "They did not fully explore the limits of the measure of justice: 'And the people were like murmurers' (Num. 11:1).
   D. "What is written is not 'murmurers,' but only, 'like murmurers.'"
   E. "'The princes of Judah are like those who remove the landmark' (Nos. 5:10).
   F. "What is written is not 'remove,' but 'like those who remove.'
   G. "'For Israel is like a stubborn heifer' (Hos. 4:16).
   H. "What is written is not 'a stubborn heifer,' but 'like a stubborn heifer.'
   I. "And the Attribute of Justice did not go to extremes against them.
   J. "What is written here is not 'an enemy' but 'like an enemy.'"

As above.

LAMENTATIONS RABBAH LXI.I.

1. A. "The Lord has become like an enemy:"
   B. Said R. Aibu, "They did not fully explore the limits of the measure of justice, so the measure of justice did not go to extremes against them.
   C. "They did not fully explore the limits of the measure of justice: 'And the people were like murmurers' (Num. 11:1).
   D. "What is written is not 'murmurers,' but only, 'like murmurers.'"
   E. "'The princes of Judah are like those who remove the landmark' (Nos. 5:10).
   F. "What is written is not 'remove,' but 'like those who remove.'
   G. "'For Israel is like a stubborn heifer' (Hos. 4:16).
   H. "What is written is not 'a stubborn heifer,' but 'like a stubborn heifer.'
   I. "And the Attribute of Justice did not go to extremes against them.
   J. "What is written here is not 'an enemy' but 'like an enemy.'"

As above.

LAMENTATIONS RABBAH CXIII.I.

2. A. Seven transgressions did the Israelites commit on that day: they murdered [1] a priest, [2] prophet, [3] judge, [4] they spilled innocent blood, [5] they blasphemed the divine name, [6] they imparted uncleanness to the courtyard, and it was, furthermore, [7] a Day of Atonement that coincided with the Sabbath.
   B. When Nebuzaradan came in, he saw the blood of Zechariah begin to drip. He said to them, "What sort of blood is this dripping blood?"
   C. They said to him, "It is the blood of oxen, rams, and sheep that we offered on the altar."
   D. He forthwith sent and brought oxen, rams, and sheep and slaughtered them in his presence, but the blood continued to drip.
   E. He said to them, "If you tell the truth, well and good, but if not, I shall comb your flesh with iron combs."
   F. They said to him, "What shall we tell you? He was a prophet who rebuked us. We conspired against him and killed him. And lo, years have passed, but his blood has not stopped seething."
   G. He said to them, "I shall appease it."
   H. He brought before him the great sanhedrin and the lesser sanhedrin and killed them, [until their blood mingled with that of Zechariah: "Oaths are imposed and broken, they kill and rob, there is nothing but adultery and license, one deed of blood after another (Hos. 4:2)].

As above.

LAMENTATIONS RABBAH CXVII:I.

1. A. "Our eyes failed, ever watching vainly for help:"
   B. What did the Ten Tribes do?
   C. They sent oil to Egypt and imported grain, which they sent to Assyria.
   D. For they said, "If the enemy comes against us, [one or the other of] these will help us."
   E. That is in line with this verse: "And they make a covenant with Assyria and oil is exported to Egypt" (Hos. 12:1).
   F. So when the enemy came against them, they sent to Pharaoh Neccho and said to him, "Send us some of your troops."
   G. Pharaoh was on a sea-voyage.
   H. The Holy One, blessed be He, made a gesture to the skeletons [of the Egyptians drowned in the Red Sea in the time of Moses], and they floated up to the top.
   I. [The Egyptians] said to one another, "What are these skeletons?"
   J. He said to them, "The forebears of this people rebelled against yours, and they went and drowned them in the sea."
   K. They said, "If that is how they behaved towards our forebears, are we going to help them?!"

        L. They forthwith turned back: "Behold, Pharaoh's army, which has come forth to help you, will return to Egypt, to their own land" (Jer. 37:7).
        M. Accordingly: "in our watching we watched for a nation which could not save."

Hosea condemns the Ten Tribes' commerce with Assyria and Egypt.

LAMENTATIONS RABBAH CXXVIII.
    1. A. "We have given the hand to Egypt and to Assyria to get bread enough:"
        B. What did the Ten Tribes do?
        C. They sent oil to Egypt and imported grain, which they sent to Assyria.
        D. For they said, "If the enemy comes against us, [one or the other of] these will help us."
        E. That is in line with this verse: "And they make a covenant with Assyria and oil is exported to Egypt" (Hos. 12:1).

As above.

THE FATHERS ACCORDING TO RABBI NATHAN

THE FATHERS ACCORDING TO RABBI NATHAN IV:II.
    1. A. ...**on the Torah**: how so?
        B. "For I desire mercy and not sacrifice, and the knowledge of God rather than burnt offerings" (Hos. 6:6):
        C. On the basis of this statement we learn that the burnt offering is the most desired offering of all, because the burnt offering is entirely consumed on the altar fires [and yields nothing for either the priest or the farmer who brought the beast, hence it is a mark of total generosity to the altar].
        D. As it is said, "And the priest shall make the whole smoke on the altar" (Lev. 1:9)

Hosea 6:6 shows that the burnt offering is the most valued of all offerings.

THE FATHERS ACCORDING TO RABBI NATHAN IV:V.
    1. A. ...**on deeds of loving kindness:** how so?
        B. Lo, Scripture says, "For I desire mercy and not sacrifice, [and the knowledge of God rather than burnt offerings]" (Hos. 6:6).
        C. To begin with the world was created only on account of loving kindness.
        D. For so it is said, "For I have said, the world is built with loving kindness, in the very heavens you establish your faithfulness" (Ps. 89:3).

Hos. 6:6 proves that the world rests on deeds of loving kindness.

THE FATHERS ACCORDING TO RABBI NATHAN IV:V.
2. A. One time [after the destruction of the Temple] Rabban Yohanan ben Zakkai was going forth from Jerusalem, with R. Joshua following after him. He saw the house of the sanctuary lying in ruins.
B. R. Joshua said, "Woe is us for this place which lies in ruins, the place in which the sins of Israel used to come to atonement."
C. He said to him, "My son, do not be distressed. We have another mode of atonement, which is like [atonement through sacrifice], and what is that? It is deeds of loving kindness.
D. "For so it is said, 'For I desire mercy and not sacrifice, [and the knowledge of God rather than burnt offerings]' (Hos. 6:6)."

Hos. 6:6 proves that acts of loving kindness replace sacrifices in the Temple, now that the Temple is destroyed.

THE FATHERS ACCORDING TO RABBI NATHAN XXIII:IV.
1. A. He [Nehorai] used to say, "He who studies the Torah in his youth — to what is he likened? To a calf subdued when young, as it is said, Ephraim is a heifer well broken, that loves to thresh (Hos. 10:11).
B. "But he who studies the Torah only in his old age — to what is he likened? To a full-grown cow that has been subdued only in its old age, as it is said, 'For Israel is stubborn as a rebelling old beast' (Hos. 4:16)."

Hos. 10:11, 4:16 indicate that it is preferable to study the Torah in one's youth, rather than beginning in old age.

THE FATHERS ACCORDING TO RABBI NATHAN XXIII:IV.
4 A. He who repeats Mishnah-traditions and forgets them is like a woman who gives birth and then buries her children,
B. as it is said, "Yes, though they bring up their children, yet I will bereave them that there be not a man left" (Hos. 9:12).
C. Read the letters that are pronounced I will bereave them to sound like I will cause them to forget.

Hos. 9:12 shows that God makes people forget the Torah they have studied, as a penalty for bad conduct.

THE FATHERS ACCORDING TO RABBI NATHAN XXXVII:VII.
1. A. Seven attributes serve before the throne of glory.
B. And these are they: wisdom, righteousness, loving-kindness, mercy, truth, peace,

    C.   as it is said, "And I will betroth you to me for ever, yes, I will betroth you to me in righteousness, justice, loving-kindness, compassion. And I will betroth you to me in faithfulness and you shall know the Lord" (Hos. 2:21-22).
    D.   R. Meir says, "Why does Scripture state, and you shall know the Lord ? It is to teach you that any person in whom are these traits knows the mind of the Omnipresent."

Hos. 2:21-22 shows that a person who has the traits of righteousness, justice, and so on knows the mind of God.

THE FATHERS ACCORDING TO RABBI NATHAN XXXIV:IX.

1. A.   In ten upward stages the Presence of God departed, from one place to the next: from the ark cover to the cherub, from the cherub to the threshold of the temple-building; from the threshold of the temple to the two cherubim; from the two cherubim to the roof of the sanctuary; from the roof of the sanctuary to the wall of the temple court; from the wall of the temple court to the altar; from the altar to the city; from the city to the Temple mount; from the temple mount to the wilderness.
    K.   And then to on high: "I will go and return to my place" (Hos. 5:15).

As above.

6

Hosea in the Bavli

i. Berakhot

Bavli Berakhot 1:1 III.

26. A. Said R. Helbo said R. Huna, "For whoever arranges a regular place for praying, the God of Abraham is a help, and when he dies, they say for him, 'Woe for the humble man, woe for the pious man, one of the disciples of Abraham, our father.'
    B. "And how do we know in the case of Abraham, our father, that he arranged a regular place for praying?
    C. "For it is written, 'And Abraham got up early in the morning on the place where he had stood' (Gen. 19:27).
    D. "'Standing' refers only to praying, for it is said, 'Then Phinehas stood up and prayed' (Ps. 106:30)."
    E. Said R. Helbo to R. Huna, "He who leaves the synagogue should not take large steps."
    F. Said Abbayye, "That statement applies only when one leaves, but when he enters, it is a religious duty to run [to the synagogue].
    G. "For it is said, 'Let us run to know the Lord' (Hos. 6:3)."
    H. Said R. Zira, "When in the beginning I saw rabbis running to the lesson on the Sabbath, I thought that the rabbis were profaning the Sabbath. But now that I have heard what R. Tanhum said R. Joshua b. Levi said,
    I. "namely, 'A person should always run to take up a matter of law, and even on the Sabbath, as it is said, "They shall walk after the Lord who shall roar like a lion [for he shall roar, and the children shall come hurrying]" (Hos. 11:10),' I too run."

Hos. 6:3 signals that one should run to the synagogue, that is to the Lord. Hos. 11:10 delivers the same message.

Bavli Berakhot 1:1 III.
37. A. And R. Yohanan said in the name of R. Yosé, "Better is one self-reproach that a person sets in his own heart [on account of what he has done] than a great many scourgings.
   B. "For it is said, 'And she shall run after her lovers... then shall she say [in her heart], I shall go and return to my first husband, for then it was better for me than now' (Hos. 2:9)."
   C. And R. Simeon b. Laqish said, "It is better than a hundred scourgings,
   D. "as it is said, 'A rebuke enters deeper into a man of understanding than a hundred stripes into a fool' (Prov. 17:10)."

Hos. 3:9 indicates that self-reproach is to be preferred to the reproach of others.

Bavli Berakhot 5:1 I.
28. A. And R. Eleazar said, "Moses spoke insolently toward the height [God], as it is said, 'And Moses prayed to the Lord' (Num. 11:2).
   B. "Do not read 'to the Lord' but [shifting a letter] 'against the Lord.'"
   C. For so in the house of R. Eliezer b. Jacob people pronounce the letter alef as an ayin and an ayin as an alef [both silently]. [That explains B.]
   D. The house of R. Yannai say, "Proof [that it was God's fault] derives from the following: 'And enough gold' (Deut. 1:1)."
   E. What is the meaning of "enough gold"?
   F. They say in the house of R. Yannai, "This is what Moses said before the Holy One, blessed be he, 'Lord of the age, it was on account of the silver and gold that you lavished upon Israel until they said, "Enough," that caused them to make the golden calf.'"
   G. They say in the house of R. Yannai, "A lion roars not over a basket of straw but over a basket of meat."
   H. Said R. Oshaia, "The matter may be compared to the case of a man who had a cow that was thin but had good limbs. [To fatten it] he fed it lupines, and it bucked.
   I. "He said to it, 'What made you buck against me? It was only the lupines that I fed you.'"
   J. Said R. Hiyya bar Abba said R. Yohanan, "The matter may be compared to the case of a man who had a son. He washed him, anointed him, gave him food and drink, and hung a purse around his neck and sat him at the door of a whorehouse. What could the son do so as not to sin?"
   K. Said R. Aha son of R. Huna said R. Sheshet, "That is in line with what people say: 'Full stomach, bad impulse,' as it is said, 'When they were fed, they became full, they were filled and their heart was exalted, therefore they have forgotten me' (Hos. 13:6)."

6. Hosea in the Bavli

Hos. 13:6 supports the proposition that people rebel against God when they feel secure and prosperous.

BAVLI BERAKHOT 5:1 I.
27. A. Said R. Hama b. R. Hanina, "Were it not for these three verses of Scripture [Simon, p. 195, n. 6: which show that God is responsible for the evil impulse], the feet of (the enemies of) Israel should be moved [for Israel would bear the blame for its sinfulness].
B. "One: 'Whom I have wronged' (Mic. 4:6).
C. "The second: 'Behold as the clay in the potter's hand, so are you in my hand, house of Israel' (Jer. 18:6).
D. "The third: 'I will take out of your flesh the heart of stone, and give you a heart of flesh' (Ez. 36:26).
E. R. Papa said, "The matter derives from here: 'And I will put my spirit within you and cause you to walk in my statutes' (Ex. 36:27). [So God causes one thing or the other.]"
L. R. Nahman said, "Proof derives from the following: 'Then your heart was lifted up and you forgot the Lord' (Deut. 8:14)."
M. Rabbis say, "Proof derives from the following: 'And they shall have eaten their fill and gotten fat and turned to other gods' (Deut. 31:20)."
N. If you prefer, I can derive proof from the following: "But Jeshurun waxed fat and kicked" (Deut. 32:15).
O. Said R. Samuel bar Nahmani said R. Jonathan, "How do we know that the Holy One, blessed be he, retracted and conceded that Moses was right?
P. "As it is said, 'And [I] multiplied to her silver and gold which they used for Baal' (Hos. 2:10)."

God caused Israel's sin, Hos. 2:10.

BAVLI BERAKHOT 6:1 I.
5. A. R. Hanina bar Pappa contrasted these verses: "It is written, 'Therefore I will take back my grain in its time' (Hos. 2:11), and it is further written, 'And you shall gather in your grain' (Deut. 11:14).
B. "There is no contradiction between the two verses. One speaks of a time in which the Israelites carry out the will of the Omnipresent. The other speaks of a time in which the Israelites do not carry out the will of the Omnipresent."

When Israel carries out God's will, it prospers, and when not, not, Hos. 2:11.

BAVLI BERAKHOT 6:5-6 VI.
7. A. Said R. Zutra bar Tobiah said Rab, "How do we know that people are supposed to say a blessing over a good scent?

B. "As it is said, 'Let the whole of the soul praise the Lord' (Ps. 150:6).
C. "What is it from which the soul, and not the body, derives pleasure? One must say, it is a good smell."
D. And R. Zutra bar Tobiah said Rab said, "The young men of Israel are destined to give forth a good smell like Lebanon.
E. "For it is said, 'His branches shall spread, and his beauty shall be as the olive tree, and his fragrance as Lebanon' (Hos. 14:7)."

Hos. 14:7 praises Israelite youth.

BAVLI BERAKHOT 9:1-5 I.
30. A. Said R. Joshua b. Levi, "He who in a dream sees a river, when he gets up should say, 'Behold I will extend peace to her like a river' (Is. 66:12). [This he should do] lest some other verse should come to mind before that one, such as, 'For distress will come in like a river' (Is. 59:19).
B. "He who in a dream sees a bird, when he gets up should say, 'As birds hovering, so will the Lord of hosts protect' (Is. 31:5). [This he should do] lest some other verse should come to mind before that one, such as, 'As a bird that wanders from her nest, so is a man who wanders from his place' (Prov. 27:8).
C. "He who in a dream sees a pot, when he gets up should say, 'Lord, you will establish peace for us' (Is. 26:12), lest some other verse should come to mind before that one, such as 'Set on the pot, set it on' (Ez. 24:3).
D. "He who in a dream sees grapes, when he gets up should say, 'I found Israel like grapes in the wilderness' (Hos. 9:10), lest some other verse should come to mind before that one, such as, 'Their grapes are grapes of wrath' (Deut. 32:32).
E. "He who in a dream sees a mountain, when he gets up should say, 'How beautiful upon the mountains are the feet of the messenger of good tidings' (Is. 52:7), lest some other verse should come to mind before that one, such as, 'For the mountains will I take up a weeping and wailing' (Jer. 9:9).
F. "He who in a dream sees a horn, when he gets up should say, 'And it shall come to pass in that day that a great horn shall be blown' (Is. 27:13), lest some other verse should come to mind before that one, such as, 'Blow you the horn of Gibeah' (Hos. 5:8).
G. "He who in a dream sees a dog, when he gets up should say, 'But against any of the children of Israel shall not a dog whet his tongue' (Ex. 11:7), lest some other verse should come to mind before that one, such as, 'Yes, the dogs are greedy' (Is. 56:11).
H. "He who in a dream sees a lion, when he gets up should say, 'The lion has roared, who will not fear' (Amos. 3:8), lest another verse should come to mind first, such as, 'A lion is gone up from his thicket' (Jer. 4:7).

6. Hosea in the Bavli

I. "He who in a dream sees [himself] shaving, when he gets up should say, 'And Joseph shaved himself and changed his raiment' (Gen. 41:14), lest another verse should come to mind before that one, such as, 'If I be shaven, then my strength will go from me' (Jud. 16:17).

J. "He who in a dream sees a well, when he gets up should say, 'A well of living waters' (Song. 4:15), lest another verse should come to mind first, such as, 'As a cistern wells with her waters, so she wells with her wickedness' (Jer. 6:7).

K. "He who in a dream sees a reed, when he gets up should say, 'A bruised reed shall he not break' (Is. 52:3), lest another verse should come to mind first, such as, 'Behold you rely upon the staff of this bruised reed' (Is. 36:6)."

Hos. 5:8 is to be avoided if one sees a horn in a dream.

BAVLI BERAKHOT 9:2 VII.

1. A. For lightning, one says, "Blessed is he whose strength and power fill the world" [M. 9:2]:
B. What is lightning?
C. Said Raba, "A flash of light."
D. And said Raba, "A single flash of light, white light, blue light, clouds rising in the west, clouds coming from the south, two clouds that rise facing one another — all signify trouble."
E. What difference does such an omen make?
F. So that one should pray for mercy.
G. And that rule applies to these phenomena appearing at night, but if they come by day, they mean nothing.
H. Said R. Samuel bar Isaac, "Clouds that come by day have no significance [Simon: do not portend a good fall of rain], for it is said, 'Your goodness is as a morning cloud' (Hos. 6:4)."
I. Said R. Pappa, to Abbayye, "But lo, people say, 'When you open your door to find rain, ass-driver, put down your sack and sleep on it'" [Simon, p. 368, n. 4: because corn will be cheap on account of abundant rain].' [So would that not mean morning clouds bring rain?]"
J. There is no contradiction. One saying speaks of a case in which the clouds are thick, the other, light.

Hos. 6:4 means morning clouds bring rain.

II. SHABBAT

BAVLI SHABBAT 5:4 XII.

11. A. At what point was the merit accruing from the patriarchs exhausted?

B. Said Rab, "From the time of Hosea b. Beeri: 'And now will I discover her lewdness in the sight of her lovers, and none shall deliver her out of my hand' (Hos. 2:12).

C. Said Samuel, "From the time of Hazael: 'And Hazael king of Syria oppressed Israel all the days of Jehoahaz' (2 Kgs. 13:22); 'But the Lord was gracious unto them and had compassion upon them and had respect for them, because of the covenant with Abraham, Isaac and Jacob and would not destroy them, neither did he cast them from his presence' (2 Kgs. 13:23) — until now."

D. R. Joshua b. Levi said, "From the time of Elijah: 'And it came to pass at the time of the offering of the evening whole-offering, that Elijah the prophet came near and said, O Lord the God of Abraham, Isaac and Israel let it be known this day that you are God in Israel and that I am your servant and that I have done all these things at your word' (1 Kgs. 18:36)."

E. R. Yohanan said, "From the time of Hezekiah: 'Of the increase of his government and of peace there shall be no end, upon the throne of David and upon his kingdom, to establish it and to uphold it with judgment and with righteousness from henceforth and even for ever; the zeal of the Lord of hosts shall perform this' (Isa. 9:6)."

Hosea marks the end of the merit accruing from the patriarchs, so Hos. 1:12.

BAVLI SHABBAT 9:4 II.

4. A. Said R. Hiyya bar Abba said R. Yohanan, "It was quite appropriate for our father Abraham to go down to Egypt in iron chains, but the accumulated heavenly favor saved him from such a fate: 'I drew them with the cords of a man, with bands of love, and I was to them as they that take off the yoke on their jaws and I laid meat before them' (Hos. 11:4)."

Hos. 11:4 speaks of Abraham in Egypt.

BAVLI SHABBAT 22:2 II.

2. A. In session before R. Yohanan were R. Hiyya bar Abba and R. Assi, and R. Yohanan was in session but dozing off. Said R. Hiyya bar Abba to R. Assi, "How come the chickens in Babylonia are fat?"

B. He said to him, "Go to the wilderness of Gaza, and I'll show you chickens fatter than they."

C. "How come the festivals in Babylonia are so joyful?"

D. "Because they are so poor."

E. "How come the disciples of sages in Babylonia are so clearly designated as such in their garments?"

F. "Because they really are not masters of the Torah."

6. Hosea in the Bavli

G. "How come gentiles lust?"
H. "Because they eat disgusting and creeping things."
I. At that moment R. Yohanan woke up and said to them, "Little ones, didn't I say to you, 'Say to wisdom, you are my sister' (Prov. 7:4) — if a matter is as clear to you as the fact that your sister is forbidden to marry you, say it, and if not, don't say it."
J. They said to him, "Then let the master say to us some of the answers to these questions: How come the chickens in Babylonia are fat?"
K. "Because they didn't go into exile: 'Moab has been at ease from his youth and he has settled on his lees, neither has he gone into captivity, therefore his taste remains in him and his scent is not changed' (Jer. 48:11)."
L. And how do we know that they went into exile here?
M. As has been taught on Tannaite authority: R. Judah says, "For fifty two years, nobody passed through Judea: 'For the mountains will I take up a weeping and wailing and for the pastures of the wilderness a lamentation, because they are burned up so that none passes through... both the fowls of the heaven and the beast are fled, they are gone' (Jer. 9:9) — and the numerical value of the word for beast is fifty-two."
N. Said R. Jacob said R. Yohanan, "All of them returned, however, except for the [Freedman:] colias of the Spaniards."
O. For said Rab, "The drains of Babylonia carry water down to En Etam."
P. But these, since their spine is not firm, could not go up.
Q. "How come the festivals in Babylonia are so joyful?"
R. "Because they were not subject to the curse in this language: 'I will also cause all her mirth to cease, her feasts, her new moons, her Sabbaths, and all her solemn assemblies' (Hos. 2:13), and further, 'Your new moons and your appointed feasts my soul hates, they are a trouble to me' (Isa. 1:14)."
S. What is the meaning of they are a trouble to me?
T. Said R. Eleazar, "Said the Holy One, blessed be He, 'It doesn't suffice for the Israelites that they are sinning before me, but that they impose on me the trouble of deciding which evil decree I am supposed to bring upon them.'"
U. Said R. Isaac, "There is not a single festival on which a harassing troop doesn't come upon Sepphoris."
V. And said R. Hanina, "There is not a single festival on which there doesn't come to Tiberias a general with his [Freedman:] suite and centurions."
W. "How come the disciples of sages in Babylonia are so clearly designated as such in their garments?"
X. "Because they are not where they come from, as people say, 'In my own town, my name is enough; away from home, my clothing.'"
Y. "In days to come shall Jacob take root, Israel shall blossom and bud" (Isa. 27:6) —

Z. R. Joseph stated as a Tannaite statement: "This refers to the disciples of sages who are in Babylonia, who wreathe blossoms and flowers around the Torah."
AA. "How come gentiles lust?"

The festivals in Babylonia are joyful because abroad Israelites are not subject to the curse of Hos. 2:13.

BAVLI SHABBAT III.
1. A. **And the priests cast lots on a festival day for [which priest gets which part of] Holy Things, but not for the portions:**
   B. What is the meaning of **but not for the portions**?
   C. Said R. Jacob son of Jacob's daughter, "...**but not on festivals for the portions** means, but not for shares of sacrifices made on the weekday."
   D. Well, that's pretty obvious!
   E. What might you otherwise have thought? Since it is written, "For your people are like the priests who quarrel" (Hos. 4:4), even the portions of weekdays, too, [may be subject to a lottery, to keep the priests from quarreling]. So we are informed that that is not the case.

Hos. 4:4 refers to the contentious priests, who are kept from quarreling by the use of lots.

III. ERUBIN
I find nothing relevant.

IV. PESAHIM

BAVLI PESAHIM 2:5 VIII.
12. A. And on what basis do we maintain that the word for pancakes denotes something of considerable value?
    B. Because it is written, "And he dealt among all the people, even among the whole multitude of Israel, both to men and women, to every one a cake of bread and a good piece of meat and a pancake" (2 Sam. 6:19), on which R. Hanan bar Abba said, "A piece of meat refers to a sixth of a bullock, and a pancake refers to one made with a sixth of an ephah of flour."
    C. And he differs from Samuel, for said Samuel, "The word under discussion here as pancake refers to a cask of wine: 'And love casks of grapes' (Hos. 3:1)."

Hos. 3:1 supplies philological data.

6. Hosea in the Bavli

BAVLI PESAHIM 6:1-2 I.

2. A. "And it shall be at that day says the Lord that you will call my 'My man,' and not 'My master'" (Hos. 2:18) —
   B. Said R. Yohanan, "Like a bride in the household of her father-in-law, not like a bride in the household of her father."
3. A. "We have a little sister, and she has no breasts" (Song 8:8):
   B. R. Yohanan said, "This refers to Elam, which had sufficient inherited merit to learn but didn't have sufficient inherited merit to teach."
4. A. "I am a wall and my breasts are like towers" (Song 8:10).
   B. Said R. Yohanan, "'I am a wall' refers to the Torah, 'and my breasts are like towers' refers to disciples of the sages."
   C. And Raba said, "'I am a wall' refers to the community of Israel, 'and my breasts are like towers' refers to houses of assembly and houses of study."
5. A. Said R. Zutra bar Tobiah said Rab, *"What is the meaning of the verse of Scripture,* 'We whose sons are as plants grown up in their youth, whose daughters are as corner pillars carved after the fashion of the Temple' (Ps. 144:12)? 'We whose sons are as plants grown up in their youth' refers to Israelite youngsters, who have never tasted the flavor of sin. '…whose daughters are as corner pillars carved aft her the fashion of the Temple' refers to Israelite girls, who seal their doors to save them for their husbands, and so Scripture says, 'and they shall be filled like the basins, like the corners of the altar' (Zech. 9:15). *And if you wish, I shall say that the same proposition derives from here:* 'Whose garners are full, affording all manner of store' (Ps. 144:13). 'carved after the fashion of the Temple' (Ps. 144:12) — to both the one and the other is regarded by Scripture as though the Temple were built in their times."
7. A. "Gomer:"
   B. said Rab, "For everybody finished up on her."
   C. "'Daughter [87B] of Diblaim:'
   D. "woman of bad name daughter of a woman of bad name."
   E. And Samuel said, "She was sweet in everybody's mouth as a cake of figs."
   F. And R. Yohanan said, "Because everybody 'walked' on her as a cake of figs is pressed down."
8. A. Another interpretation: "Gomer:"
   B. Said R. Judah, "It is because they wanted to destroy the capital of Israel in her time."
   C. R. Yohanan said, "They despoiled and finished it up: 'For the king of Aram destroyed them and made them like the dust in threshing' (2 Kgs. 13:7)."
9. A. "And she conceived and bore him a son. And the Lord said to him, Call his name Jezreel, for yet a little while and I will visit the blood of Jezreel on the house of Jehu and will cause to cease the

kingdom of the house of Israel. And it shall come to pass at that day that I will break the bow of Israel in the valley of Jezreel.' And she conceived again, and bore a daughter, and he said to him, 'Call her name Lo ruhamah' [she has not obtained compassion], for I will no more have compassion upon the house of Israel, that I should in any wise pardon them...and she conceived and bore a son, and he said, Call his name Lo-ammi [not my people], for you are not my people and I will not be yours'" (Hos. 1:3-6, 8-9):

B. After two sons and a daughter were born to him, said the Holy One, blessed be he to Hosea, "Shouldn't you have learned the lesson from your lord, Moses? As soon as I spoke with him, he desisted from sexual relations with his wife. You too, desist from sexual relations with her."

C. He said to him, "Lord of the world, I have children by her, and I can't expel her or divorce her."

D. Said to him the Holy One, blessed be he, "Now you, with a whore for a wife and with children of harlotry, and not knowing whether your children are yours or belong to someone else, are the way you are, then Israel, who really are my children, the children of those whom I have favored, Abraham, Isaac, and Jacob; who are one of the four possessions that I have acquired in this world" —

E. the Torah is one possession: "The Lord acquirement me as the beginning of his way" (Prov. 8:22);

F. "heaven and earth are one possession: "God Most High who possesses heaven and earth" (Gen. 14:19);

G. the Temple is one: "This mountain, which his right hand has acquired" (Ps. 78:54);

H. Israel is one: "This people that you have gotten" (Ex. 15:16) —

I. — "and you can use such language as, ' exchange them for some other nation.'?!"

J. When he realized that he had sinned, he sought mercy for himself. Said to him the Holy One, blessed be he, "Instead of seeking mercy for yourself, seek mercy for Israel, for I have made three decrees against them on account of you."

K. He went and sought mercy, and he annulled the decrees.

L. He began to bless them: "Yet the number of the children of Israel shall be as the sand of the sea...and it shall come to pass that, instead of that which was said unto them, You are not my people, it shall be said unto them, you are the children of the living God. And the children of Judah and the children of Israel shall be gathered together. And I will sow her to me in the land and I will have compassion upon her that has not obtained compassion and I will say to them that were not my people, you are my people" (Hos. 2:1-2, 25).

10. A. Said R. Yohanan, "Woe to a government that buries the one who possesses it, for you don't have a single prophet who didn't outlive four kings in his own lifetime: 'The vision of Isaiah the son of

6. Hosea in the Bavli

Amoz, which he saw concerning Judah and Jerusalem in the days of Uzziah, Jotham, Ahaz, and Hezekiah, kings of Judah' (Is. 1:1)."

11. A. Said R. Yohanan, "On what basis did Jeroboam son of Joash, king of Israel, have the unearned grace of being counted with the kings of Judah? Because he didn't accept gossip against Amos.
    B. "How do we know that he was counted with them? 'The word of the Lord that came to Hosea son of Beeri in the days of Uzziah, Jotham Ahaz, and Hezekiah, kings of Judah' Hos. 1:1).
    C. "And how do we know that he didn't accept gossip? 'Then Amaziah priest of Beth el sent to Jeroboam king of Israel, saying, Amos has conspired against you' (Amos 7:10); 'for thus Amos said, 'Jeroboam shall die by the sword' (Amos 7:11). Said Jeroboam, 'God forbid, that that righteous man could have said any such thing! But if he did say it, what can I do to him, since the Presence of God said it to him.'"

12. A. Said R. Eleazar, "Even at the time of the wrath of the Holy One, blessed be he, he remembers mercy: 'for I will no more have compassion upon the house of Israel' (Hos. 1:6)."
    B. R. Yosé bar Hanina said, "It derives from here: 'that I should in any wise pardon them' (Hos. 1:6)."

13. A. And said R. Eliezer, "The Holy One, blessed be he, exiled the Israelites among the nations only so that converts should join them: 'And I will sow her unto me in the land' (Hos. 2:25). Certainly someone sows a seah of seed to harvest many kor of seed."
    B. R. Yohanan derived the same proposition from the following: "And I will have compassion upon her who has not obtained compassion" (Hos. 2:25).

14. A. Said R. Yohanan in the name of R. Simeon b. Yohai, "What is the meaning of the verse of Scripture: 'Don't slander a servant to his master, lest he curse you and you be found guilty' (Prov. 30:10)? And it is written, 'a generation that curse their father and do not bless their mother' (Prov. 30:11)? Is the sense, because they curse their father and don't bless their mother, don't slander? But the sense is, even if the slaves are a generation that curse their father and don't bless their mother, don't slander them. On what basis do we know that fact? From Hosea."

THE EXILE AND HOSEA'S PROPHECY

15. A. Said R. Oshayya, "What is the meaning of the verse of Scripture: 'Even the righteous acts of his ruler in Israel' (Judges 5:11)? The Holy One, blessed be he, did an act of righteousness with Israel when he scattered them among the nations."
    B. *That is in line with what a certain heretic said to R. Hanina, "We are better than you. Concerning you it is written, 'for Joab and all Israel remained there six months, until he had cut off every male in Edom' (1 Kgs. 11:16), while you have been with us many years and we haven't done a thing to you."*
    C. He said to him, "If you like, let a disciple deal with you."

- D. R. Oshayya dealt with him. *He said to him, "It is because you don't know how to behave. If you want to destroy all of them, they're not all among you, being scattered. If you want to destroy those who are among you, then you'll be called a kingdom of murderers."*
- E. *He said to him, "By the Roman capitol! We worry about this when we lie down, and we worry about this when we get up"* [Freedman: how to destroy you without incurring odium].
- 16. A. *R. Hiyya taught on Tannaite authority, "What is the meaning of the verse of Scripture:* 'God understood her way and he knew her place' (Job 28:23)? The Holy One, blessed be he, knew that the Israelites wouldn't be able to take the Romans' persecution, so he drove them to Babylonia."
- 17. A. And said R. Eleazar, "The Holy One, blessed be he, exiled Israel to Babylonia only because it is as deep as hell: 'I shall ransom them from the power of the netherworld, I shall redeem them from death' (Hos. 13:14)."
  - B. R. Hanina said, "It is because their language is near the language of the Torah."
  - C. R. Yohanan said, "It is because he sent them back to their mother's house. The matter may be compared to the case of someone who got made at his wife. Where does he send her? To her mother's house."
  - D. *That's in line with what R. Alexandri stated:* "Three went back to the place where they were planted, and these are they: Israel, the wealth of Egypt, and the writing of the tablets.
  - E. "Israel: as we just said.
  - F. "the wealth of Egypt: 'And it came to pass in the fifth year of King Rehoboam, that Shishak king of Egypt came up against Jerusalem and he took away the treasures of the house of the Lord' (1 Kgs. 14:25).
  - G. "and the writing of the tablets: 'And I broke them before your eyes' (Dt. 9:17)."
- 18. A. *A Tannaite statement:*
  - B. The tablets broke, and the letters flew up.
- 19. A. Ulla said, "They were sent into exile so that they might eat **[88A]** dates and have the free time to get busy with the Torah."
- 20. A. *Ulla came to Pumbedita. They offered him a basket of dates. He said to them, "How many of these do you get for a zuz?"*
  - B. *"Three for a zuz."*
  - C. *"A basketful of honey for a zuz, and yet the Babylonians don't engage in the study of the Torah?!"*
  - D. *That night the dates upset his belly. He said, "A basketful of deadly poison costs a zuz in Babylonia, and yet the Babylonians study the Torah?!"*
- 21. A. And said R. Eleazar, "What's the meaning of the verse of Scripture, 'And many people shall go and say, Come and let's go up to the

6. Hosea in the Bavli

mountain of the Lord, to the house of the god of Jacob' Is. 2:3)? The God of Jacob, not the God of Abraham or Isaac? But we shall not be like Abraham, in whose regard 'mountain' is written: as it is said to this day, in the mountain where the Lord is seen' (Gen. 22:14), nor like Isaac, in regard to whom 'field' is written, 'And Isaac went out to meditate in the field at eventide' (Gen. 24:63), but let us be like Jacob, who called him 'home,' 'and he called the name of that place Beth El' [God is a home]' (Gen. 28:19)."

22. A. Said R. Yohanan, "The ingathering of the exiles is as great as the day on which heaven and earth were created: 'And the children of Judah and the children of Israel shall be gathered together, and they shall appoint themselves one head and shall go up out of the land, for great shall be the day of Jezreel' (Hos. 2:2), and 'and there was evening and there was morning, one day' (Gen. 1:4)."

A large composite takes up fundamental doctrines of Hosea.

v. YOMA

BAVLI YOMA 2:1-2 III.

1. A. And if the two came at the same time, the one in charge says to them, "Choose up [by raising a finger]:"
   B. A Tannaite statement:
   C. "Put forth your fingers for the count."
   D. But let him count them by heads?
   E. The fact before us supports the view of R. Isaac, for said R. Isaac, "It is forbidden to count out Israelites by number, even for the purpose of carrying out a religious duty. For it is written, 'And he numbered them with pebbles [bezeq]' (1 Sam. 11:8)."
   F. Objected R. Ashi, "On what basis do you insist that the language, 'with pebbles' refers to something that is broken, maybe it is a place name, in line with the usage, 'And they found Adoni-Bezeq in Bezeq' (Judges 1:5)?"
   G. Rather, proof for the stated proposition derives from the following verse" "And Saul summoned the people and numbered them with sheep" (1 Sam. 15:4)."
   H. Said R. Eleazar, "Whoever counts out Israelites violates a negative commandment, as it is said, 'Yet the number of the children of Israel shall be as the sand of the sea, which cannot be measured' (Hos. 2:1)."
   I. R. Nahman bar Isaac said, "He violates two negative commandments: 'Which cannot be measured nor numbered.'"
   J. Said R. Samuel bar Nahmani, "R. Jonathan contrasted verses of Scripture in the following way: 'It is written, "Yet the number of the children of Israel shall be as the sand of the sea" (Hos. 2:1), and it is written, "Which cannot be numbered" (Hos. 2:1). How

so? There is in fact no conflict. The one speaks of the time at which Israel carries out the will of the Omnipresent, the other speaks of a time in which they do not carry out the will of the Omnipresent.'"
K. Rab said in the name of Abba Yosé b. Dosetai, "There is no conflict. The one speaks of counting them by mortal man, the other, counting them by Heaven."

Hos. 2:1 says the Israelites will be as numerous as the sand of the sea and that they cannot be numbered. On the one side they carry out the will of God, on the other they do not.

BAVLI YOMA 3:11 V.

5. A. And said R. Eleazar, "Out of the blessing that a righteous man gives you can infer the curse for the wicked, and from the curse that a wicked man gives you may infer the blessing for the righteous.
   B. "Out of the blessing that a righteous man gives you can infer the curse for the wicked: For I have known him to the end that he may command' (Gen. 18:19), and then, 'And the Lord said, Verily the cry of Sodom and Gomorrah is great' (Gen. 13:15).
   C. ."..., and from the curse that a wicked man gives you may infer the blessing for the righteous: Now the men of Sodom were wicked and sinners against the Lord exceedingly' (Gen. 13:20), 'And the Lord said to Abram, after Lot was separated from him...all the land that you see, to you will I give it' (Gen. 13:15)."
6. A. And said R. Eleazar, "Even on account of a single righteous man is the world created, 'And God saw the light that it was for one who is good' (Gen. 1:4), and good refers only to the righteous, 'Say you of the righteous that he is the good one' (Is. 3:10)."
7. A. And said R. Eleazar, "Whoever forgets a single matter of what he has learned brings about exile for his children: 'Seeing that you have forgotten the Torah of your God, I also will forget your children' (Hos. 4:6)."
   B. R. Abbahu said, "They bring him down from his greatness: 'Because you have rejected knowledge, I also will reject you, that you shall be no priest to me' (Hos. 4:6)."
8. A. Said R. Hiyya bar Abba said R. Yohanan, "A righteous man does not take his leave from the world before another righteous man like him is created: 'The sun rises, and the sun goes down' (Qoh. 1:5).
   B. "Before Eli's sun set, Samuel of Ramah's sun shone: 'and the lamp of God was not yet gone out, and Samuel was laid down' (1 Sam. 3:3)."
9. A. Said R. Hiyya bar Abba said R. Yohanan, "The Holy One, blessed be he, saw that the righteous are few. He went and planted some of them in every generation: 'For the pillars of the earth are the Lord's, and he has set the world upon them' (1 Sam. 2:8)."

Hos. 4:6 means that if the Israelites forget the Torah, their children will go into exile.

BAVLI YOMA 3:11 V.
7. A. And said R. Eleazar, "Whoever forgets a single matter of what he has learned brings about exile for his children: 'Seeing that you have forgotten the Torah of your God, I also will forget your children' (Hos. 4:6)."
   B. R. Abbahu said, "They bring him down from his greatness: 'Because you have rejected knowledge, I also will reject you, that you shall be no priest to me' (Hos. 4:6)."

As above.

BAVLI YOMA 8:1-2 II.
1. A. **...to (1) eat, (2) drink, [(3) bathe, (4) put on any sort of oil, (5) put on a sandal, (6) or engage in sexual relations]:**
   B. As to these five afflictions, to what do they correspond?
   C. Said R. Hisda, "They correspond to the five afflictions mentioned in the Torah, as follows: 'And on the tenth day' Num. 29:7), 'howbeit on the tenth day' (Lev. 23:27), 'a Sabbath of solemn rest' (Lev. 23:32), 'it is a Sabbath of solemn rest' (Lev. 16:31), 'and it shall be unto you' (Lev. 16:29)."
   D. But these are five, and our Mishnah lists six!
   E. Drinking is encompassed within eating.
   F. For said R. Simeon b. Laqish, "'How on the basis of Scripture do we know that drinking falls into the category of eating? As it is said, "And you shall eat before the Lord your God in the place which he shall choose for a dwelling place for his name, the tithe of your grain, your wine" (Dt. 14:23). Now wine of course is drunk, and yet Scripture says, 'you shall eat...'"'
   G. But perhaps Scripture refers to elaiogaron [a sauce that contains wine which is a food, and so is eaten, not drunk, but perhaps drinking is in general not classified as an act of eating]?
   H. For said Rabbah bar Samuel, "Elaiogaron is juice of beet roots, oxygaron is juice of any other boiled vegetables."
   I. Rather, said R. Aha bar Jacob, "Proof that drinking falls into the category of eating derives from this verse: 'And you shall bestow the money for whatever your soul desires, for oxen or sheep or fine or strong drink...and you shall eat there' (Dt. 14:26). Now wine here certainly means wine, and yet it is written, 'and you shall eat there'!"
   J. But perhaps here too Scripture refers to elaiogaron!
   K. But "strong drink" is stated as well, something that can inebriate!
   L. Perhaps what is meant is Keilah-figs, for it has been taught on Tannaite authority:

M. If one ate pressed figs from Keilah, or drank honey or milk, and went into the sanctuary and performed an act of divine service, [76B] he is flogged.
N. Rather, derive the rule by verbal analogy established through the use of "strong drink" in the case of the Nazirite. Just as in that context, we find that "strong drink" means wine, so in the present context, strong drink means wine.
O. But does "strong drink" refer to wine? And has it not been taught on Tannaite authority:
P. He who takes a vow not to drink string drink is forbidden to drink any kind of sweet drink but may use wine.
Q. But isn't it wine? Surely it is written, "And strong drink makes the maids flourish" (Zech. 9:17), something that derives from strong drink makes maids flourish.
R. But isn't it written, "And your vats shall overflow with strong drink" (Prov. 3:10)?
S. Your vats will overflow with what is derived from strong drink.
T. But it is written, "Harlotry, wine, and strong drink take away the heart" (Hos. 4:11).
U. Rather, everybody concurs that strong drink is classified as wine, but when it comes to vows, we must be guided by the usages of everyday speech.
V. Then why would it be called wine, and why would it be called strong drink?
W. It is called wine because it brings lamentation into the world, and strong drink because one who uses it is impoverished. [The letters for wine yield "woe" and of strong drink yield "poor."]

Hos. 4:11 condemns harlotry and wine and strong drink.

VI. SUKKAH

BAVLI SUKKAH 4:9 V:

8. A. A Tannaite authority of the house of R. Anan taught, "What is the sense of Scripture's statement, "The roundings of your thighs" (Song 7:2)?
B. "Why are the teachings of Torah compared to the thigh?
C. "It is to teach you that, just as the thigh is kept hidden, so teachings of Torah are to be kept hidden."
D. That is in line with what R. Eleazar said, "What is the sense of the verse of Scripture, "It has been told you, O man, what is good, and what the Lord requires of you: only to do justly, to love mercy, and to walk humbly with your God" (Mic. 6:8)?
E. "'To do justly' refers to justice.
F. "'To love mercy' refers to doing deeds of loving kindness.
G. "'And to walk humbly with your God' refers to taking out a corpse for burial and bringing the bride in to the marriage-canopy.

6. Hosea in the Bavli

H. "And is it not a matter of argument a fortiori:
I. "Now if, as to matters which are ordinarily done in public, the Torah has said, "To walk humbly," matters which are normally done in private, all the more so [must they be done humbly and in secret, that is, the giving of charity is done secretly]."
J. Said R. Eleazar, "Greater is the one who carries out an act of charity more than one who offers all the sacrifices.
K. "For it is said, "To do charity and justice is more desired by the Lord than sacrifice" (Prov. 21:3)."
L. And R. Eleazar said, "An act of loving kindness is greater than an act of charity.
M. "For it is said, "Sow to yourselves according to your charity, but reap according to your loving kindness" (Hos. 10:12).
N. "If a man sows seed, it is a matter of doubt whether he will eat a crop or not. But if a man harvests the crop, he most certainly will eat it."
O. And R. Eleazar said, "An act of charity is rewarded only in accord with the loving kindness that is connected with it.
P. "For it is said, "Sow to yourselves according to your charity, but reap according to your loving kindness" (Hos. 10:12)."

Hos. 10:12 teaches that an act of loving kindness is greater than an act of charity, and governs the reward for charity is proportionate with the loving kindness that accompanies the act of charity.

BAVLI SUKKAH 5:2 II:

12. A. R. Huna contrasted the following verses of Scripture: "It is written, "For the spirit of harlotry has caused them to err" (Hos. 4:12) [thus the cause is external to the person].
B. "But it also is written, "[For the spirit of harlotry] is within them" (Hos. 5:4).
C. "In the beginning, it caused them to err, but in the end, it is within them."
D. Said Raba, "In the beginning one calls it a passer-by, then a guest, and finally, a man [of the household].
E. "For it is said, 'And there came a passer-by to the rich man, and he spared to take of his own flock and of his own herd, to dress for the guest [no longer passer-by]," and [at the end] the verse states, "But he took, the poor man's lamb and dressed it for the man [now a household member] who had come to him' (2 Sam. 12:4)."

Hos. 4:12 indicates that the cause of harlotry is external to the person, but Hos. 5:4 that it is internal. These are harmonized.

BAVLI SUKKAH 5:2 II:
13. A. Said R. Yohanan, "There is in man a small organ, which makes him feel hungry when he is sated,
B. "and makes him feel sated when he is hungry,
C. "as it is said, 'When they were starved, they became full' (Hos. 13:6)."

Hos. 13:6 refers to the "small organ that makes a man feel hungry when he is sated, and sated when he is hungry."

VII. TAANIT

BAVLI TAANIT 1:1-2
[II.9][A] Said R. Samuel bar Nahmani said R. Jonathan, "Three men put forward their petition improperly, two were answered, nonetheless, in a proper way, and one they answered not in a proper way, and these are they: Eliezer, the servant of Abraham, Saul son of Qish, and Jephtha of Gilead.
[B] "Eliezer, the servant of Abraham: 'So let it come to pass that the girl to whom I shall say, Let down your pitcher that I may drink, and who shall say, Drink and I will provide water for your camels — let her be the one whom you have chosen for your servant, Isaac. By this I shall know that you have shown trustworthy love to my master' (Gen. 24:14) — now it is possible that she might have been lame or blind. Nonetheless, he was answered in a proper way, and Rebecca was chosen for him.
[C] "Saul son of Qish: 'And it shall be that the man who kills him — the king will enrich him with great wealth and will give him his daughter' (1 Sam. 17:25) — [the successful warrior] might have been inappropriate as a slave or a mamzer, but he too was answered properly, and David was chosen for him.
[D] "and Jephtha of Gilead: 'If you will give the Ammonites into my hand, then whoever comes forth from the doors of my house to meet me, when I return victorious from the Ammonites, shall be the Lord's, and I will offer him up for a burnt offering' (Judges 11:31) — now it is possible that what he said would apply even to an unclean thing [which cannot be offered up], but he was answered not in an appropriate way. His daughter was chosen for him!"
[E] That is in line with what the prophet said to Israel, "Is there no balm in Gilead? Is there no physician there" (Jer. 8:22) [why was there no solution to Jephtha's situation? A sage could have remitted the vow.]
[F] And it is written, "Which I did not command nor of which I ever spoke, nor which ever entered my mind" (Jer. 19:5):
[G] "Which I did not command: this refers to the sacrifice of the son of Mesha, king of Moab: 'Then he took his eldest son that should

6. Hosea in the Bavli

have reigned in his place and offered him for a burnt offering" (2 Kgs. 3:27).

[H] "nor of which I ever spoke:" this refers to the daughter of Jephtha.

[I] "nor which ever entered my mind:" this refers to Isaac, the son of Abraham.

[J] Said R. Berekhiah, "So too the community of Israel asked in an inappropriate manner, but the Holy One, blessed be he, responded in an appropriate manner, as it is said, 'And let us know, really try to know the Lord, his going forth is sure as the morning, and he will come to us as the rain' (Hos. 6:3). Said to her the Holy One, blessed be he, 'My daughter, you have petitioned for something that sometimes is besought and sometimes is not besought, but I, I shall be for you something that is besought at all times, as it is said, "I shall be as dew to Israel" (Hos. 14:6).'

[K] "And further she asked in an inappropriate manner. She said before him, 'Lord of the world, "Set me as a seal upon your heart, as a seal upon your arm" (Song 8:6). Said to her the Holy One, blessed be he, 'My daughter, you have petitioned for something that sometimes can be seen and sometimes cannot be seen. But I will make of you something that can be seen all the time: "Behold, I have graven you upon the palms of my hands"' (Is. 49:16)."

Hos. 6:3 has Israel ask for rain, which may or may not be a benefit, but Hos. 14:6 has God respond with dew, which is always a benefit.

BAVLI TAANIT 1:2E-H

[I.3] [A] And said R. Nahman to R. Isaac, "What is the meaning of the verse of Scripture, 'The Holy One is in your midst, and I will not come into the city' (Hos. 11:9). [Can it possibly mean,] because the Holy One is in your midst, I shall not come into the city?!"

[B] He said to him, "This is what R. Yohanan said, 'Said the Holy One, blessed be he, "I shall not come into the heavenly Jerusalem until I enter the earthly Jerusalem."'"

[C] And is there really a heavenly Jerusalem?

[D] Indeed there is, for it is written, "Jerusalem that is built up like a city that is well-joined all together [above and below]" (Ps. 122:3).

Hos. 11:9 is interpreted to mean that God will not enter the heavenly Jerusalem until he enters the earthly one.

BAVLI TAANIT 1:2E-H

[I.6] [A] And said R. Nahman to R. Isaac, "What is the meaning of the verse of Scripture, 'And it came to pass, when Samuel got old' (1 Sam. 8:1). But did Samuel ever get that old? Lo, he reached only fifty-two, for said a master, 'If someone died at the age of fifty-two, that is the death of Samuel the Ramathite.'"

[B] He said to him, "This is what R. Yohanan said, 'Samuel aged prematurely, for it is written, "I am sorry that I set up Saul to be king" (1 Sam. 15:11). He said before Him, "Lord of the world, you have treated me as equivalent to Moses and Aaron, for it is written, 'Moses and Aaron are among his priests and Samuel among those who call upon his name' (Ps. 99:6). Then, just as in the case of Moses and Aaron, nothing that they ever did came to naught in their lifetimes, so let nothing that I have ever done come to nothing in my lifetime." Said the Holy One, blessed me he, "So what am I supposed to do? Should Saul die? Samuel would never permit it. Should Samuel die young? People will draw the wrong conclusions about him [thinking he has died by extirpation by reason of sins]. Should neither Saul nor Samuel die? But the time has come for the reign of David to commence, and one reign cannot impinge]upon another even by so much as a hair's breadth." Said the Holy One, blessed be he, I will make him prematurely old." And that is in line with what is written, "Now Saul was sitting in Gibeah under the tamarisk tree in Ramah" (1 Sam. 22:6). And what has Gibeah to do with Ramah? But it is to say to you, what caused Saul to sit in Gibeah for two and a half years? It was the prayer of Samuel of Ramah.""'

[C] So then does one man get shunted aside on account of another?

[D] Indeed so, for said R. Samuel bar Nahmani said R. Jonathan, "What is the meaning of the verse of Scripture, 'Therefore have I hewed them by the prophets, I have slain them by the words of my mouth' (Hos. 6:5)? What is said is not, by their deeds," but rather, "by the words of my mouth," which proves that one man get shunted aside on account of another.

Hos. 6:5 indicates that one man gets shunted aside on account of another one.

BAVLI TAANIT 1:2E-H

[I.14] [A] Said R. Abbahu, "What is the meaning of the word rebi'ah [former rain]? It is that which fructifies the ground."

[B] That is in accord with R. Judah, for said R. Judah, "Rain is the husband of the earth, as it is said, 'For as the rain falls and the snow from heaven and does not return there except as it waters the earth and makes it bring forth and bud' (Is. 55:10)."

[C] And said R. Abbahu, "As to the first rain, it should fall hard enough to penetrate a handbreadth deep into the soil, and the second should be enough to water the earth so that it can be shaped into a stopper for a cask."

[D] Said R. Hisda, "Rain that has fallen hard enough to water the earth so that it can be shaped into a stopper for a cask is not subject to the consideration, 'He will shut up the heavens' (Dt. 11:17)."

6. Hosea in the Bavli

[E] And said R. Hisda, "If rain came down prior [to the time for reciting, in the Shema,' the words,] 'And he will shut up,' signifies that that consideration does not apply."

[F] Said Abbayye, "We have made such a statement only in the case in which the rain has come down prior to the reference in the language of the Shema' to 'he will shut up' in the evening recitation of the Shema', but if it fell before the time for reciting those words in the Shema' of the morning, then the curse may still pertain."

[G] For said R. Judah bar Isaac, "Morning clouds have no substance, as it is written, 'O Ephraim, what shall I do to you, for your goodness is as the morning cloud' (Hos. 6:4)."

[H] Said R. Pappa to Abbayye, "But people say, 'If it rains when the gates are opened, put down your sack, ass driver, and go to sleep'" [there will be plenty of rain and the crops will be abundant and prices will fall, so moving food from place to place will bring no profit]."

[I] There is no contradiction between the two allegations, the one case speaks of heavens that are overcast with thick clouds, the other, light ones [which are insubstantial.]

Hos. 6:4 compares the goodness of Ephraim to a morning cloud, which is transient.

BAVLI TAANIT 1:4-5

[I.9] [A] Said Samuel, "Whoever sits in a fast [for self-affliction] is called a sinner."

[B] He concurs with the thinking of the following Tannaite authority, for it has been taught on Tannaite authority:

[C] R. Eleazar Haqqappar BeRabbi says, "Why does Scripture say, 'and make atonement for him for he has sinned by reason of the soul' (Num. 6:11)? Now, against what soul has this one sinned? But he has caused himself distress by abstaining from wine. And does that not yield an argument a fortiori: if this one, who has caused himself only the distress that comes from giving up wine is called a sinner, he who causes himself distress by abstaining from anything whatsoever — all the more so does he sin!"

[D] R. Eleazar says, "He is called 'holy,' as it is said, 'He shall be holy, he shall let the locks of the hair of his head grow long' (Num. 6:5). Now if this one, who has caused himself distress only in one matter, is called holy, he who causes himself distress in any matter whatsoever — how much the more so!"

[E] Now facing Samuel is the contradictory fact, then, that he is called holy!

[F] That refers to the matter of growing the hair long.

[G] And from the perspective of R. Eleazar, lo, he is called a sinner [and not holy]!

[H] That refers to the fact that he contracts corpse uncleanness.

[I] But has not R. Eleazar said, "One should always weigh himself [11B] as though the Holy One is dwelling within him: 'The Holy One in the midst of you and I will not come in fury' (Hos. 11:9)" [Rabinowitz: Eleazar holds the view that the divine is ever present in man. How then could a man who fasts be called holy, seeing that he humiliates God through his fasting.]

[J] There is no contradiction. The one speaks of a person who can endure self-affliction, the other, one who cannot.

Hos. 11:9 indicates that God is ever present in man.

BAVLI TAANIT 4:6-7

[XXIV.2] [A] R. Isaac bar Giori sent word in the name of R. Yohanan, "Even though they have said that flax garments are not subject to the prohibition against laundry work, still, it is forbidden to wear them [if they are freshly washed] in the week in which the ninth of Ab falls."

[B] Said Rab, "They have taught that rule only to cover the days before the ninth of Ab, but as to the days after the ninth of Ab [in that same week], it is permitted to wear them."

[C] Samuel said, "Even on the days after the ninth of Ab, it is forbidden to wear them."

[D] An objection was raised: In the week in which the ninth of Ab falls, it is forbidden to get a haircut or to launder clothing, but on Thursday that is permitted because of the honor owing to the Sabbath. How so? If the ninth of Ab fell on Sunday, it is permitted to do laundry all that week. If it fell on Monday, Tuesday, Wednesday, or Thursday, on the days prior to the ninth of Ab it is forbidden to do so, on those afterward, it is permitted. If it fell on Friday, it is permitted to wash clothing on Thursday on account of the honor owing to the Sabbath. And if he did not do laundry on Thursday, it is permitted to do laundry on Friday from the afternoon service onward.

[E] Abbayye ridiculed this rule, and some say, R. Aha bar Jacob [did so].

[F] If the ninth of Ab coincided with a Monday or a Thursday, three men recite read [from the Torah], and of these the third reads the prophetic lesson. If it coincides with a Tuesday or a Wednesday, one person reads from the Torah and also reads the prophetic portion.

[G] R. Yosé says, "Under all circumstances three persons read, and of these the third reads the prophetic lesson.

[H] Now does the foregoing not refute the position of Samuel ["Even on the days after the ninth of Ab, it is forbidden to wear them" vs. "If it fell on Monday, Tuesday, Wednesday, or Thursday, on the days prior to the ninth of Ab it is forbidden to do so, on those afterward, it is permitted"]?

6. Hosea in the Bavli

[I] Samuel will tell you, "It is a conflict of Tannaite authorities, for it has been taught on Tannaite authority: 'If the ninth of Ab coincides with the Sabbath, and so if the eve of the ninth of Ab coincides with the Sabbath, one eats and drinks as needed and puts on his table a meal as gargantuan as what Solomon ate in his day. And it is forbidden to get a hair cut or to wash one's clothing from the New Moon to the fast,' the words of R. Meir. R. Judah says, 'The entire month is forbidden [for getting hair cuts and washing clothing].' Rabban Simeon b. Gamaliel says, 'Forbidden is only that week alone.' And it has further been taught on Tannaite authority: 'And one observes the laws of mourning from the new moon to the fast,' the words of R. Meir. R. Judah says, 'All that entire month is forbidden.' Rabban Simeon b. Gamaliel says, 'Forbidden is only that week alone.'" [Judah and Simeon b. Gamaliel forbid washing cloths after the ninth of Ab, thus sustaining Samuel's position.]

[J] Said R. Yohanan, "All three authorities interpret the same verse of Scripture: 'I will also cause all her mirth to cease, her feasts, her new moons, and her Sabbaths' (Hos. 2:13) —

[K] "Now the one who says, 'From the new moon to the fast' [30A] rests his position on 'her feasts.'

[L] "The one who says, 'All that entire month is forbidden' rests his position on 'her new moons.'

[M] "And the one who says, 'That week alone' rests his position on 'her Sabbaths.'"

[N] Said Raba, "The decided law accords with the position of Rabban Simeon b. Gamaliel,"

[O] And said Raba, "The decided law accords with the position of R. Meir."

[P] And both decisions yield the more lenient ruling, and it was necessary to articulate them both. For had we been told, "The decided law accords with R. Meir," one might have supposed that that is so even from the advent of the new moon of Ab. So we are informed that the decided law accords with Rabban Simeon b. Gamaliel. And if we had been informed only that the decided law accords with Rabban Simeon b. Gamaliel, one might have thought that that is so even after the ninth of Ab itself. So we are informed that in that aspect the decided law accords with R. Meir.

Treated as a datum of Halakhah, Hos. 2:13 is given three different interpretations.

VIII. MEGILLAH

BAVLI MEGILLAH INTERPRETATION OF ESTHER CHAPTER THREE I:
    1. A.   "After these things..."

B. After what?
C. Said Raba: "After The Holy One, Blessed Be He, created the cure for the illness.
D. For said Resh Laqish: The Holy One, Blessed Be He, does not smite Israel unless he creates 'for them a cure first, as is said, 'When I cure Israel, the sin of Ephraim will become clear" (Hos. 7:1).
E. But this is not true of the nations of the world. [First] He smites them, and afterwards he creates for them the cure, as is said, "And the Lord will smite Egypt, smiting and then curing them" (Is. 19:22).

Hos. 7:1 indicates that God first creates a cure and then smites the sinner.

BAVLI MEGILLAH INTERPRETATION OF ESTHER CHAPTER THREE X.
2. BBB. And what is the relationship between Josiah and the altar in Beth El?
CCC. Rather this teaches that Josiah ruled over them.
DDD. Rav Nahman said: ["This is learned] from here: 'Judah also will bring in the harvest, when I cause my people to return from captivity' (Hos. 6:11)."

Josiah ruled in Beth El, so Hos. 6:11.

BAVLI MEGILLAH 2:1 I.
5. DD. And when the exiles have been gathered [together in the holy land], judgment will be rendered against the evildoers, as is said, ." ..and I will return (ve-ashivah) my hand on you, and I will purify your dross as with lye [following New JPS]" (Is. 1:25).
EE. And it is written, ." ..and I will restore (ve-ashivah) your judges as in the beginning" (Is. 1:26).
FF. And when judgment has been rendered against evildoers, the heretics will be eliminated, and the spiteful sinners with them, as is said, ." ..and the breaking of the sinners and perpetual evildoers together...they will be destroyed" (Is. 1:28).
GG. And after the heretics have been eliminated, the horn of the righteous will be raised, as is written, "and I will cut off all the horns of the evildoers; the horns of the righteous will be raised" (Ps. 75:11).
HH. And [this] includes all the righteous converts [to Judaism] with the righteous, as is said, "Arise before the old, and glorify the face of an elder" (Lev. 19:32), and juxtaposed to it is, "and when a ˆ [taken here as a convert] lives with you" (Lev. 19:33).
II. And where is their horn raised? In Jerusalem, as is said, "Seek the peace of Jerusalem, those you love will remain in peace" (Ps. 122:6).

JJ. And after Jerusalem is [re]built, David comes, as is said, **[18a]** ."
..after the Israelites return and seek the Lord their God and David their king" (Hos. 3:5).

David will come when Jerusalem is rebuilt, so the sequences of events set forth at Hos. 3:5.

BAVLI MEGILLAH 3:11 I.
3. A. Said Rav Nahman: All jocularity is forbidden except jocularity [directed] at foreign worship, which is permitted, as is written, "Bel crouches, Nebo squeezes" (Is. 46:1), and [as] is written, "they squeezed [and] crouched together, but were unable to expel the load" (Is. 46:2).
B. R. Yannai said [this notion is derived] from here: "For the residents of Shomron will fear for the calves of Bet-Aven, because its people and its priests who rejoiced over it mourn for its glory, since its honor is gone"(Hos. 10:5); do not read kevodo, "his honor," read keveido, "his load."
C. Said Rav Huna bar Manoah in the name of Rav Aha the son of Rav Iqa: "An Israelite is permitted to tell a star worshiper [to] take his foreign worship and stick it up his Shin Tav."
D. Said Rav Ashi: "One who has a [justifiably] bad reputation may be disgraced with Gimmel and Shin.
E. "And one who has a good reputation may be praised; and one who praised him, blessings will rest on his head. "

Hos. 10:5 illustrates the rule that jocularity is permitted only against idolatry.

ix. MOED QATAN

BAVLI MOED QATAN 3:'1-2 II.
43. A. Said R. Huna, "At Usha they made this ordinance: 'The principal of the court who went astray — they do not excommunicate him, but say to him, 'Save your dignity and stay home' (2 Kgs. 14:10). If he went astray again, then they excommunicate him because of the profanation of the Divine Name [involved in his action].'"
B. That differs from the view of R. Simeon b. Laqish, for said R. Simeon b. Laqish, "A disciple of a sage who turned sour is not to be humiliated in public: 'Therefore you shall stumble in the day, and the prophet also shall stumble with you in the night' (Hos. 4:5). Cover it up in darkness."

Hos. 4:5 refers to a disciple of a sage who went astray; that should be concealed and not made public.

x. Hagigah

I found no reference to Hosea.

xi. Besah

I found no relevant items.

xii. Rosh Hashanah

Bavli Rosh Hashanah 2:4

[III.4.A] [Referring to the locales listed at M. R.H. 2:4] said R. Yohanan, "Between each [place and the next] were eight parasangs."
B. How much distance was there [in all, from the Mount of Olives to Bet Baltin]?
C. Thirty two [parasangs].
D. But, lo, now there is a greater [distance]!
E. Said Abbayye, "[This is because] the [direct] roads have been closed],
F. "as it is written, 'Therefore I will hedge up her way with thorns [...so that she cannot find her paths] (Hos. 2:6).'"
G. R. Nahman bar Isaac said, "We know the direct roads have been closed] from this [verse], as it is written [Lam. 3:9: 'He has blocked my ways with hewn stones, he has made] my paths crooked.'"

Hos. 2:6 explains why the distance from the Mount of Olives to the specified location has become greater.

Bavli Rosh Hashanah 4:1 I.

2. A. **It is taught on Tannaite authority** [see M. Tam.
K. Said Abbayye, "[For] two [days] it will be desolate, as it says [Hos. 6:2]: 'After two days he will revive us; [on the third day he will raise us up, that we may live before him].'"

God resurrects the dead on the third day, Hos. 6:2.

Bavli Rosh Hashanah 4:4 I.

6. A. Said R. Judah bar Idi said R. Yohanan, "The divine presence [Shekhinah] made ten journeys [in leaving the land and people of Israel prior to the destruction of the first Temple]. [That is, "The Divine Presence left Israel by ten stages" (Simon, p. 147)]. [This we know from] Scripture. And corresponding to these [stages], the Sanhedrin was exiled [successively to ten places of banishment]. [This we know from] tradition."
B. The divine presence [Shekhinah] made ten journeys [in leaving Israel prior to the destruction of the first Temple]. [This we know from] Scripture: [It went] (1) from the ark-cover to the cherub;

6. Hosea in the Bavli

[delete: and from (one) cherub to the (other) cherub;] (2) and from the cherub to the threshold [of the Holy-of-Holies]; (3) and from the threshold to the [Temple-] court; (4) and from the court to the altar; (5) and from the altar to [Temple-] roof; (6) and from the roof to wall; (7) and from the wall to the city; (8) and from the city to the mountain; (9) and from the mountain to the wilderness; (10) and from the wilderness it ascended and dwelled in its place [in heaven]—as it is said [Hos. 5:15]: "I will return again to my place, [until they acknowledge their guilt and seek my face]."

C. From the ark-cover to the cherub; [delete: and from (one) cherub to the (other) cherub;] (2) and from the cherub to the threshold [of the Holy-of-Holies]—as it is written [Ex. 25:22, proving that the original location of the divine presence was above the ark-cover]: "There I will meet with you, and [from above the ark-cover, from between the two cherubim that are upon the ark of the testimony], I will speak with you." And [showing that, later, the divine presence had moved to the cherub] it is written [II Sam. 22:11]: "He rode on a cherub and flew." And [proving that the divine presence then moved to the threshold] it is written [Ez. 9:3]: "Now the glory of the God of Israel had gone up from the cherubim on which it rested to the threshold of the house." (3) And from the threshold to the [Temple-] court—as it is written [Ez. 10:4]: "And the house was filled with the cloud, and the court was full of the brightness of the glory of the Lord." (4) And from the court to the altar—as it is written [Am. 9:1]: "I saw the Lord standing beside the altar." (5) And from the altar to [Temple-] roof— as it is written [Prov. 21:9]: "It is better to live in a corner of the roof [than in a house shared with a contentious woman]." (6) And from the roof to wall—as it is written [Am. 7:1: "He showed me]: behold, the Lord was standing beside a wall built with a plumb line." (7) And from the wall to the city—as it is written [Micah 6:9]: "The voice of the Lord cries to the city." (8) And from the city to the mountain—as it is written [Ez. 11:23]: "And the glory of the Lord went up from the midst of the city and stood upon the mountain which is on the east side of the city." (9) And from the mountain to the wilderness—as it is written [Prov. 21:19]: "It is better to live in a land of wilderness [than with a contentious and fretful woman]." (10) And from the wilderness it ascended and dwelled in its place [in heaven]—as it is said [Hos. 5:15]: 'I will return again to my place, [until they acknowledge their guilt and seek my face].'

D. Said R. Yohanan, "For sixth months, the divine presence waited on Israel [the people] in the wilderness, hoping lest they might repent. When they did not repent, it said, 'May their souls expire.' [We know this] as it says [Job 11:2]: 'But the eyes of the wicked will fail, all means of escape will elude them, and their [only] hope will be for their souls to expire.'"

> E. "And corresponding to these [stages through which the divine presence left Israel], the Sanhedrin was exiled [successively to ten places of banishment; this we know from] tradition." [The Sanhedrin was banished] (1) from the Chamber of Hewn Stone [in the inner court of the Temple] to the market; and (2) from the market into Jerusalem [proper], and (3) from Jerusalem to Yabneh, [31b] and (4) from Yabneh to Usha, and (5) from Usha [back] to Yabneh, and (6) from Yabneh [back] to Usha, (7) and from Usha to Shefar, and (8) from Shefar to Beth Shearim, and (9) from Beth Shearim to Sepphoris, and (10) from Sepphoris to Tiberias.
> F. And Tiberias is the lowest of them all [below sea-level at the Sea of Galilee, symbolic of the complete abasement of the Sanhedrin's authority]. [We know of the lowered physical location and reduced status of the Sanhedrin] as it is said [Is. 29:4]: 'And deep from the earth you shall speak.'
> G. [Proposing a different description of the banishment of the Sanhedrin] R. Eleazar says, "There were [only] six [places of] banishment, as it says [Is. 26:5]: 'For (1) he has brought low the inhabitants of the height, the lofty city. (2) He lays it low, (3) lays it low (4) to the ground, (5) he casts it (6) to the dust.'"
> H. Said R. Yohanan, "And from there are destined to be redeemed, as it says [Is. 52:2]: 'Shake yourself from the dust; arise!'"

Hos. 5:15 indicates that God will abandon the Temple and Jerusalem and return to Heaven.

BAVLI ROSH HASHANAH 4:6C-E

> [I.1] A. Sovereignty verses [that speak of punishment]: [Verses] such as [Ez. 20:33]: "As I live, says the Lord God, surely with a mighty hand and an outstretched arm, and with wrath poured out, I shall be king over you."
> B. And even though [indicating that this verse does not describe a totally pessimistic future] R. Nahman said, "Let the Holy One be as angry as all this with us, just that he should [eventually] redeem us"—[despite this fact], since [the verse] was said in anger, it is not recited at the beginning of the year.
> C. [What does M. R.H. 4:6C mean by] Remembrance verses [that speak of punishment]? **[Verses] such as [Ps. 78:39]: "And he remembered that they are but flesh [a wind that passes and comes not again]."**
> D. [What does M. R.H. 4:6C mean by] Shofar verses [that speak of punishment]? **[Verses] such as [Hos. 5:8, which refers to the use of the shofar to sound an alarm when God acts as Israel's enemy]: "Blow the horn in Gibeah."**

Hos. 5:8 refers to the sounding of the shofar as an alarm.

XIII. YEBAMOT

BAVLI YEBAMOT 1:3-4 II.
- 26. A. Said R. Judah said R. Assi, "A gentile who betrothed an Israelite woman at this time — they take account of the possibility of the validity of the betrothal, since he might derive from the Ten Tribes."
  - B. But lo, whatever falls from a mixed lot is assumed to have fallen from the majority thereof!
  - C. The statement speaks of places in which the ten tribes took up residence, for said R. Abba bar Kahana, "'And he put them in Halah and in Habor, on the river of Gozan, and the cities of the Medes' (2 Kgs. 18:11) — 'Halah' — this is Halwan; 'Habor' — this is Adiabene; 'the river of Gozan' — this is in Ginzaq; 'the cities of the Medes' — these are Hamdan and the neighboring towns." Others say, "Nihar and its neighboring towns."
  - D. What are the neighboring towns?
  - E. Samuel said, "Karak, Moshki, Hidqi, and Dumqia."
  - F. Said R. Yohanan, "All of these places that have been listed are listed so as to invalidate betrothals between their residents and Israelite women. But when I stated this before Samuel, he said to me, '"Your son" Dt. 7:4) who comes from an Israelite woman is called your son, but your son who is descended from a gentile woman is classified as not your son but her son."
  - G. But lo, there are daughters too! And said Rabina, "From this one may infer that the son of your daughter by a gentile is regarded as your son."
  - H. There is a tradition that the women of that generation were rendered barren.
  - I. There are those who say: "When I stated this before Samuel, he said to me, 'They did not leave that place until they declared them to be entirely gentiles: "They have dealt treacherously against the Lord, for they have begotten strange children" (Hos. 5:7).'"

Hos. 5:7 indicates that the Ten Tribes completely assimilated among the gentiles and ceased to be Israelites.

BAVLI YEBAMOT 1:3-4 II.
- 29. A. What is the etymology of Harpania?
  - B. Said R. Zira, "A mountain to which everybody turns." [The words just now given are built of the consonants of the name, Harpania.]
  - C. In a Tannaite formulation it has been stated: Anyone who did not know which family he derived from or which tribe would turn there.
  - D. Said Raba, "And it is deeper than Sheol: 'I shall ransom them from the power of the nether world, I shall redeem them from death' (Hos. 13:14) — but as to these, that which renders them invalid is beyond all remedy.

      E.   "The invalidity of Harpania is on account of that of Meshan, that of Meshan on account of that of Tarmod, that of Tarmod on account of the slaves of Solomon.

      F.   "That is in line with what people say: The little qab-measure and the big one roll down to Sheol, and from Sheol to Tarmud, and from Tarmud to Meshan, and from Meshan to Harpania."

Hos. 13:14 indicates that while God redeems people from the netherworld and from death, those from Harpania are beyond redemption.

BAVLI YEBAMOT 6:5 I.

1. A.   [**An ordinary priest should not marry a sterile woman, unless he already has a wife and children**:] Said the exilarch to R. Huna, "How come? Surely it is because of the consideration of being fruitful and multiplying! But then are only priests subject to the commandment of being fruitful and multiply, while Israelites are not so commanded [that only the priest should be listed here, when the rule pertains to everybody]?"

    B.   He said to him, "It is because he wanted to insert into the Tannaite formulation the further clause: **R. Judah says, [61B] 'Even though he has a wife and children, he should not marry a sterile woman, because she is the whore (Lev. 21:7) referred to in the Torah.'** Since only priests are subject to that consideration but Israelites are not, only **priest** was mentioned in the opening clause."

    C.   Said R. Huna, "What is the scriptural basis for the position of R. Judah? 'And they shall eat and not have enough, and they shall commit harlotry but shall not increase' (Hos. 4:10) — any sexual relations that are not aimed at producing children are nothing more than fornication."

Hos. 4:10 proves that any sexual relations that are not aimed at producing children are nothing more than fornication

BAVLI YEBAMOT 12:1-2 II.

12. A.   There was a min [Christian] who said to Rabban Gamaliel, "You are a people the master of which has performed the rite of removing the shoe [severing his connection (Slotki)], for it is written, 'With their flocks and with their herds they shall go to seek the Lord but they shall not find them, he has drawn off the shoe from them' (Hos. 5:6)."

    B.   He said to him, "You jerk! Is it written, 'he has drawn off the shoe for them'? It is written, 'he has drawn off the shoe from them.' Now if the levir drew off the shoe from the levirate widow, would such an act be valid?"

Hos. 5:6 indicates to the *min* that the Israelites have been subjected to the rite of *halisah* and are not validly married to God.

XIV. KETUBOT

BAVLI KETUBOT 5:8 III.
1. A. And one pays over to her a half-qab of pulse, a half-log of oil, and a qab of dried figs or a maneh of fig cake:
   B. So how about wine? That supports R. Eleazar for said R. Eleazar, [65A] "They do not provide an allowance for the woman for wine."
   C. And if you cite the verse, "I will go after my lovers, who give me my bread and my water, my wool and my flax, my oil and my drink" (Hos. 2:7) [including wine], this refers to things that a woman lusts after, and what are they? They are really jewelry.

Hos. 2:7 says women lust after jewelry.

BAVLI KETUBOT 7:4-5 I.
2. A. "Then I was in his eyes as one that found peace" (Song 8:10) —
   B. Said R. Yohanan, "Like a bride found flawless by her father-in-law's house, who is anxious to go home and tell her success in her father's household."
I.3. A. "And it shall be at that day says the Lord that you will call me 'My man,' and not 'My master'" (Hos. 2:18) —
   B. Said R. Yohanan, "Like a bride in the household of her father-in-law, not like a bride in the household of her father."

Hos. 2:18 promises that Israel will be at home with God like a bride who succeeds in her father-in-law's house.

XV. NEDARIM

I find nothing that pertains.

XVI. NAZIR

BAVLI NAZIR 4:1-2
[I.2] [A] Said Rabbah bar bar Hannah said R. Yohanan, "What is the meaning of the verse of Scripture, 'For the paths of the Lord are straight, that the righteous shall pass along them, but the transgressors will stumble in them' (Hos. 14:10)? The matter may be compared to the case of two men who roasted their Passover offerings. One of them ate it for the sake of performing the religious duty, and the other one ate it to stuff himself with a big meal. The one who ate it for the sake of performing a religious duty — 'the righteous shall pass along them.' And as to the one who ate it to stuff himself with a big meal — 'but the transgressors will stumble in them'"

B. Said to him R. Simeon b. Laqish, "But do you really call him a wicked person? Granted that he did not carry out a religious duty in the best possible way, still, has he not eaten his Passover offering as he is supposed to? Rather, the matter may be compared to the case of two men. This one has his wife and sister with him in the house, and that one has his wife and his sister with him in the house [in the darkness of the night]. One of them had a sexual encounter with his wife, while the other had a sexual encounter with his sister. The one who had the sexual encounter with his wife — 'the righteous shall pass along them.' And as to the one who had a sexual encounter with his sister.— 'but the transgressors will stumble in them'"

C. But are the cases comparable to the verse of Scripture? Scripture speaks of a single path in which righteous and wicked walk, but here there are two paths [one being legal the other not]. Rather, the matter may be compared to the case of Lot and his two daughters. Those who had sexual relations to carry out a religious duty [to be fruitful and multiply] — "the righteous shall pass along them." And as to the one who had sexual relations in order to perform a transgression — "but the transgressors will stumble in them"

D. But maybe he too had in mind to fulfill the commandment?

Hos. 4:10 distinguishes action for the sake of carrying out a religious imperative from action for personal gratification.

BAVLI NAZIR 4:3

[I.3] [A] Said R. Yohanan, "The entire verse of Scripture is formulated to express the intention of committing a transgression, as it is said, 'And Lot lifted his eyes and saw the entire plain of the Jordan that it was well watered' (Gen. 13:10).

F. "[The sense of 'lifted' derives from, 'And his master's wife lifted her eyes toward Joseph and said, Lay with me' (Gen. 39:7).

G. "'...his eyes...:' 'And Samson said, Take her for me, as she is beautiful in my eyes' (Jud. 14:3).

H. "'And saw...:' 'And Shechem, son of Hamor...saw her and took her and lay with her and abused her' (Gen. 34:2).

I. "'the entire plain of the Jordan...:' 'For a whore can be had for the price of a loaf of bread' (Prov. 6:326). [The Hebrew words for plain and loaf being the same.]

J. "'that it was well watered...:' 'I will go after my lovers, who provide my bread and water, my wool and flax, my oil and my drink' (Hos. 2:7)."

K. But wasn't he drunk anyhow, so he really was forced into the act!

L. A Tannaite statement in the name of R. Yosé b. R. Honi, "Why are there dots about the word 'and' in the verse, 'and when the elder daughter arose' (Gen. 19:33)? It tells you that when she lay down

6. Hosea in the Bavli

with him, he didn't know what was going on, but when she got up, he knew."
M. So what was he supposed to do? What was was.
N. The point is that the next night, he shouldn't have gotten drunk [so as to get involved with the younger daughter].

Hos. 2:7 shows that Gen. 13:10 refers to committing a transgression.

XVII. SOTAH

BAVLI SOTAH 7:5 XI.1

13. A. [Reverting to 4.A,] what did Judah do?
    B. It is in accord with that which has been taught on Tannaite authority:
    C. R. Meir says, "When the Israelites stood at the sea, the tribes argued with one another, with this one saying, 'I shall go down to the sea first,' and that one saying, 'I shall go down to the sea first.'
    D. "The tribe of Benjamin jumped forward [37A] and went down to the sea first, as it is said, 'There is little Benjamin, their ruler' (Ps. 68:17). Do not read, 'their rules' but 'descended into the sea.'
    E. "Then the princes of the tribe of Judah threw stones at them, as it is said, 'The princes of Judah stoned them' (Ps. 68:27).
    F. "For that reason Benjamin, the righteous, attained such merit as to be made the host of the All-Mighty, as it is said, 'He dwells between his shoulders' (Deut. 33:12). [God, in the temple, dwells in Benjamin's land.]"
    G. Said R. Judah to [Meir], "That is not how things happened. Rather, this one was saying, 'I shall not go down to the sea first,' and that one was saying, 'I shall not go down to the sea first. Nahshon b. Aminadab jumped forward and went down to the sea first, as it is said, 'Ephraim compasses me about with falsehood, and the house of Israel with deceit, but Judah yet rules with God' (Hos. 12:1)."
    H. In his regard it is explained in tradition, "Save me, O God, for the waters have come into my soul. I sink in deep mire, where there is no standing" (Ps. 69:2-3).
    I. "Let the water-flood not overwhelm me, nor let the deep swallow me up" (Ps. 69:16):
    J. At that time, Moses was praying at his own good time. Said to him, the Holy One, blessed be he, "My dear ones are drowning in the sea, and you are taking your own good time in prayer before me?!"
    K. He said to him, "Lord of the world, what can I do?"
    L. He said to him, "Speak to the children of Israel, that they go forward, and lift up your rod and stretch out your hand" (Ex. 14:15-16).
    M. Therefore Judah attained such merit as to be made ruler in Israel, as it is said, "Judah became his sanctuary, Israel his dominion" (Ps. 114:2).

N. What is the reason that "Judah became his sanctuary and Israel his dominion"? Because "the sea saw him and fled" (Ps. 114:3).

Hos. 12:1 refers to Israel at the sea, when Judah carried out an act of faith in God.

BAVLI SOTAH 7:8 V.

4. A. Said R. Jeremiah bar Abba, "There are four categories who will not receive the face of the Presence of God:
B. "The category of scoffers, flatterers, liars, and slanderers.
C. "The category of scoffers, as it is written, 'He has stretched out his hand against scorners' (Hos. 7:5).
D. "The category of flatterers, as it is written, 'For a flatterer shall not come before him' (Job. 13:16).
E. "The category of liars, as it is written, 'He who speaks lies shall not be established in my sight' (Ps. 101:7).
F. "The category of slanderers, as it is written, 'For you are not a God who has pleasure in wickedness; evil will not dwell with you' (Ps. 5:5). 'You are righteous, O Lord, and evil will not dwell in your house.' [Ps. 5 addresses slander.]"

Hos. 7:5 shows that scoffers will not see God.

BAVLI SOTAH V.

1. A. Since it says, I will not punish your daughters when they commit whoredom, etc. [M. 9:9D].
B. What is the purpose of adding, "Since it says..."?
C. If you should propose that his own sin [will impede the use of the water], but the sin of his sons and daughters will not, then come and take note:
D. "I will not punish your daughters when they commit whoredom, nor your daughters-in-law when they commit adultery" (Hos. 4:14).
E. And should you say that the transgression of a man's wife will matter, but the transgression of an unattached woman will not, come and take note:
F. "For they themselves go apart with whores" (Hos. 4:14).
G. What is the meaning of the phrase, "And the people that does not understand shall be overthrown" (Hos. 4:14)?
H. Said R. Eleazar, "Said the prophet to Israel, 'If you are strict with ourselves, the water will put your wives to the test, and if not, the water will not put your wives to the test.'"

Hos. 4:14 shows that the sins of the sons and daughters impede the working of the bitter water, not only the sins of the husband himself. Indeed, the same consideration extends to transgression with an unattached woman.

6. Hosea in the Bavli

BAVLI SOTAH 9:12 V.

4. A. Said R. Ilai, son of Yebarekhia, "If there are two disciples of sages who live in the same town and are not easy with one another in the law, one will die and the other will go into exile,
   B. "as it is said, 'That the manslaughter may flee there, who slays his neighbor without knowledge' (Deut. 4:42).
   C. "'Knowledge' refers only to Torah, as it is said, 'My people are destroyed for lack of knowledge' (Hos. 4:6)."

Hos. 4:6 speaks of knowledge of the Torah.

XVIII. GITTIN

BAVLI GITTIN 1:1 I.

31. A. They sent word to Mar Uqba, "How on the basis of Scripture do we know that it is forbidden to sing?"
    B. He underlined and wrote the verse, "'Do not rejoice, Israel, as do the peoples, for you have gone astray from your God' (Hos. 9:1)."
    C. Shouldn't he send him the following verse: "They shall not drink wine with music, strong drink shall be better to them who drink it" (Isa. 24:9)?
    D. Had he sent that verse, one might have concluded that what is forbidden is the use of musical instruments, but not a cappella singing; from the other verse I derive that fact.

Hos. 9:1 indicates that it is forbidden to sing.

BAVLI GITTIN 3:8 III.

6. A. Raba and R. Nahman bar Isaac were in session. R. Nahman bar Jacob was coming by them enthroned in a gilt carriage, wearing a purple cloak. Raba went to greet him, R. Nahman bar Isaac didn't go to greet him. He said, "Perhaps he's a member of the exilarch's household. Raba needs them, I don't."
   B. When he saw R. Nahman bar Jacob coming, he showed his arm, saying, "The south wind is blowing."
   C. Said Raba, "This is what Rab said, 'When this wind blows, a woman miscarries,' and Samuel said, 'Even a pearl in the sea rots,' and R. Yohanan said, 'Even the semen in a woman's womb putrefies.'"
   D. Said R. Nahman bar Isaac, "All three of them interpret the same verse of Scripture: 'Though he be fruitful among his brothers, an east wind shall come, and the breath of the Lord coming up from the wilderness, his spring shall become dry, and his fountain shall be dried up; he shall spoil the treasure of all pleasant vessels' (Hos. 13:15). 'His spring' is the woman's womb; 'his fountain shall be dried up' refers to the semen in the woman's womb; 'the treasure of all pleasant vessels' refers to the pearl in the sea."

- E. Said Raba, "He's from Sura, where they read verses of Scripture very closely."
- F. What is the meaning of "though he be fruitful among his brothers" (Hos. 13:15)?
- G. Said Raba, "Even [32A] the pin in the handle of the plough loosens."
- H. R. Joseph said, "Even a peg in a wall loosens."
- I. R. Aha bar Jacob said, "Even a cane in a wicker basket loosens."

Hos. 13:15 refers to the bad effect of the south wind.

Bavli Gittin 5:6 I.

25. A. [57B] Said R. Hiyya bar Abin said R. Joshua b. Qorha, "A certain elder from the people of Jerusalem told me:
- B. "'In this valley Nebuzaradan, chief slaughterer, killed two million one hundred thousand, and in Jerusalem, nine hundred forty thousand on one stone, until their blood went and mixed with that of Zechariah, carrying out the verse, "Blood touches blood" (Hos. 4:2).'"
- C. [Nebuzaradan] saw the blood of Zechariah boiling. He said to them, "What is this?"
- D. They said to him, "It is the blood of the sacrifices, that has been poured out."
- E. He said to them, "Come and let us bring [animal blood to make a comparison to see whether they are alike or not alike]." He slaughtered an animal and the blood was not like [that which was boiling].
- F. He said to them, "Explain it to me, and if not, I shall comb your flesh with iron combs."
- G. They said to him, "What should we tell you! This one was a prophet among us, and he rebuked us on account of matters having to do with Heaven. We ganged up against him and killed him. And lo, for many years his blood has not come to rest."
- H. He said to them, "I shall be the one to appease him." He brought the great sanhedrin and the lesser sanhedrin and killed them over him, but [the blood] did not come to rest. He brought young men and women, but the blood did not come to rest. He brought schoolchildren and killed them over him, but still the blood did not come to rest. He drew near [the blood] and said, "Zechariah, Zechariah, I have destroyed the best of them. Do you want me to kill them all?"
- I. When he said this to him, forthwith the blood came to rest.
- J. He said to himself, "Now if they, who killed only a single person, were treated in such a way, that man [I] – what will come of him?"
- K. He fled, sent his instructions to his household [giving over his property to his family], and then converted [to Judaism].

6. Hosea in the Bavli

Hos. 4:2 refers to the blood of Zechariah, which disfigured the Temple.

BAVLI GITTIN 5:8 I.
9. A. Said R. Eleazar, "As to the Torah, the larger part is in writing, and the smaller part is oral: 'Though I wrote for him the major portion of my law, they were counted a strange thing' (Hos. 8:12)."
   B. And R. Yohanan said, "The larger part was oral, the smaller part in writing: 'For orally, these words...' (Ex. 34:27)."
   C. And as to the other party, isn't it written, "Though I wrote for him the major portion of my law"?
   D. That is an expression of astonishment, namely, should I have written down for him the major portion of my law?! Even now, isn't it regarded by him as a strange thing?!
   E. And as to the other party, isn't it written, "For orally, these words..."?
   F. That is because it is a formidable task to learn them.

Hos. 8:12 refers to the oral Torah.

BAVLI GITTIN 7:1 I.
7. A. ["And the house when it was being built was made of stone made ready at the quarry; neither hammer nor axe nor any tool of iron was heard in the house while it was being built" (1 Kgs. 6:7):] He said to the rabbis, "So what should I do?"
   B. They said to him, "Well, there is a king of worm called the shamir, which Moses brought for cutting the stones of the ephod."
   C. He said to them, "Where is it found?"
   D. They said to him, "Bring a male and a female demon and tie them together; maybe they'll know and tell you."
   E. He brought a male and female demon and tied them together. They said to him, "We don't know where it is, but maybe Ashmodai, prince of the demons, knows."
   F. He said to them, "So where is he?"
   G. They said to him, "He is in such-and-so mountain. He dug a pit there, which he fills with water and covers with a stone and seals with his seal. Every day he goes up to Heaven and studies in the academy in Heaven, then he comes back down to earth and studies in the academy on earth, then he goes and examines his seal, opens the pit, drinks from it, and closes it and seals it again and goes away."
   H. [Solomon] sent Benaiahu, son of Jehoiada, there and gave him a chain on which the Divine Name was engraved and a ring on which the Divine Name was engraved and fleeces of wool and bottles of wine. Benaiahu went and dug a pit lower down the hill and let the water flow into it and stopped up the hole with the wool fleece; then he dug a pit higher up and poured the wine into it and filled up the pits. He went and sat on a tree. When Ashmodai came, he

looked at the seal, opened the pit, and found it full of wine. He said, "It is written, 'Wine is a mocker, strong drink a brawler, and whoever errs through it is not wise' (Prov. 20:1), and, 'Whoredom and wine and new wine take away understanding' (Hos. 4:11). So I won't drink it."

I. He got thirsty, couldn't hold back, drank and got drunk, and fell asleep. Benaiahu came and threw a chain over him and locked it. When he woke up, he struggled. Benaiahu said to him, "The Name of your Master is on you, the Name of your Master is on you."

J. As he was dragging him along, he came to a palm tree and rubbed against it and brought it down. He came to a house and brought it down. He came to the hut of a certain widow. She came out, [68B] and she looked for him and bent down so as not to touch him, and broke a bone. He said, "That's in line with the verse, 'A soft tongue breaks the bone' (Prov. 25:15)."

K. He saw a blind man who had lost his way and put him on the right road.

L. He saw a drunken man losing his way and put him on the right road.

M. He saw a wedding procession celebrating and he wept.

N. He heard a man say to a shoemaker, "Make me a pair of shoes to last for seven years," and he laughed.

O. He saw a diviner practicing divination and he laughed.

P. When they got to Jerusalem, they didn't take him to see Solomon for three days.

Hos. 4:11 condemns wine drinking, it takes away understanding.

XIX. QIDDUSHIN

BAVLI QIDDUSHIN 1:1 VI.

10. A. Further, in session they said, "Lo, in regard to what R. Judah said Samuel said, 'Whoever doesn't know the essentials of writs of divorce and betrothals should not get involved in them,' said R. Assi said R. Yohanan, 'And such folk are more of a problem to the world than the generation of the flood, for it has been stated, "By swearing, lying, killing, stealing, and committing adultery, they spread forth and blood touches blood"' (Hos. 4:2)."

B. How does that verse bear the alleged implication?

C. It is in line with the way in which R. Joseph interpreted the verse in his translation, "They beget children by their neighbors' wives, piling evil upon evil."

Hos. 4:2 refers to the result of adultery.

6. Hosea in the Bavli

BAVLI QIDDUSHIN 1:1 VI.
- 9. A. When R. Assi died, rabbis assembled to collect his traditions. Said one of the rabbis, R. Jacob by name, "This is what R. Assi said R. Mani said, 'Just as a woman may not be acquired with less than a penny, so real estate cannot be acquired for less than a penny.'"
  - B. They said to him, "But hasn't it been taught on Tannaite authority: Even though a woman may not be acquired with less than a penny, real estate can be acquired for less than a penny?"
  - C. He said to them, "When that Tannaite ruling was set forth, it had to do with barter, for it has been taught on Tannaite authority: Transfer of title may take place with a utensil even though the utensil is not worth a penny."
  - D. [Reverting to A:] "And it is written, 'Therefore shall the land mourn and everyone who dwells therein shall languish, with the beasts of the field and the fowl of heaven, yes the fish of the sea also shall be taken away' (Hos. 4:3). By contrast, with respect to the generation of the flood, there was no decree against the fish of the sea: 'Of all that was in the dry land died' (Gen. 7:22) – but not the fish in the sea; here even the fish in the sea are covered."
  - E. But might one say that that penalty was inflicted only when all of the sins listed were committed [not only adultery]?
  - F. Don't imagine it! For it is written, "For because of swearing the land mourns" (Jer. 23:10) [a single crime suffices (Freedman)].
  - G. Well, maybe swearing stands on its own terms, and the others combined on theirs?
  - H. **[13B]** Is it written, "and they spread forth"? What is written is, "they spread forth."

Hos. 4:3 speaks of the removal of the fish of the sea, but Gen. 7:22 omits that category of life.

BAVLI QIDDUSHIN 1:1 V.
- 2. A. Isi taught as a Tannaite statement: "So, too, are women exempt from the prohibition of baldness" (Lev. 21:5).
  - B. What is the scriptural basis for Isi's view?
  - C. This is how he expounds the matter: "'You are sons of the Lord your God, you shall not cut yourselves nor make any baldness between your eyes for the dead, for you are a holy people to the Lord your God' (Deut. 14:1) – sons, but not daughters, in the matter of baldness.
  - D. "You maintain that it is in respect to baldness. But maybe it is in respect to cutting yourselves?
  - E. "When Scripture says, 'for you are a holy people to the Lord your God,' cutting is covered. So how do I interpret the sense of 'sons,' but not daughters? It is in respect to baldness.
  - F. "Well, why do you prefer to extend the law to cutting and to exclude from the law the matter of baldness?

G. "I extend the law to cutting, which is possible both where there is hair and where there is none, but I exclude the matter of baldness, which pertains only instead of hair."

H. But why not say: "sons and not daughters" in regard to both baldness and cutting, and the phrase, "for you are a holy people to the Lord your God," pertains to an incision [Lev. 21:5: Priests are not to make any incision]?

I. Isi takes the view that incisions and cuttings [36A] are the same thing.

J. Said Abbayye, "This is the scriptural basis for the position of Isi: He derives a verbal analogy from the appearance in both contexts of the phrase, 'sons of Aaron,' in regard to baldness [both at Deut. 14:1-2, for Israelites, and Lev. 21:5, for priests]. Just as in the one case, women are exempt, so in the other, women are exempt."

K. But if we assume that Scripture refers to the entire matter in making reference to "the sons of Aaron," then let Scripture just fall silent, and the exemption of women I would derive from an argument a fortiori, as follows: If in the case of priests, for whom Scripture has provided an abundance of religious duty, yield the argument, "sons of Aaron" and not daughters of Aaron, then a fortiori the same rule should apply to ordinary Israelites!

L. But if it were not for the verbal analogy, I might have said that the matter is interrupted [so that "sons of Aaron" does not refer to "they shall not shave"]. So here too, why not say that the matter is interrupted, and, so far as the argument resting on the verbal analogy, it is required for another purpose altogether, namely, for that which has been taught on Tannaite authority:

M. **"They shall not make tonsures [upon their heads, nor shave off the edges of their beards, nor make any cuttings in their flesh]:"**

N. **Might one suppose that for making four or five tonsures, one should be liable only on one count?**

O. **Scripture refers to "tonsure" in the singular, so imposing liability for each cut.**

P. **"Upon their heads:"**

Q. **What is the point of Scripture here?**

R. **Since it is said, "[You are the sons of the Lord your God: You shall not cut yourselves nor make any baldness on your foreheads for the dead" (Deut. 14:1),**

S. **one might have thought that liability is incurred only for a cut on the forehead.**

T. **How do we know that the prohibition extends to the entire head?**

U. **Scripture says, "upon their heads,"**

V. **to encompass the entire head.**

W. **Might one suppose that in the case of priests, for whom Scripture has specified numerous supererogatory commandments, liability extends to each cut and also to the entire head,**

X. while for ordinary Israelites, for whom Scripture has not specified supererogatory commandments, liability should be incurred only on one count for however many cuts and only for a cut on the forehead?

Y. Scripture refers to "tonsure" in several passages [here and at Deut. 14:1, here speaking of the priests, there speaking of Israelites as well], so establishing grounds for the following analogy:

Z. Just as in the case of "cutting" stated with reference to priests, liability is incurred for each cut and is incurred for a cut on any part of the head as much as on the forehead, so for "cut" spoken of in connection with an Israelite, liability is incurred for each cut and is incurred for a cut on any part of the head as much as on the forehead.

AA. And just as "cutting" stated with reference to an Israelite imposes liability only if it is made for a deceased, so "cutting" stated with reference to priests imposes liability only if it is made for a deceased [Sifra CCXII:I.1-3].

BB. [Abbayye responds:] "If so, Scripture should write "baldness" [in abbreviated form. Why say "baldness" in a fully spelled out form]? It is to yield both points."

CC. Said Raba, "This is the scriptural basis for the position of Isi: He derives how the consideration of the phrase 'between your eyes' applies from the case of phylacteries. Just as in the latter case, women are exempt, so here, too, they are exempt."

DD. And how come Raba doesn't state matters as does Abbayye?

EE. Because he doesn't see any point in the variation of spellings of the word for baldness.

FF. And how come Abbayye doesn't state matters as does Raba?

GG. He will say to you, "The matter of phylacteries themselves derives from this very passage, namely: Just as in that context 'between the eyes' means, a place where a bald spot can be made, which is the upper part of the head, so here too, the place at which phylacteries are located is the upper part of the head."

HH. Now in regard to both Abbayye and Raba, how do they deal with the phrase, "you are sons" [since they make the same point on the basis of other language altogether]?

II. They require it in line with that which has been taught on Tannaite authority:

JJ. "You are children of the Lord your God. You shall not gash yourselves or shave the front of your heads because of the dead. For you are a people consecrated to the Lord your God: The Lord your God chose you from among all other peoples on earth to be his treasured people" (Deut. 14:1-2):

KK. R. Judah says, "If you conduct yourselves in the way good children do, then you are children, and if not, you are not children [of the Lord your God]."

LL. R. Meir says, "One way or another, 'You are children of the Lord your God.'"
MM. And so Scripture says, "Yet the number of the children of Israel shall be as the sand of the sea...it shall be said to them, 'You are the children of the living God'" (Hos. 2:1) [B.'s version: "They are sottish children" (Jer. 4:22); "They are children in whom is no faith" (Deut. 32:20), "A seed of evil doers, sons that deal corruptly" (Isa. 1:4), then Hos. 2:1] [Sifré Deut. XCVI:IV.1].
NN. Why all these further verses?
OO. If you should reply, then only when they are foolish are they classified as sons, but not when they lack faith, come and take note: "They are children in whom is no faith" (Deut. 32:20).
PP. If you should reply, then only when they have no faith they are classified as sons, but when they serve idols they are not classified as sons, then come and hear: "A seed of evil doers, sons that deal corruptly" (Isa. 1:4).
2. And should you say, well, they're called sons that act corruptly, but not good sons, then come and hear: "Yet the number of the children of Israel shall be as the sand of the sea...it shall be said to them, 'You are the children of the living God'" (Hos. 2:1).

Hos. 2:1 confirms that the Israelites are God's children, in line with the promise of numerous descendants.

BAVLI QIDDUSHIN 4:1-2 V.
3. A. Said Rabbah bar R. Adda said Rab, "Whoever marries a woman for money will have children who are unworthy: 'They have dealt treacherously against the Lord, for they have produced strange children' (Hos. 6:7). And lest you think, at least the money is there, Scripture states, 'Now shall the new moon devour them with their portions' (Hos. 5:7). And lest you think, his, not hers, the language that is used refers to both: 'Their portions.' And lest you think that that is only after a long period, Scripture is explicit: 'The new moon.'"
B. How does this make the point?
C. Said R. Nahman bar Isaac, "A new month comes, the old month goes, and their money is lost."

The strange children of Hos. 6:7 are illegitimate because the couple married for money, hence the wrong intention was involved in their action.

BAVLI QIDDUSHIN 4:1-2 V.
6. A. Said R. Judah said Samuel, "Four hundred slaves" – some say, "four thousand slaves" – did Pashur son of Immer have, and they all became mixed up with the priesthood, so every priest who shows arrogance derives only from them."

6. Hosea in the Bavli

B. Said Abbayye, "And all of them live within the wall of Nehardea."

C. And [Judah] differs from R. Eleazar, for said R. Eleazar, "If you see a priest who is brazen, don't entertain suspicions about his origins, for it is said, 'Your people are like the contentious ones in the priesthood' (Hos. 4:4)."

Hos. 4:4 characterizes brazen priests as authentic to the priesthood.

XX. BABA QAMMA

BAVLI BABA QAMMA 1:4K-N I.

8. A. Said R. Yohanan in the name of R. Simeon b. Yohai, "What is the meaning of the verse of Scripture, 'Happy are you who sow beside all waters, that send forth the feet of the ox and the ass' (Isa. 32:20)? Whoever is devoted to the Torah and to doing deeds of grace, has the merit of inheriting two tribes: 'Blessed are you that sow.' And 'sowing' speaks of acts of charity, 'Sow to yourselves in charity, reap in kindness' (Hos. 10:12). Water stands for the Torah: 'everyone that thirsts, come to the water' (Isa. 55:1)."

B. "Here is worthy of the inheritance of two tribes," Joseph: "Joseph is a fruitful bough, whose branches run over the wall" (Gen. 49:22); and Issachar, "Issachar is a strong ass" (Gen. 49:14).

C. Some say, "His enemies will fall before him: 'With them he shall push the people together to the ends of the earth' (Deut. 33:17)."

D. He is worthy of understanding like Issachar, "which were men who had understanding of the times, to know what Israel out to do" (1 Chr. 12:12).

Hos. 10:12 speaks of acts of charity when it uses the language of sowing and reaping.

XXI. BABA MESIA

BAVLI BABA MESIA 3:6 II.

4. A. Whether a captive that has been taken prisoner does or does not take over the management of his property is a dispute between Tannaite authorities as well, for it has been taught on Tannaite authority:

B. **He who takes over the estate of a captive is not removed from it. Not only so, but if he heard a report that the ones assumed to have died and left the estate are coming back, if he went ahead and plucked up produce from the ground in any measure at all, lo, this one is rewarded for his promptness.**

C. **What is meant by such an estate of a captive? It is any one whose father or brothers or one of those who leave him an inheritance went overseas, and he heard that they had died, and he entered into his inheritance.**

D. He who takes over a forsaken estate is removed from it. What is an abandoned estate? It is any one whose father or brothers or one of those who leave him an inheritance went overseas, and he has not heard that they had died, and he entered into his inheritance. [Tosefta: It is any estate, the death of the owner of which has not been reported, but into which one nevertheless has entered for purpose of inheritance.]
　　E. Rabban Simeon b. Gamaliel says, "I have heard that an abandoned estate is equivalent to a captive's estate."
　　F. He who takes over an abandoned estate — they retrieve it from his possession. What is an abandoned estate? It is any one whose father or brothers or one of those who leave him an inheritance is here, but we do not know where he has gone. [Tosefta: And in all of them, they estimate the value for restoring what is misappropriated as if the one who took over the estate had been in the status of a tenant farmer. What is abandoned property? Any of which the location of the owner is not known [T. Ketubot 8:3A-L].
　　G. What is the difference between the one kind, which is called "abandoned," and the other, which is called [39A] "forsaken"?
　　H. "Abandoned" is against one's will: "But the seventh year you shall let it rest and abandon it" Ex. 23:11), that is, by royal decree.
　　I. "'Forsaken' is done voluntarily: "The mother shall be forsaken of her children" (Hos. 10:15).

Hos. 10:15 provides a philological fact.

XXII. BABA BATRA

BAVLI BABA BATRA 1:5 III.
4. A. R. Nahman bar R. Hisda collected the head tax [karga] from rabbis. Said to him R. Nahman bar Isaac, "You have violated the rules of the Torah, the Prophets, and the Writings.
　　B. "The Torah: 'Although he loves the peoples, all his saints are in your hand' (Deut. 33:3).
　　C. "Said Moses before the Holy One, blessed be He, 'Lord of the world, even when you love the peoples, may all his holy ones be in your hand.'"
　　D. "And they are cut at your feet" (Deut. 33:3) —
　　E. R. Joseph repeated as a Tannaite statement: "This refers to the disciples of sages who cut their feet as they wander from town to town and province to province to study Torah."
　　F. "They shall receive of your words" (Deut. 33:3) —
　　G. this refers to how they discuss the statements of God.
　　H. "The Prophets: 'Yes, though they repeat Tannaite traditions among the nations, now I shall gather them and a few of them shall be free from the burden of kings and princes' (Hos. 8:10)."

6. Hosea in the Bavli

    I. Said Ulla, "This verse is stated in the Aramaic language, namely: if all of them repeat Tannaite traditions, I shall gather them even now, and if only a few of them do so, those at the very least shall be exempt from the burdens of king and princes."
    J. "The Writings: 'It shall not be lawful to impose upon them minda, belo, and halak' (Ezra 7:24), and said R. Judah, 'Minda refers to the king's tax, belo, the poll tax, and halach, the corvée.'"

Hos. 8:10 means that if the Israelites repeat Tannaite traditions in the exile, God will gather them in and some of them will be tax-exempt.

BAVLI BABA BATRA 1:6 IV.

7. A. Let's consider:
    B. Hosea came first: "God spoke first to Hosea" (Hos. 1:2).
    C. But did he speak first of all with Hosea? And were there not any number of prophets from Moses to Hosea?
    D. And said R. Yohanan, "He was the first of the group of four prophets who prophesied at that time: Hosea, Isaiah, Amos, and Micah."
    E. So should not Hosea come first?
    F. Well, since his prophesies are written down along with those of Haggai, Zechariah, and Malachi, and since Haggai, Zechariah, and Malachi are designated as the conclusion of prophecy, he is reckoned along with them.
    G. So why not write out his prophecy on its own and put it first?
    H. Well, his scroll is so small that if copied on its own it might get lost.

Hos. 1:2 claims that Hosea was the first of the prophets, though there were many prior to him. He was first of the group, Isaiah, Amos, Micah, Hosea.

BAVLI BABA BATRA 5:1 IV.

28. A. Rabbah said R. Yohanan said, "The Holy One, blessed be He, is destined to make a banquet for the righteous out of the meat of Leviathan: 'Companions will make a banquet of it' (Job 40:30). The meaning of 'banquet' derives from the usage of the same word in the verse, 'And he prepared for them a great banquet and they ate and drank' (2 Kgs. 6:23)."
    B. "'Companions' can refer only to disciples of sages, in line with this usage: 'You that dwells in the gardens, the companions hearken for your voice, cause me to hear it' (Song 8:13). The rest of the creature will be cut up and sold in the markets of Jerusalem: 'They will part him among the Canaanites' (Job 40:30), and 'Canaanites' must be merchants, in line with this usage: 'As for the Canaanite, the balances of deceit are in his hand, he loves to oppress' (Hos. 12:8). If you prefer: 'Whose merchants are princes, whose traffickers are the honorable of the earth' (Isa. 23:8)."

Hos. 12:8 indicates that by "Canaanite" is meant merchant.

BAVLI BABA BATRA 5:10-11 III.
12. A. Our rabbis have taught on Tannaite authority:
    B. They do not make the strike thick on one side and thin on the other.
    C. They do not make the strike with a single quick movement, because striking in that way brings loss to the seller and advantage to the buyer, nor very slowly, since this is a loss to the buyer but a benefit to the seller.
    D. In regard to all of these shady practices, said Rabban Yohanan b. Zakkai, "Woe is me if I speak, woe is me if I do not speak. If I speak, then sharpers will learn from me, and if I don't speak, then the sharpers will say, 'The disciples of sages haven't got the slightest idea what we are doing.'"
III.13. A. The question was raised: "So did he speak of them or didn't he?"
    B. Said R. Samuel bar R. Isaac, "He did speak of them: 'For the ways of the Lord are right, and the just walk in them; but transgressors stumble therein' (Hos. 14:10)."

Hos. 14:10 indicates that Yohanan ben Zakkai did speak of the sharp practices.

XXIII. SANHEDRIN

BAVLI SANHEDRIN 4:5 V.
7. A. And R. Judah said Rab said, "The first Man was a min.
   B. "For it is said, 'And the Lord God called to Adam and said to him, where are you' (Gen. 3:9), meaning, 'Where has your heart gone?'"
   C. Said R. Isaac, "He drew out his foreskin [to obliterate the mark of circumcision].
   D. "Here it is written, 'But like Adam, they have transgressed the covenant' (Hos. 6:7), and it is written further, 'He has broken my covenant' (Gen. 17:14)."
   E. R. Nahman said, 'He denied the very principle [that God ruled]. Here it is written, 'They have transgressed the covenant' (Hos. 6:7), and elsewhere it is written, 'Because they forsook the covenant of the Lord their God' (Jer. 22:9) [speaking of belief in God's rule]."

Hos. 6:7 proves that Israel and Adam are comparable, and both have transgressed the covenant.

BAVLI SANHEDRIN 7:5 I.
3. W. Surely "God" refers to courts of justice, for it is written, "And the householder will come near to God" (Ex. 22:7).

6. Hosea in the Bavli

    X. But on what basis do we conclude that, "And he commanded" refers to idolatry?
    Y. R. Hisda and R. Isaac bar Abedimi: One said, "'They have turned aside quickly out of the way which I commanded them; they have made them a molten calf' (Ex. 32:8)."
    Z. The other said, "'Ephraim is oppressed and broken in judgment, because he willingly walked after the commandment' (Hos. 5:11) [in which context, 'commandment' speaks of idolatry]."
    AA. What is at issue between them?
    BB. At issue is the case of an idolater who made an idol but did not bow down to it.
    CC. In the view of him who has said that [the prohibition of gentiles' idol-worship is in the verse,] "They have made them a golden calf,"] one is liable from the time of the making of the idol [even without worshipping it].
    DD. In the view of him who has said that the source of the prohibition is in the verse, "Because he willingly walked after the commandment," one is liable only after he has followed the idol and worshipped it.

Hos. 5:11 proves that "commandment" refers to idolatry in particular.

BAVLI SANHEDRIN 7:6 IV.

3. A. Said R. Nahman, "Any form of mockery is forbidden except for mockery of idolatry, which is permitted. For it is written, 'Bel bows down. Nebo stoops... they stoop, they bow down together, they could not deliver the burden' (Is. 46:1). And it is written, 'They have spoken: the inhabitants of Samaria shall fear because of the calves of Beth Aven; for the people therefore shall mourn over it, and the priests thereof that rejoiced on it for the glory thereof, which is departed from it' (Hos. 10:5). Do not read 'its glory' but 'his weight.'"

Hos. 10:5 indicates that it is permitted to mock idolatry.

BAVLI SANHEDRIN 7:6 IV.

4. A. Said R. Isaac, "What is the meaning of the following verse of Scripture: 'And now they sin more and more and have made for themselves molten images of their silver and idols in their image' (Hos. 13:2)?
    B. "What is the meaning of 'idols in their image'? This teaches that each one of them made an image of his god and put it in his pocket. When he called it to mind, he took it out of his pocket and embraced it and kissed it."
    C. What is the meaning of, "Let the men that sacrifice kiss the calves" (Hos. 13:2)?

- D. Said R. Isaac of the house of R. Ammi, "The servants of the idols would look enviously at wealthy men. They would starve the calves and make images of [the rich men] and set them up at the side of the cribs and then bring the calves out. When the calves would see the men, they would run after them and nuzzle them. [The servants] would say to the men, 'The idol wants you. Let him come and sacrifice himself to him.' [Freedman, p. 433, n. 7: Thus the verse is translated: They sacrifice themselves in their homage to the calves.]"
- E. Said Raba, "Then the verse, 'Let the men that sacrifice kiss the calves' should read, 'Let the calves kiss the men that sacrifice.'"
- F. Rather said Raba, "'Whoever sacrifices his son to an idol would have the priest say to him, "You have offered a great gift to it. Come and kiss it."'"

Hos. 13:2 is worded to show that each one had an idol in his image, which he caressed. The Israelites worshipped their idols.

BAVLI SANHEDRIN 11:1-2 I.

32. A. Said R. Eleazar, "Every authority who leads the community serenely will have the merit of leading them in the world to come, as it is said, 'For he who has mercy on them shall lead them, even by springs of water shall he guide them' (Is. 49:10)."
- B. And said R. Eleazar, "Great is knowledge, for it is set between two names [lit. letters] [of God], as it is written, 'For a God of knowledge is the Lord' (1 Sam. 2:3)."
- C. And said R. Eleazar, "Great is the sanctuary, for it is set between two names [of God], as it is written, 'You have made for yourself, O Lord, a sanctuary, O Lord, your hands have established it' (Ex. 15:17)."
- D. To this view R. Ada Qarhinaah objected, "Then how about the following: 'Great is vengeance, for it is set between two names [of God], as it is written, 'O God of vengeance, O Lord, O God of Vengeance, appear' (Ps. 94:1)."
- E. He said to him, "In context, that is quite so, in line with what Ulla said."
- F. For Ulla said, "What purpose is served by these two references to 'appear'? One speaks of the measure of good, the other, the measure of punishment."
- G. And said R. Eleazar, "In the case of any man who has knowledge it is as if the house of the sanctuary had been built in his own time, for this [knowledge] is set between two names of [God], and that [the Temple] likewise is set between two names of [God]."
- H. And said R. Eleazar, "Any man in whom there is knowledge in the end will be rich, for it is said, 'And by knowledge shall the chambers be filled with all precious and pleasant riches' (Prov. 24:4)."

6. Hosea in the Bavli

I. And said R. Eleazar, "It is forbidden to have pity on any man in whom there is no knowledge, as it is said, 'For it is a people of no understanding; therefore he that made them will not have mercy upon them, and he that formed them will show them no favor' (Is. 27:11)."

J. And said R. Eleazar, "Whoever gives his bread to someone who does not have knowledge in the end will be afflicted with sufferings, for it is said, 'They who eat your bread have laid a wound under you, there is no understanding in him' (Obad. 1:7), and the word for 'wound' can mean only suffering, as it is written, 'When Ephraim saw his sickness and Judah his suffering' [using the same word] (Hos. 5:13)."

K. And said R. Eleazar, "Any man who has no knowledge in the end will go into exile, as it is said, 'Therefore my people have gone into exile, because they have no knowledge' (Is. 5:13)."

3. And said R. Eleazar, "Any house in which words of Torah are not heard by night will be eaten up by fire, as it is said, 'All darkness is hid in his secret places; a fire not blown shall consume him; he grudges him that is left in his tabernacle' (Job 20:26).

Hos. 5:13 provides philological data.

BAVLI SANHEDRIN 11:1-2 I.

80. A. Said Ulla, "Ammon and Moab were bad neighbors of Jerusalem.
B. "When they heard the prophets prophesying the destruction of Jerusalem, they sent word to Nebuchadnezzar, 'Go out and come here.'
C. "He said, 'I am afraid that they will do to me what they did to those who came before me.'
D. "They sent to him, '"For the man is not at home" (Prov. 7:19), and "man" can refer only to the Holy One, blessed be he, as it is said, "The Lord is a man of war" (Ex. 15:3).'
E. "He replied, 'He is nearby and he will come.'
F. "They sent to him, '"He has gone on a far journey" (Prov. 7:19).'
G. "He sent to them, 'There are righteous men there, who will pray for mercy and bring him back.'
H. "They sent to him, '"He has taken a bag of money with him" (Prov. 7:20), and "money" refers only to the righteous, as it is said, "So I bought her to me for fifteen pieces of silver and for a homer of barley and a half-homer of barley" (Hos. 3:2).'
I. "He sent word to them, 'The wicked may repent and pray for mercy and bring him back.'
J. "They sent to him, 'He has already set a time for them, as it is said, "And he will come home at the day appointed" (Prov. 7:20), and "day appointed" can refer only to time, as it is said, "In the time appointed on our solemn feast day" (Ps. 81:1,3).'

K. "He sent word to them, 'It is winter, and I cannot make the trip because of the snow and rain.'
L. "They sent to him, 'Come through the mountains [if need be]. For it is said, "Send you a messenger to the ruler of the earth [that he may come] by way of the rocks to the wilderness to the mountain of the daughter of Zion" (Is. 16:1).'
M. "He sent to them, 'If I come, I shall not have a place in which to make camp.'
N. "They sent word to him, 'Their cemeteries are superior to your palaces, as it is written, "At that time, says the Lord, they shall bring out the bones of the king of Judea and the bones of his princes and the bones of the priests and the bones of the prophets and the bones of the inhabitants of Jerusalem, out of their graves. And they shall spread them before the sun and the moon and all the host of heaven, whom they have loved and whom they have served and after whom they have walked" (Jer. 8:1-2).' [Freedman, p. 654, n. 1: The great burial vaults will be cleared out to give shelter to Nebuchadnezzar's army.]"

Hos. 3:2 shows that "money" refers to th righteous.

BAVLI SANHEDRIN 11:1-2 I.
88. A. Said R. Qattina, "The world will exist for six thousand years and be destroyed for one thousand,
B. "as it is said, 'And the Lord alone shall be exalted in that day' (Is. 2:11)."
C. Abbayye said, "It will be desolate for two thousand years, as it is said, 'After two days will he revive us, in the third day, he will raise us up and we shall live in his sight' (Hos. 6:2)."
D. It has been taught on Tannaite authority in accord with the view of R. Qattina:
E. Just as at the advent of the Sabbatical Year the world will lie fallow for one out of seven years.
F. so it is with the world. A thousand years will the world lie fallow out of seven thousand years,
G. as it is said, "And the Lord alone shall be exalted in that day" (Is. 2:11), and Scripture says, "A Psalm and song for the Sabbath Day" (Ps. 92:1) — a day that is wholly the Sabbath.
H. And Scripture says, "For a thousand years in your sight are but as yesterday when they are past" (Ps. 90:4). [A day stands for a thousand years.]

Hos. 6:2 speaks of a thousand years as a day and has the world desolate for two thousand years but revived in the third thousand.

6. Hosea in the Bavli

BAVLI SANHEDRIN 11:1-2 VII.
7. A. It is written, "And the revolters are profound to make slaughter, though I have been a rebuke of all of them" (Hos. 5:2):
   B. Said R. Yohanan, "Said the Holy One, blessed be he, 'They have gone deeper than I did. I said, "Whoever does not go up to Jerusalem for the Festival transgresses an affirmative requirement," but they have said, "Whoever does go up to Jerusalem for the festival will be stabbed with a sword."'"

Hos. 5:2 clarifies the matter of the pilgrimage to Jerusalem.

BAVLI SANHEDRIN 11:1-2 VIII.
3. A. "Yes, their altars are as heaps in the furrows of the fields" (Hos. 12:12):
   B. Said R. Yohanan, "You have no furrow in the whole of the land of Israel in which Ahab did not set up an idol and bow down to it."

Hos. 12:12 refers to the idolatry of Ahab.

BAVLI SANHEDRIN 11:1-2 X.
4. A. Said R. Hisda said R. Jeremiah bar Abba, "What is the meaning of the following verse: 'I went by the field of the slothful and by the vineyard of the man void of understanding. And lo, it was all grown over with thorns and nettles had covered the face thereof, and the stone wall thereof was broken down' (Prov. 24:30-31)?
   B. "'I went by the field of the slothful' — this speaks of Ahaz.
   C. "'And by the vineyard of the man void of understanding' — this speaks of Manasseh.
   D. "'And lo, it was all grown over with thorns' — this refers to Amon.
   E. "'And nettles had covered the face thereof' — this refers to Jehoiakim.
   F. "'And the stone wall thereof was broken down' — this refers to Zedekiah, in whose time the Temple was destroyed.
   G. And said R. Hisda said R. Jeremiah bar Abba, "There are four categories who will not receive the face of the Presence of God:
   H. "The categories of scoffers, flatterers, liars, and slanderers.
   I. "The category of scoffers, as it is written, 'He has stretched out his hand against scorners' (Hos. 7:5).
   J. "The category of flatterers, as it is written, 'He who speaks lies shall not be established in my sight' (Job. 13:16).
   K. "The category of liars, as it is written, 'He who speaks lies shall not be established in my sight' (Ps. 101:7).
   L. "The category of slanderers, as it is written, 'For you are not a God who has pleasure in wickedness; evil will not dwell with you' (Ps. 5:5). 'You are righteous, O Lord, and evil will not dwell in your house [Ps. 5 addresses slander.]"

M. And said R. Hisda said R. Jeremiah bar Abba, "What is the meaning of the verse, 'There shall nor evil befall you, neither shall any plague come near your dwelling'(Ps. 91:10)?
N. "'There shall not evil befall you' means that the evil impulse will not rule over you.
O. "'Neither shall any plague come near your dwelling' means that, when you come home from a trip, you will never find that your wife is in doubt as to whether or not she is menstruating."
P. "Another matter: 'There shall not evil befall you' means that bad dreams and fantasies will never frighten you.
Q. "'Neither shall any plague come near your dwelling' means that you will not have a son or a disciple who in public burns his food [that is, teaches something heretical].'
R. "Up to this point is the blessing that his father had given him.
S. "From this point forward comes the blessing that his mother had given to him: 'For he shall give his angels charge over you, to keep you in all your ways. They shall bear you in their hands ... You shall tread upon the lion and the adder' (Ps. 91:10).
T. "Up to this point is the blessing that his mother gave him.
U. "From this point onward comes the blessing that heaven gave him:
V. "'[103B] Because he has set his love upon me, therefore will I deliver him. I will set him on high, because he has known my name. He shall call upon me, and I will answer him. I will be with him in trouble. I will deliver him and honor him. With long life will I satisfy him and show him my salvation' (Ps. 91:14-16)."

Hos. 7:5 shows that scoffers will not be received by God.

BAVLI SANHEDRIN 11:1-2 XI.

21. A. "And now, behold, I go to my people; come and I shall advise you what this people shall do to your people in the end of days" (Num. 24:24):
B. Rather than saying, "This people to your people," it should say, "Your people to this people." [Freedman, p. 723, n. 4: He advised the Moabites to ensnare Israel through unchastity. Thus he was referring to an action by the former to the latter, while Scripture suggests otherwise.]
C. Said R. Abba, "It is like a man who curses himself but assigns the curse to others. [Scripture alludes to Israel but refers to Moab.]
D. "[Balaam] said to [Balak], 'The God of these people hates fornication, and they lust after linen [clothing, which rich people wear]. Come and I shall give you advice: Make tents and set whores in them, an old one outside and a girl inside. Let them sell linen garments to them.'
E. "He made tents for them from the snowy mountain to Beth Hajeshimoth [north to south] and put whores in them, old women outside, young women inside.

6. Hosea in the Bavli

F. "When an Israelite was eating and drinking and carousing and going out for walks in the market, the old lady would say to him, 'Don't you want some linen clothes?'

G. "The old lady would offer them at true value, and the girl would offer them at less.

H. "This would happen two or three times, and then [the young one] would say to him, 'Lo, you are at home here. Sit down and make a choice for yourself.' Gourds of Ammonite wine would be set near her. (At this point the wine of gentiles had not yet been forbidden to Israelites.) She would say to him, 'Do you want to drink a cup of wine?'

I. "When he had drunk a cup of wine, he would become inflamed. He said to her, 'Submit to me.' She would than take her god from her bosom and said to him, 'Worship this.'

J. "He would say to her, 'Am I not a Jew?'

K. "She would say to him, 'What difference does it make to you? Do they ask anything more from you than that you bare yourself?' But he did not know that that was how this idol was served.

L. "'And not only so, but I shall not let you do so until you deny the Torah of Moses, your master!'

M. "As it is said, 'They went in to Baal-peor and separated themselves unto that shame, and their abominations were according as they loved' (Hos. 9:10)."

Hos. 9:10 condemns the Israelites for worshiping Baal-peor.

BAVLI SANHEDRIN 11:3 I.

4. A. It has been taught on Tannaite authority:

B. R. Simai says, "It is said, 'I shall take you to me for a people' (Ex. 6:7), and it is said, 'And I will bring you in [to the land]' (Ex. 6:7).

C. "Their exodus from Egypt is compared to their entry into the land. Just as, when they came into the land, they were only two out of the original six hundred thousand [only Caleb and Joshua], so when they left Egypt, there were only two out of six hundred thousand."

D. Said Raba, "So it will be in the times of the Messiah, as it is said, 'And she shall sing there, as in the days of her youth, and as in the days when she came up out of the land of Egypt' (Hos. 2:17)."

Hos. 2:17 indicates that the pattern of the liberation from Egypt will be repeated in the Messiah's age.

XXIV. MAKKOT

BAVLI MAKKOT 2:6A-F I:

2. A. [How come] the three cities in Transjordan were the same as the three cities for the land of Israel [since so many more people lived in the land of Israel]?

B. Said Abbayye, "In Gilead there were lots of murderers, [10A] as it is written, 'Gilead is a city of those who work iniquity and is covered with footprints of blood' (Hos. 6:8)."

Hos. 6:8 condemns Gilead for murder.

BAVLI MAKKOT 2:6A-F I:
4. A. How come some are further apart at one side and closer together at the other [following the reading of Lazarus]?
B. Said Abbayye, "In Shechem too there were lots of murderers, as it is written, 'And as troops of robbers wait for a man, so does the company of priests murder in the way toward Shechem' (Hos. 6:9)."

Hos. 6:9 condemns Shechem for murder.

XXV. ABODAH ZARAH

BAVLI ABODAH ZARAH 1:1 I.
11. A. That is in line with what R. Abba said, "What is the meaning of the verse, 'Though I would redeem them, yet they have spoken lies against me' (Hos. 7:23)? 'I said that I would redeem them through [inflicting a penalty] on their property in this world, so that they might have the merit of enjoying the world to come, "yet they have spoken lies against me" (Hos. 7:23).'"
I.12.A. That is in line with what R. Pappi in the name of Raba said, "What is the meaning of the verse, 'Though I have trained [and] strengthened their arms, yet they imagine mischief against me' (Hos. 7:15)?
B. Said the Holy One, blessed be He, I thought that I would punish them with suffering in this world, so that their arm might be strengthened in the world to come, "yet they have spoken lies against me" (Hos. 7:23).'"

Hos. 7:14, 23 show that Israel had a change to suffer in this world and to gain the world to come, but gave up that chance and spoke lies against God.

BAVLI ABODAH ZARAH 1:1 I.
33. A. Said R. Yohanan in the name of R. Benaah, "What is the meaning of the verse of Scripture, 'Happy are you who sow beside all waters, that send forth the feet of the ox and the ass' (Isa. 32:20)? 'Happy are you, O Israel, when you are devoted to the Torah and to doing deeds of grace, then their inclination to do evil is handed over to them, and they are not handed over into the power of their inclination to do evil.
B. "For it is said, 'Happy are you who sow beside all waters.' For what does the word 'sowing' mean, if not 'doing deeds of grace,'

6. Hosea in the Bavli

in line with the use of the word in this verse: 'Sow for yourselves in righteousness, reap according to mercy' (Hos. 10:12), and what is the meaning of 'water' if not Torah: 'Oh you who are thirsty, come to the water' (Isa. 55:1)."
- C. As to the phrase, "that send forth the feet of the ox and the ass:"
- D. it has been taught by the Tannaite authority of the household of Elijah:
- E. "A person should always place upon himself the work of studying the Torah as an ox accepts the yoke, and as an ass, its burden."

Hos. 10:12 contributes the meaning of the word "sowing" in an exegetical context.

BAVLI ABODAH ZARAH 1:7 II.

19. A. Said R. Eleazar, "As to him who scoffs, affliction will come upon him: 'Now therefore do you not scoff, lest your punishment be made severe' (Isa. 28:22)."
    B. Said Raba to rabbis, "By your leave, I beg you not to scorn, so that suffering not come upon you."
    C. Said R. Qattina, "Whoever scorns will find his sustenance diminished: 'He withdraws his hand in the case of scoffers' (Hos. 7:5)."
    D. Said R. Simeon b. Laqish, "Whoever scorns falls into Gehenna: 'A proud and haughty man, scoffer is his name, works for arrogant wrath' (Prov. 21:24), and 'wrath' means only Gehenna: 'That day is a day of wrath' (Zeph. 1:15)."
    E. Said R. Oshaia, "Whoever takes pride falls into Gehenna: "A proud and haughty man, scoffer is his name, works for arrogant wrath' (Prov. 21:24), and 'wrath' means only Gehenna: 'That day is a day of wrath' (Zeph. 1:15)."
    F. Said R. Hanilai b. Hanilai, "Whoever scoffs brings annihilation upon the world: 'Now therefore do not be scoffers, lest your affliction be made severe, for an annihilation wholly determined have I heard' (Isa. 28:22).
    G. Said R. Eleazar, "It is hard, since it starts with 'afflict' and ends up with 'annihilation.'"

Hos. 7:5 warns that one who scoffs will lose his sustenance.

XXVI. HORAYOT

BAVLI HORAYOT 3:3 I:

7. A. Said Rabbah bar bar Hannah said R. Yohanan, "What is the meaning of the verse of Scripture, 'For the paths of the Lord are straight, that the righteous shall pass along them, but the transgressors will stumble in them' (Hos. 14:10)? The matter may be compared to

the case of two men who roasted their Passover offerings. One of them ate it for the sake of performing the religious duty, and the other one ate it to stuff himself with a big meal. The one who ate it for the sake of performing a religious duty — 'the righteous shall pass along them.' And as to the one who ate it to stuff himself with a big meal — 'but the transgressors will stumble in them'"

B. Said to him R. Simeon b. Laqish, "But do you really call him a wicked person? Granted that he did not carry out a religious duty in the best possible way, still, has he not eaten his Passover offering as he is supposed to? Rather, the matter may be compared to the case of two men. This one has his wife and sister with him in the house, and that one has his wife and his sister with him in the house. One of them had a sexual encounter with his wife, while the other had a sexual encounter with his sister. The one who had the sexual encounter with his wife — 'the righteous shall pass along them.' And as to the one who had a sexual encounter with his sister.— 'but the transgressors will stumble in them'"

C. But are the cases comparable to the verse of Scripture? Scripture speaks of a single path in which righteous and wicked walk, but here there are two paths [one being legal the other not]. Rather, the matter may be compared to the case of Lot and his two daughters. Those who had sexual relations to carry out a religious duty [to be fruitful and multiply] — "the righteous shall pass along them." And As to the one who had sexual relations in order to perform a transgression — "but the transgressors will stumble in them"

D. But maybe he too had in mind to fulfill the commandment?

E. Said R. Yohanan, "The entire verse of Scripture is formulated to express the intention of committing a transgression, as it is said, 'And Lot lifted his eyes and saw the entire plain of the Jordan that it was well watered' (Gen. 13:10).

F. "[The sense of 'lifted' derives from, 'And his master's wife lifted her eyes toward Joseph and said, Lay with me' (Gen. 39:7).

G. "'...his eyes....:' 'And Samson said, Take her for me, as she is beautiful in my eyes' (Jud. 14:3).

H. "'And saw...:' 'And Shechem, son of Hamor...saw her and took her and lay with her and abused her' (Gen. 34:2).

I. "'the entire plain of the Jordan...:' 'For a whore can be had for the price of a loaf of bread' (Prov. 6:326). [The Hebrew words for plain and loaf being the same.]

J. "'that it was well watered...:' 'I will go after my lovers, who provide my bread and water, my wool and flax, my oil and my drink' (Hos. 2:7)."

K. But wasn't he drunk anyhow, so he really was forced into the act!

L. A Tannaite statement in the name of R. Yosé b. R. Honi, "Why are there dots about the word 'and' in the verse, 'and when the elder daughter arose' (Gen. 19:33)? It tells you that when she lay down

6. Hosea in the Bavli

with him, he didn't know what was going on, but when she got up, he knew."
M. So what was he supposed to do? What was was.
N. The point is that the next night, he shouldn't have gotten drunk [to get involved with the younger daughter.

Hos. 14:10 distinguishes between the attitude that animates a single action, whether to perform a religious duty or to serve one's own interest. Hos. 2:7 treats "well watered" as a metaphor for sexual promiscuity.

XXVII. SHEBUOT

BAVLI SHEBUOT 6:1-4 I:
3. A. Our rabbis have taught on Tannaite authority:
B. The oath of witnesses and judges is said also in any language.
C. They say to him, "Know that [39A] the whole world trembled on the day on which it was said, "You shall not take the name of the Lord your God in vain" (Ex. 20:7).
D. And with reference to all transgressions that are listed in the Torah, it is written, "And he shall be acquitted," but with reference to this one it is written, "And he shall not be acquitted."
E. In regard to all the transgressions that are mentioned in the Torah, they exact retribution from the man himself, but in this case they exact retribution from him and from his relatives, as it is said, "Suffer not your mouth to bring your flesh into guilt" (Qoh. 5:5), and "flesh" refers only to a relative, as it is said, "From your flesh do not hide yourself" (Is. 58:7).
F. In regard to all transgressions that are mentioned in the Torah, they exact retribution from the man himself, but with reference to this one, they exact retribution from the man and from the entire world, so that the transgression of the entire world is blamed on him, since it is said, "Swearing and lying...therefore does the land mourn, and every one who dwells therein does languish" (Hos. 4:2-3) [T. Sot. 7:1A, 7:2A-M]..
G. But might one suppose that that is the case only if he does all of them [killing, stealing, committing adultery]?
H. Perish the thought! For it is written, "Because of swearing the land mourns" (Jer. 23:10) and further, "therefore does the land mourn and every one that dwells therein does languish" (Hos. 4:3) [because of swearing the land mourns, therefore every inhabitant languishes because of swearing (Silverstone)].

Hos. 4:3 says the land languishes because of swearing.

XXVIII. ZEBAHIM

BAVLI ZEBAHIM 9:7 III:

5. A. And said R. Inyani bar Sasson, "Why are the passages that concern the sacrificial offerings [Lev. 7] and concerning the priestly vestments [Lev. 8] set side by side? It is to tell you: just as the sacrifices effect atonement, so do the priestly vestments effect atonement.
   B. "The coat effects atonement for the shedding of blood: 'And they killed a he goat and dipped the coat in the blood' (Gen. 37:31).
   C. "The underpants atoned for lewdness: 'And you shall make them linen breeches to cover the flesh of their nakedness' (Ex. 28:42).
   D. "The miter effected atonement for arrogance."
   E. (How do we know that?
   F. Said R. Hanina, "Let an article of clothing that is worn high up come and effect offence for holding one's nose in the air.")
   G. "The girdle effected atonement for impure meditations of the heart, corresponding to the place at which it was located.
   H. "The breastplate effected atonement for neglecting the civil laws: 'And you shall make a breastplate of judgment' (Ex. 28:15).
   I. "The ephod effected atonement for idolatry: 'without ephod there are teraphim' (Hos. 3:4).
   J. "The robe effected atonement for slander."
   K. (How do we know that?
   L. Said R. Hanina, "Let an article that carries sound [being fringed with bells] come and effect atonement for a sin that is committed through making sound [gossip].")
   M. "The headplate effected atonement for brazenness: 'And it shall be upon Aaron's forehead' (Ex. 28:38), and of brazenness it is written, 'Yet you had a harlot's forehead' (Jer. 3:3)."

Hos. 3:4 shows that the ephod atoned for idolatry.

XXIX. MENAHOT

BAVLI MENAHOT 11:3-5 IV:

11. A. And said R. Simeon b. Laqish, "A disciple of a sage who turned sour is not to be humiliated in public: 'Therefore you shall stumble in the day, and the prophet also shall stumble with you in the night' (Hos. 4:5).
    B. "Cover it up in darkness."

Hos. 4:5 indicates that when the prophet stumbles, it is at night, when no one sees.

XXX. HULLIN

I find nothing relevant.

XXXI. BEKHOROT

I notice nothing that pertains.

XXXII. ARAKHIN

BAVLI ARAKHIN 3:4 I.
13. A. The tunic of the priesthood achieves atonement for the sin of bloodshed, for it is written [in Scripture], "And they dipped the tunic in the blood" (Gen. 37:31).
   B. The pants achieve atonement for fornication, as it is written in Scripture, "And he made linen trousers to cover the flesh of their nakedness" (Ex. 28:42).
   C. The miter achieves atonement for arrogance, and that view is in accord with that which R. Hanina said.
   D. For R. Hanina said, "Let that which is set high up come and achieve atonement for a deed that was haughty."
   E. The girdle achieves atonement for the sin of sinful thoughts of the heart [Jung], that is, where [the garment itself] is located [that is, broad enough to cover the heart].
   F. The breastplate achieves atonement for [error] in legal decisions, as it is written, "And you shall make a breastplate of judgment" (Ex. 28:15).
   G. The ephod achieves atonement for idolatry, as it is written [in Scripture], "And without ephod or teraphim" (Hos. 3:4 [Jung, p. 92, n. 5: "Because there was no ephod, there were teraphim (idols)"].
   H. The robe achieves atonement for slaughter.

As above.

BAVLI ARAKHIN 9:6 IV.
33. A. And did they count out years of release and Jubilee years [as claimed above]?
   B. If, after the tribe of Reuben, the tribe of Gad, and the half-tribe of Manasseh went into exile, the Jubilee years were annulled, could Ezra, concerning whom it is written [in Scripture], "The whole congregation together was [merely] forty two thousand three hundred sixty" (Ezra 2:64), have counted them? [Surely there were too few Israelites to justify taking up the count of years of release and of Jubilee years, as will now be demonstrated, and that would indicate that they did not in fact count the years of release and Jubilees].

C. For it has been taught on Tannaite authority: Once the tribe of Reuben, the tribe of Gad, and the half-tribe of Manasseh, went into exile, Jubilee years were annulled, as it is said, "And you shall proclaim liberty throughout the land to all the inhabitants thereof" (Lev. 25:10).

D. [The meaning of the proof text is this:] When all of its inhabitants are in it [you shall proclaim liberty], and not when part of them have gone into exile.

E. Is it possible, [furthermore,] to suppose that the Jubilee year would be celebrated when the Israelites were on the Land but were confused among one another, with the tribe of Benjamin located in Judah and the tribe of Judah in Benjamin? [That is how things were in Ezra's day.]

F. Scripture says, "To all its inhabitants," meaning, when its inhabitants are in good order and not when they are mixed together. [Accordingly, in the time of Ezra the Israelites surely could not have counted out years of release and Jubilee years.]

G. Said R. Nahman bar Isaac, "They counted out the Jubilees [only] in order to consecrate the years of release [which continued to apply. Jung: "Though the Jubilees had been abolished, years of release were still observed, consequently they had to count the Jubilees in order to be able to observe the years of release in their proper time. For the year of Jubilee was not included in the seven years-cycle. They therefore had to know when the year of Jubilee arrives to be able to fix the next year of release, which was to be the eighth year following the year of Jubilee."]

H. [33A] That view poses no problem to rabbis, who take the view that the fiftieth year does not count [among the years of release, as explained by Jung].

I. But in the opinion of R. Judah, who holds that the fiftieth year is counted as part both [the preceding cycle of seven years and also the ensuing cycle of seven years], why do I have [to continue to count the Jubilee]? Surely it suffices to count out the years of release.

J. It assuredly follows that the cited statement is not in accord with R Judah.

K. But [vs. A] did they not count out years of release and Jubilee years? For is it not written, "At the end of seven years you shall let go every man his brother who is a Hebrew, who has been sold to you" (Jer. 34:14).?

L. And in this connection we queried as follows: "[Why is it written] 'at the end of seven years'? Is it not written, 'He shall serve you six years' (Deut. 15:12)?"

M. And in response to this query, R. Nahman bar Isaac said, "'Six years' [applies] to the one who had been sold, and 'seven' to the one whose ear had been pierced [Ex. 21:6, such a one continues to the Jubilee. If he had served for seven years, and the eighth was a

Jubilee, he would go forth free.]" [Jeremiah spoke of the time of Zedekiah, after Sennacherib had exiled the north tribes. So the law of the year of Jubilee did remain valid in his time, contrary to the earlier statements.]

N. But was not [Jeremiah's statement] intended as a denunciation, that is, the prophet meant to say, "Did you send them forth?"

O. [Such a solution is impossible, for] is it not written, "And they obeyed and sent them forth" (Jer. 34:10). [It follows that the response just given is contrary to the facts.]

P. Rather, said R. Yohanan, "Jeremiah brought them back, and Josiah, son of Amon, ruled over them."

Q. How do we know that they returned? For it is written [in Scripture], "For the seller shall not return to that which is sold" (Ezek. 7:13). Is it possible [to imagine] that the Jubilee had already been annulled and yet the prophet [Ezekiel] should prophesy that it would be annulled in the future [as is his message at Ezek. 7:13]?

R. [Accordingly, the Jubilees were in effect, and that was because, as] the passage teaches, Jeremiah brought them back. [So A is wrong and K is right.]

S. And how do we know that Josiah ruled over them? Since it is written, "Then he said, What monument is that which I see? And the men of the city told him, It is the sepulchre of the man of God, who came from Judah and proclaimed these things that you have done against the altar of Beth El" (2 Kgs. 23:17).

T. What was Josiah doing at Beth El, unless when Jeremiah brought them back, Josiah was ruling over them?

U. R. Nahman bar Isaac said, "Proof comes from this passage: 'Also, Judah, there is a harvest appointed for you when I return the exiles of my people' (Hos. 6:11). [Jung: "Reading for kazir (harvest) kazin (prince, ruler). The letters r and n interchange... the meaning of the passage thus is given as: 'From Judah' (whose king Josiah was first) was a king appointed for thee (O Israel).'"]

Hos. 6:11 is read to indicate that the Judeans had a king appointed for them wen the exiles were returned.

XXXIII. TEMURAH

I found nothing.

XXXIV. KERITOT

I found nothing.

xxxv. Meilah

I found nothing.

xxxvi. Tamid

I found nothing.

xxxvii. Niddah

I found nothing.

STUDIES IN JUDAISM
TITLES IN THE SERIES
PUBLISHED BY UNIVERSITY PRESS OF AMERICA

Judith Z. Abrams
The Babylonian Talmud: A Topical Guide, 2002.

Roger David Aus
Matthew 1-2 and the Virginal Conception: In Light of Palestinian and Hellenistic Judaic Traditions on the Birth of Israel's First Redeemer, Moses, 2004.

My Name Is "Legion": Palestinian Judaic Traditions in Mark 5:1-20 and Other Gospel Texts, 2003.

Alan L. Berger, Harry James Cargas, and Susan E. Nowak
The Continuing Agony: From the Carmelite Convent to the Crosses at Auschwitz, 2004.

S. Daniel Breslauer
Creating a Judaism without Religion: A Postmodern Jewish Possibility, 2001.

Bruce Chilton
Targumic Approaches to the Gospels: Essays in the Mutual Definition of Judaism and Christianity, 1986.

David Ellenson
Tradition in Transition: Orthodoxy, Halakhah, and the Boundaries of Modern Jewish Identity, 1989.

Paul V. M. Flesher
New Perspectives on Ancient Judaism, Volume 5: Society and Literature in Analysis, 1990.

Marvin Fox
Collected Essays on Philosophy and on Judaism, Volume One: Greek Philosophy, Maimonides, 2003.

Collected Essays on Philosophy and on Judaism, Volume Two: Some Philosophers, 2003.

Collected Essays on Philosophy and on Judaism, Volume Three: Ethics, Reflections, 2003.

Zev Garber
Methodology in the Academic Teaching of Judaism, 1986.

Zev Garber, Alan L. Berger, and Richard Libowitz
Methodology in the Academic Teaching of the Holocaust, 1988.

Abraham Gross
Spirituality and Law: Courting Martyrdom in Christianity and Judaism, 2005.

Harold S. Himmelfarb and Sergio DellaPergola
Jewish Education Worldwide: Cross-Cultural Perspectives, 1989.

William Kluback
The Idea of Humanity: Hermann Cohen's Legacy to Philosophy and Theology, 1987.

Samuel Morell
Studies in the Judicial Methodology of Rabbi David ibn Abi Zimra, 2004.

Jacob Neusner
Amos in Talmud and Midrash, 2006.

Ancient Israel, Judaism, and Christianity in Contemporary Perspective, 2006.

The Aggadic Role in Halakhic Discourses: Volume I, 2001.

The Aggadic Role in Halakhic Discourses: Volume II, 2001.

The Aggadic Role in Halakhic Discourses: Volume III, 2001.

Analysis and Argumentation in Rabbinic Judaism, 2003.

Analytical Templates of the Bavli, 2006.

Ancient Judaism and Modern Category-Formation: "Judaism," "Midrash," "Messianism," and Canon in the Past Quarter Century, 1986.

Canon and Connection: Intertextuality in Judaism, 1987.

Chapters in the Formative History of Judaism. 2006

Dual Discourse, Single Judaism, 2001.

The Emergence of Judaism: Jewish Religion in Response to the Critical Issues of the First Six Centuries, 2000.

First Principles of Systemic Analysis: The Case of Judaism within the History of Religion, 1988.

The Halakhah and the Aggadah, 2001.

Halakhic Hermeneutics, 2003.

Halakhic Theology: A Sourcebook, 2006.

The Hermeneutics of Rabbinic Category Formations, 2001.

Hosea in Talmud and Midrash, 2006.

How Important Was the Destruction of the Second Temple in the Formation of Rabbinic Judaism? 2006.

How Not to Study Judaism, Examples and Counter-Examples, Volume One: Parables, Rabbinic Narratives, Rabbis' Biographies, Rabbis' Disputes, 2004.

How Not to Study Judaism, Examples and Counter-Examples, Volume Two: Ethnicity and Identity versus Culture and

Religion, How Not to Write a Book on Judaism, Point and Counterpoint, 2004.

How the Halakhah Unfolds: Moed Qatan in the Mishnah, ToseftaYerushalmi and Bavli, 2006.

The Implicit Norms of Rabbinic Judaism. 2006.

Intellectual Templates of the Law of Judaism, 2006.

Is Scripture the Origin of the Halakhah? 2005.

Israel and Iran in Talmudic Times: A Political History, 1986.

Israel's Politics in Sasanian Iran: Self-Government in Talmudic Times, 1986.

Jeremiah in Talmud and Midrash: A Source Book, 2006.

Judaism in Monologue and Dialogue, 2005.

Major Trends in Formative Judaism, Fourth Series, 2002.

Major Trends in Formative Judaism, Fifth Series, 2002.

Messiah in Context: Israel's History and Destiny in Formative Judaism, 1988.

Micah and Joel in Talmud and Midrash, 2006.

The Native Category - Formations of the Aggadah: The Later Midrash-Compilations - Volume I, 2000.

The Native Category - Formations of the Aggadah: The Earlier Midrash-Compilations - Volume II, 2000.

Paradigms in Passage: Patterns of Change in the Contemporary Study of Judaism, 1988.

Parsing the Torah, 2005.

Praxis and Parable: The Divergent Discourses of Rabbinic Judaism, 2006.

Rabbi Jeremiah, 2006.

Reading Scripture with the Rabbis: The Five Books of Moses, 2006.

The Religious Study of Judaism: Description, Analysis and Interpretation, Volume 1, 1986.

The Religious Study of Judaism: Description, Analysis, Interpretation, Volume 2, 1986.

The Religious Study of Judaism: Context, Text, Circumstance, Volume 3, 1987.

The Religious Study of Judaism: Description, Analysis, Interpretation, Volume 4: Ideas of History, Ethics, Ontology, and Religion in Formative Judaism, 1988.

Struggle for the Jewish Mind: Debates and Disputes on Judaism Then and Now, 1988.

The Talmud Law, Theology, Narrative: A Sourcebook, 2005.

Talmud Torah: Ways to God's Presence through Learning: An Exercise in Practical Theology, 2002.

Texts Without Boundaries: Protocols of Non-Documentary Writing in the Rabbinic Canon: Volume I: The Mishnah, Tractate Abot, and the Tosefta, 2002.

Texts Without Boundaries: Protocols of Non-Documentary Writing in the Rabbinic Canon: Volume II: Sifra and Sifré to Numbers, 2002.

Texts Without Boundaries: Protocols of Non-Documentary Writing in the Rabbinic Canon: Volume III: Sifré to Deuteronomy and Mekhilta Attributed to Rabbi Ishmael, 2002.

Texts Without Boundaries: Protocols of Non-Documentary Writing in the Rabbinic Canon: Volume IV: Leviticus Rabbah, 2002.

A Theological Commentary to the Midrash - Volume I: Pesiqta deRab Kahana, 2001.

A Theological Commentary to the Midrash - Volume II: Genesis Raba, 2001.

A Theological Commentary to the Midrash - Volume III: Song of Songs Rabbah, 2001.

A Theological Commentary to the Midrash - Volume IV: Leviticus Rabbah, 2001.

A Theological Commentary to the Midrash - Volume V: Lamentations Rabbati, 2001.

A Theological Commentary to the Midrash - Volume VI: Ruth Rabbah and Esther Rabbah, 2001.

A Theological Commentary to the Midrash - Volume VII: Sifra, 2001.

A Theological Commentary to the Midrash - Volume VIII: Sifré to Numbers and Sifré to Deuteronomy, 2001.

A Theological Commentary to the Midrash - Volume IX: Mekhilta Attributed to Rabbi Ishmael, 2001.

Theological Dictionary of Rabbinic Judaism: Part One: Principal Theological Categories, 2005.

Theological Dictionary of Rabbinic Judaism: Part Two: Making Connections and Building Constructions, 2005.

Theological Dictionary of Rabbinic Judaism: Part Three: Models of Analysis, Explanation, and Anticipation, 2005.

The Theological Foundations of Rabbinic Midrash, 2006.

Theology of Normative Judaism: A Source Book, 2005.

Theology in Action: How the Rabbis of the Talmud Present Theology (Aggadah) in the Medium of the Law (Halakhah). An Anthology, 2006

The Torah and the Halakhah: The Four Relationships, 2003.

The Unity of Rabbinic Discourse: Volume I: Aggadah in the Halakhah, 2001.

The Unity of Rabbinic Discourse: Volume II: Halakhah in the Aggadah, 2001.

The Unity of Rabbinic Discourse: Volume III: Halakhah and Aggadah in Concert, 2001.

The Vitality of Rabbinic Imagination: The Mishnah Against the Bible and Qumran,2005.

Who, Where and What is "Israel?": Zionist Perspectives on Israeli and American Judaism, 1989.

The Wonder-Working Lawyers of Talmudic Babylonia: The Theory and Practice of Judaism in its Formative Age, 1987.

Jacob Neusner and Ernest S. Frerichs
New Perspectives on Ancient Judaism, Volume 2: Judaic and Christian Interpretation of Texts: Contents and Contexts, 1987.

New Perspectives on Ancient Judaism, Volume 3: Judaic and Christian Interpretation of Texts: Contents and Contexts, 1987.

Jacob Neusner and James F. Strange
Religious Texts and Material Contexts, 2001.

David Novak and Norbert M. Samuelson
Creation and the End of Days: Judaism and Scientific Cosmology, 1986.
Proceedings of the Academy for Jewish Philosophy, 1990.

Risto Nurmela
The Mouth of the Lord Has Spoken: Inner-Biblical Allusions in Second and Third Isaiah, 2006.

Aaron D. Panken
The Rhetoric of Innovation: Self-Conscious Legal Change in Rabbinic Literature, 2005.

Norbert M. Samuelson
Studies in Jewish Philosophy: Collected Essays of the Academy for Jewish Philosophy, 1980-1985, 1987.

Benjamin Edidin Scolnic
Alcimus, Enemy of the Maccabees, 2004.

If the Egyptians Drowned in the Red Sea Where are Pharaoh's Chariots?: Exploring the Historical Dimension of the Bible, 2005.

Rivka Ulmer
Pesiqta Rabbati: A Synoptic Edition of Pesiqta Rabbati Based upon all Extant Manuscripts and the Editio Princeps, Volume III, 2002.

Manfred H. Vogel
A Quest for a Theology of Judaism: The Divine, the Human and the Ethical Dimensions in the Structure-of-Faith of Judaism Essays in Constructive, 1987.

Anita Weiner
Renewal: Reconnecting Soviet Jewry to the Soviet People: A Decade of American Jewish Joint Distribution Committee (AJJDC) Activities in the Former Soviet Union 1988-1998, 2003.

Eugene Weiner and Anita Weiner
Israel-A Precarious Sanctuary: War, Death and the Jewish People, 1989.

The Martyr's Conviction: A Sociological Analysis, 2002.

Leslie S. Wilson
The Serpent Symbol in the Ancient Near East: Nahash and Asherah: Death, Life, and Healing, 2001.

Made in the USA
Lexington, KY
08 May 2016